Negotiating sovereignty and human rights

MANCHESTER
1824
Manchester University Press

Negotiating sovereignty and human rights

International society and the International Criminal Court

Sibylle Scheipers

Manchester University Press
Manchester and New York
*distributed in the United States exclusively
by Palgrave Macmillan*

Published by Manchester University Press
Oxford Road, Manchester M13 9NR, UK
and Room 400, 175 Fifth Avenue, New York, NY 10010, USA
www.manchesteruniversitypress.co.uk

Distributed in the United States exclusively by
Palgrave Macmillan, 175 Fifth Avenue, New York,
NY 10010, USA

Distributed in Canada exclusively by
UBC Press, University of British Columbia, 2029 West Mall,
Vancouver, BC, Canada V6T 1Z2

British Library Cataloguing-in-Publication Data
A catalogue record for this book is available from the British Library

Library of Congress Cataloging-in-Publication Data applied for

ISBN 978 0 7190 8009 8 *hardback*

First published 2009

18 17 16 15 14 13 12 11 10 09   10 9 8 7 6 5 4 3 2 1

Typeset
by Frances Hackeson Freelance Publishing Services, Brinscall, Lancs
Printed in Great Britain
by TJ International Ltd, Padstow

Contents

Figures and tables

Figures

Tables

Acknowledgements

I am grateful to the Berlin Graduate School of Social Sciences at Humboldt University for providing me with an academic 'home' while I was writing my PhD thesis on which this book is based. In particular, I would like to thank my supervisors, Professor Herfried Münkler and Professor Klaus Eder, who generously offered their time and expertise to discuss my work with me.

During the time of my Ph.D. research, I benefited immensely from a Marie Curie Pre-doctoral Fellowship hosted by the European Research Institute at Birmingham University. I am grateful to Professor Thomas Diez, who supervised my research during that time and continued to be a source of advice and encouragement after that.

I would like to thank friends and colleagues who discussed my research with me, read various drafts and chapters of the thesis, and, most importantly, endured me during the alternating fits of euphoria and frustration that typically accompany the process of writing a Ph.D. Heiko Fritz, Bettina Renz and Daniela Sicurelli were particularly indispensible in this regard.

Also indispensable during my Ph.D. research were the scholarships I received from the Land Berlin (NAFöG) and from the European Commission/ FP 6 (Marie Curie), and the travel funds provided by the German Academic Exchange Service (DAAD).

Finally, I would like to thank my family, without whose unfailing support and encouragement this project – like so many others – would not have been possible.

Sibylle Scheipers
Oxford

Note to the reader

Please note that references are to be found both in the References and in the Appendix.

Abbreviations

ASPA	American Servicemembers' Protection Act
BIAs	Bilateral Immunity Agreements
CFSP	Common Foreign and Security Policy
CG	Convening Group
DipCon	United Nations Diplomatic Conference of Plenipotentiaries on the Establishment of an International Criminal Court
ESF	Economic Support Fund (US)
ICC	International Criminal Court
ICTR	International Criminal Tribunal for Rwanda
ICTY	International Criminal Tribunal for Yugoslavia
ILC	International Law Commission
IR	International Relations
LMG	Like-Minded Group
LRA	Lord's Resistance Army (Uganda)
NAM	Non-Aligned Movement
NGO	non-governmental organisation
OECD	Organisation for Economic Co-operation and Development
P5	Group of the permanent five members of the UN Security Council
PMC	Private Military Company
PrepCom	Preparatory Commission for the International Criminal Court
PS	Parti Socialiste (French Socialist Party)
RPR	Rassemblement pour la République (French Republican Party)
UNCHR	United Nations Commission on Human Rights
WTO	World Trade Organization

1 Introduction

Unless we are prepared to abandon every principle of growth for international law, we cannot deny that our own day has the right to institute customs and to conclude agreements that will themselves become sources of a newer and strengthened international law. International law is not capable of development by the normal processes of legislation, for there is no continuing international legislative authority. Innovations and revisions in international law are brought about by the action of governments such as those I have cited, designed to meet a change in circumstances.[1]

There is a tendency in the negotiations, occasionally, to seek to transform human rights principles and prohibitions on state practice into new criminal law principles. But this treaty-making exercise cannot become a law-making exercise. The treaty must reflect what is currently international criminal law, not what we hope or even confidently predict may one day become criminal law.[2]

The preceding quotes both represent statements by US officials concerning the role of international law and its development or, rather, continuity. The first was made by Justice Robert H. Jackson, chief prosecutor of the United States, in his opening remarks for the Nuremberg Trials in 1945; the second by David Scheffer, US Ambassador at Large for War Crimes issues at that time, with reference to the emerging International Criminal Court (ICC). The difference between the two positions seems to be dramatic at first glance: Jackson envisages international law as a highly dynamic legal field, the development of which is mainly driven by states and their governments. Scheffer, on the contrary, stresses the continuity of international law: international treaties ought to reflect custom but should not create new law.

The gap between these perspectives, however, does not derive from any major change in the political and legal culture in the United States that might have occurred in the second half of the twentieth century. Rather, it derives from the difference between the institutions referred to, namely the Nuremberg Trials and the ICC. The former represented a trial established by the Allies after the defeat of Germany in 1945. It was created to hold to account those individuals who committed major war crimes during World War II. As such, the initiators of the Nuremberg Trial fully controlled the institution they established, thus creating a tribunal based on an asymmetry: those who imposed the trial – the allied states in World War II – at the same time provided the judges, but made sure that their own citizens would not be prosecuted by the tribunal.[3]

The ICC marks a more ambitious project with regard to the enforcement of international criminal law. The independence of the prosecutor and the Court as such – both from the influences and interests of state parties and from international organisations such as the UN Security Council – was one of the major aims of its sponsors (Broomhall, 2003). Although the ICC is an institution that has been created by states and ultimately relies on state support for the enforcement of international criminal law,[4] it restricts state power and sovereignty prerogatives to a certain extent. The Rome Statute of the ICC stipulates that the Court does not replace domestic jurisdiction with regard to genocide, war crimes and crimes against humanity, but rather complements it. Cases are admissible to the ICC only if a state 'is unwilling or unable genuinely to carry out the investigation or prosecution'.[5] Nonetheless, it is the ICC chief prosecutor who decides if a state fulfilled the juridical requirements of legal prosecution when grave breaches of international criminal law occur. Moreover, the prosecutor can initiate investigations without the prior consent of the state parties or of the UN Security Council. In short, the ICC represents an unprecedented institution in the sense that it entails an 'intrusion of international criminal law into the otherwise sacrosanct domain of sovereignty' (Broomhall, 2003: 3). It was exactly this degree of independence of the ICC that gave rise to heated debates during the process of its establishment and eventually caused the US to withdraw from the Court.

During the negotiations at the UN Diplomatic Conference of Plenipotentiaries in Rome (DipCon) in 1998, several issues were contested among the participants: first, the definition of crimes within the ICC's jurisdiction; second, the role and powers of the prosecutor and third, the extent of the Court's jurisdiction (Economides, 2001; Broomhall, 2003). Each of these contested issues touches upon the question of the role and the independence of the ICC *vis-à-vis* states on the one hand and the UN Security Council on the other. The US favoured a statute that would strengthen the role of the UN Security Council and the state parties, thereby limiting the independence of the prosecutor. The Like-Minded Group (LMG), to which most EU member states belonged,[6] on the other hand, endorsed a largely independent Court that would be able to prosecute the defined crimes without relying upon the prior consent of state parties or the UN Security Council (Broomhall, 2003). The Rome Statute, adopted on the 17 July 1998, represents to a certain extent a compromise between these differing standpoints (B. Brown, 2002).

Even though the Rome Statute aimed at accommodating US reservations about the ICC while at the same time preserving the independence of the Court, the US eventually voted against it. It mainly expressed concerns about the lack of due process structures in the design of the ICC and about the possibility of prosecution of US military personnel involved in military missions abroad

(Fehl, 2004; B. Brown, 2002; Weller, 2002). Both the Clinton and the Bush administrations made various efforts to exempt US citizens from the ICC's jurisdiction, although the Bush government took a more openly hostile stance towards the Court (Broomhall, 2003; Weller, 2002). In 2001 the US withdrew from the Preparatory Commission (PrepCom), which was set up after the DipCon and charged with bringing the Court into operation, and 'unsigned' the Rome Statute in May 2002, after the number of ratifications of the Rome Statute reached 60 – the number that was necessary for the Statute in order to come into force.[7] In addition, in 2002 the US Congress adopted the American Servicemembers' Protection Act (ASPA) that prohibits US cooperation with the ICC. Moreover, it links the provision of US military aid to third states to the conclusion of Bilateral Immunity Agreements (BIAs), which rule out the extradition of US citizens to the ICC. These measures have been tightened by the adoption of the 2004 'Nethercutt Amendment' that links provisions from the US Economic Support Fund (ESF) to the conclusion of BIAs.[8]

Why did the US so fiercely oppose the ICC, thereby isolating itself from the rest of the OECD countries and making itself a target of polemic criticism, given the improbability of a prosecution of US citizens by the ICC? And why was it ultimately unsuccessful in its efforts to shape the Court according to its own preferences?

The realist explanation for the US attitude towards the ICC is as straight-forward as it is convincing: hegemonic powers try to use international legal institutions to their own ends, which are – or at least should be – largely dic-tated by their national interests. They use international law as an instrument to increase their power, but they do not bind themselves through international law in cases where this would entail a restriction of their power (Scott, 2004). With regard to the ICC, this line of reasoning is reflected in the oft-repeated argument that the US plays an exceptional role as a safeguard of global order and security and therefore would be particularly vulnerable to prosecutions of its military personnel.[9]

The liberal institutionalist explanation is similar to the realist argument, except that it takes into account that under certain circumstances international cooperation might entail joint gains. In the case of the ICC these joint gains consist in pursuing the public good of international criminal justice and of low-ering the transaction costs incurred in a system of ad hoc tribunals (such as the International Criminal Tribunal for Yugoslavia (ICTY) and the International Criminal Tribunal for Rwanda (ICTR)) (cf. Fehl, 2004). However, liberal insti-tutionalists argue that for major powers, sovereignty costs – the disadvantages that political actors have to bear by trading off parts of their sovereignty for a joint gain – are always higher than for less powerful states (Abbott and Snidal, 2000: 448). This would explain US opposition to the Court. In sum, both realist and liberal institutionalist theories hold that the US did not join the ICC because it does not correspond with their national interest as a major power.

However, these rationalist explanations have difficulty explaining why the US was not more successful in influencing the institutional design of the ICC. Both realists and liberal institutionalists predict that the institutional design of international courts and tribunals will reflect the interests of powerful states (Rudolph, 2001). In particular, this should be the case when powerful states are expected to contribute substantially more to the institution in question than other states. This clearly applied to the US and the ICC, not only with respect to financial contributions, but, more importantly, in terms of the capacity to apprehend suspects and to induce third states to cooperate with the Court. According to Korenemos *et al.* (2001: 792), lesser states will grant great powers a greater degree of control over an institution so as to ensure their participation and the vital assets and capabilities they are expected to contribute. In the case of the ICC Statute, this did not happen – the LMG and other states pushed for a vote on a Statute that only partly accommodated US concerns although the US threatened to vote against it. The potential costs of this move were obvious to many diplomats at the Rome Conference: 'We desperately, desperately, desperately want the U.S. on board. We are not sure the Court will even be workable without the U.S.', said the head of the German delegation, Hans-Peter Kaul, commenting on the final efforts in Rome to persuade the US to support the ICC Statute (quoted in Weschler, 2000: 104).

According to E. H. Carr, '[p]olitics and law are indissolubly intertwined' (1964: 165). Far from reflecting moral standards, he concluded, the law 'cannot be understood independently of [...] the political interests which it serves' (ibid: 165). While the transatlantic conflict over the ICC confirms the first of Carr's conclusions (cf. Moghalu, 2008: 126ff.), it defies the second. International law is not a mere instrument of power politics, though it is a site for power struggles. International law is often perceived as a weak legal area because it is not backed up by a central authority and largely lacks routine mechanisms of enforcement (Morgenthau, 1973: 295f.; cf. Bull, 1995: 129ff.). Compliance and enforcement are, however, but one way in which international law affects international relations. Another way in which international law impacts upon international politics is via its constitutive quality. It provides a basic order of international relations in the sense that it constitutes their basic units as well as the relations between them (cf. Reus-Smit, 2004; Finnemore and Toope, 2001: 745). The institution of sovereignty, for instance, defines statehood and at the same time provides a code of conduct among states, that is, non-intervention.[10] International law and its central concepts thus provide a structure that enables political actors to communicate about international politics. At the same time, international legal concepts are not unambiguous. They are to a certain extent open to interpretation and redefinition. In short, they are 'contested concepts' (Connolly, 1983; cf. Gallie, 1956).

This book aims to understand the US failure to impose its political preferences on the institutional design of the ICC and the subsequent transatlantic debate over the Court by exploring the discursive dynamic of this conflict.

From this perspective, the official statements and explanations of diplomats and negotiators concerning the ICC become the main focus of research, since they are not mere cloaks for power-political objectives – as realists would have it – or signals of actors' intents under conditions of scarce information – as liberal institutionalists posit. Rather, they are the main site of political power struggles. In fact, the extent to which political actors referred to international norms when justifying their political positions on the ICC is striking. Norms are defined and bound together in complex structures of meaning. By referring to them, political actors become entangled in these structures. Analysing the transatlantic conflict over the ICC from this perspective does not require giving up the concept of actors pursuing certain goals strategically. However, it does require acknowledging that they do so in a discursive space guided by certain intersubjectively shared rules that constitutes actors' identities and interests in the first place. It also implies a shift in the notion of *power*: whilst realists and liberal-institutionalists tend to perceive power as something that is at the disposal of actors, this study focuses on a form of power that is incorporated in structures rather than being tied to agents and that has an impact through 'empowering' or 'disempowering' them (Guzzini, 1993: 472; cf. also Lukes, 2005; Barnett and Duvall, 2005).

The aim of this book is to show that the dynamic of the transatlantic debate over the ICC exceeded the boundaries of a conflict based on material power interests. It developed into a debate about the normative foundations of the international order. The discursive level of the conflict had a decisive impact on the conflict outcome: the inconsistent use of shared norms of the international society, it will be argued, severely undermined US credibility in the eyes of its negotiation counterparts and thus weakened its negotiation position. The normative integration of the international society of states is arguably low, but there are some basic norms to draw upon. In the case of the transatlantic conflict over the ICC the norms of sovereignty and human rights were the most relevant. The ICC is one of the most ambitious projects within the framework of the contemporary international human rights regime. It is designed to adjudicate on a limited though fundamental range of human rights violations; namely genocide, crimes against humanity and war crimes.[11] At the same time, the establishment of the ICC touches upon the question of state sovereignty, since it affects the relationship between states and their citizens with respect to the prosecution of certain offences. The transatlantic conflict over the ICC evolved around these two norms, sovereignty and human rights. Yet it was not a clash between the two norms that gave rise to the conflict. Rather, it arose from different interpretations of their mutual relationship expressed in different discourses all of which integrated both sovereignty and human rights in a specific way.

Both sovereignty and human rights are core norms of the international society. Hedley Bull's famous concept of the international society as an 'anarchical society' (1995) implies the importance of such norms: as a society amongst states, the international society lacks the concentration of power and authority in the form of a government that could enforce order. Hence shared norms are the only available fundament for its emergence and persistence. The relationship of sovereignty and human rights, however, is often viewed as a strained one: sovereignty is regarded as a principle that gives states exclusive power over their own territory and population, whereas human rights are primarily individual in nature. Moreover, human rights are claimed to be universal, thereby transcending state borders. This constellation has led some to believe that sovereignty and human rights are inherently conflicting principles.[12] Others, by contrast, try to overcome the dichotomy between the two norms by arguing that they are closely related to each other. Their basic argument is that in recent decades, the recognition of a state's sovereignty has been made increasingly dependent on its adherence to human rights provisions and that this development should be welcomed (Wheeler, 2000; Armstrong, 1999; Barkin, 1998; Vincent, 1986). At the same time, they argue that human rights *historically* developed into the prevailing principle and that sovereignty acquires merely derivative status (Reus-Smit, 2001).[13]

The theoretical debate about the relationship between sovereignty and human rights is a useful starting point. Yet the aim of the analysis is to investigate the configuration of the two concepts empirically – to analyse how political actors construct the relationship between human rights and sovereignty in political statements and debates. This focus can be described as a 'practice as theory' approach, and as a reversal of the paradigm of critical theorising in International Relations (IR) that analyses 'theory as practice'. 'Theory as practice' characterises the paradigmatic challenge of first-generation critical scholarship in IR emerging in the early 1990s. It was based on the assumption that the theoretical concepts of orthodox IR scholarship – the state, sovereignty, security, anarchy, etc. – were not neutral categories used to analyse international politics in an 'objective' way. Rather, they structure our knowledge and are thereby constitutive of international relations as we perceive them. This first generation of critical scholarship explored 'International Relations as a discursive process, a process by which identities are formed, meaning is given, and status and privilege are accorded – a process of knowledge *as* power'. (George, 1994: 216). The 'practice as theory' approach pursued in this book follows the impetus of second generation critical theory to push the boundaries from 'intra-disciplinary critique to substantive analysis' (Price and Reus-Smit, 1998: 283). It is built on a critical reading of the theoretical debate over sovereignty and human rights (Chapter 2), but subsequently focuses on the empirical analysis of how these concepts impact upon political interactions (Chapters 3–6). The objective of this empirical analysis is not only to provide an explanation of the transatlantic conflict over the ICC, but also to feed back into our understanding of core concepts of the discipline such as statehood, sovereignty and anarchy.

The book contends that on the level of political communication, the perception of sovereignty and human rights as mutually exclusive is not viable.

Even the most confident sovereigntists[14] do not deny the relevance of human rights; they merely prefer to enforce human rights in a particular setting, that is, within the borders of sovereign states. Thus, in order to analyse political debates related to the ICC and the different concepts of order that are expressed in them in a fruitful way, it is necessary to overcome the simple dichotomy of sovereignty and human rights as it is still present in large parts of the theoretical conceptualisation of the problem. The aim is to show that the transatlantic debate about the ICC does not take the form of a conflict between adherents of competing norms – advocates of sovereignty on the one hand and proponents of human rights on the other. Rather, the debate evolved from competing concepts about the configuration of sovereignty and human rights. As mentioned above, sovereignty and human rights are 'contested concepts', the meaning of which emanates from a typical ambivalence that each concept incorporates respectively. The combination of both ambivalences in turn opens up room for different interpretations of the configuration of sovereignty and human rights.

The following chapters will provide evidence that there are four basic options for the integration of sovereignty and human rights: first, the legalistic position; second, the interventionist perspective; third, the sovereigntist point of view and fourth, the progressivist attitude. Legalism holds that human rights should be institutionalised and enforced in the framework of international or, rather, supra-state regimes to which all states have to submit equally. Interventionism endorses the view that powerful states are supposed to employ their capabilities in order to enforce human rights on a global scale. In this view, state sovereignty becomes conditional upon a state's compliance with human rights standards. Sovereigntism is based on the conviction that the sovereign state rather than supra-state institutions is the optimal framework for the implementation of human rights. Progressivists consider the delegation of the enforcement of human rights to supra-state bodies inappropriate. According to progressivism, supra-state bodies nevertheless play a role, even though their relevance does not emanate from their competences to implement human rights, but rather from the discriminatory function of access to and membership in them: a state's domestic human rights record should be decisive for its ability to participate in supra-state organisations.

The discursive dynamic that developed during the negotiation process at the DipCon in Rome and in the subsequent period of the establishment of the Court was such that the European states – considered with reference to the UK, France and Germany – mainly pursued the legalistic discourse. This discourse became hegemonic over time. The US, by contrast, was firmly opposed to this discourse and the institutional design of the ICC that it envisaged, but it faced huge difficulties in challenging the hegemonic position of legalism. US opposition to the Court was based on a combination and variation of the interventionist and the sovereigntist discourses, whereas the progressivist discourse played only a marginal role in the debates about the ICC. The fact that the US drew upon two different – and at their core incompatible – discourses decisively weakened its negotiation position. Many members of the LMG perceived the US position on the ICC as inconsistent (B. Brown, 1999: 861f.). Consistency is one of the main requirements for an actor's perceived credibility in negotiations and discursive interactions more broadly. Inconsistency – both between arguments and actions and between different arguments at different times – diminishes an actor's credibility in the eyes of its negotiation counterparts and other observers: 'actors that … are perceived to appeal to contradictory ideas to persuade a diffuse audience will lose credibility' (Schimmelfennig, 2003: 221; 2000: 65). Actors are likely to lose the discursive battle if they are perceived as violating the rules of the rhetorical game (cf. Krebs and Jackson, 2007). They will be regarded as using community norms cynically.[15]

The US simultaneous use of interventionist and sovereigntist arguments and the resulting impression of inconsistency of the US position, it will be argued, helped the legalistic discourse to acquire a hegemonic position. It is plausible to assume that the rather consistent use of legalistic arguments[16] made the Europeans appear as more reliable and ultimately more credible negotiation partners. This, it will be argued, indicates how the material balance of power between actors can be transformed once a conflict takes place in a discursive arena. Although the US was in a hegemonic position in terms of material power, it could not impose its preferences on the institutional design of the ICC. It also demonstrates that as contested concepts, norms do not have a straightforward impact on state behaviour. Rather, the contestation about their meaning and their relation opens up a space for political interaction, which is governed by particular rules. In order to prevail, actors have to play by these rules.

The book is divided into seven chapters. The following chapter discusses theoretical approaches to sovereignty and human rights and their mutual relationship. The aim is to overcome their major shortcoming, that is, the hierarchical dichotomy between sovereignty and human rights. It will be argued that both sovereignty and human rights are contested concepts. The contestation of their meaning emerges from the typical ambivalences incorporated in each concept. By combining these ambivalences, a discursive formation opens up that consists of four competing discourses, each of which claims to constitute the same object, i.e. the configuration of sovereignty and human rights. The second chapter also introduces core theoretical concepts such as discourse, discursive power and hegemony. In addition, it includes a discussion of the methodological approach.

The four subsequent chapters are devoted to the reconstruction and analysis of the four different discourses mentioned above, respectively, legalism, sovereigntism, interventionism and progressivism. Chapters 3–6 follow a similar structure: each chapter starts with an analysis of the basic narrative of the discourse in question, then moves on to the ontological features of the discourse and finally summarises the configuration of sovereignty and human rights that lies at the heart of each discourse.

The third chapter covers the legalistic discourse, which, as mentioned above, achieved a hegemonic position in the course of the debate about the ICC. The legalistic discourse draws upon the Enlightenment tradition and adopts its emphasis on progress understood as rationalisation, legalisation and the professionalisation of politics. According to legalists, the ultimate *telos* of progress in international relations consists of a just and peaceful international order that is based upon international law. Moreover, proponents of legalism hold that such an international order has to be symmetrical in the sense that all states are considered as equal regardless of their actual size and power. A specific feature of the legalistic discourse is the fact that it comprises two different strands. The first perceives the international society of states as the most vital point of reference for human rights, whereas the second puts the world society of individuals to the fore. This differentiation also affects the interpretation of sovereignty within the framework of the legalistic discourse.

The fourth chapter is devoted to the interventionist discourse. Though interventionists are aware of the relevance of international law and human rights, they oppose the legalistic idea that human rights are best enforced by professional legal bodies such as the ICC. Instead they argue that the implementation of human rights on a global scale should be left to powerful states, to which they attribute the role of *vigilantes*. *Vigilantes* are actors that enforce legal provisions on behalf of the international society, thereby substituting themselves for the central authority that the international society is lacking. Interventionists hold that the ICC in its eventual shape represents an impediment to the enforcement of human rights on a global scale rather than facilitating this task, since the Rome Statute does not reflect the exceptional role of great powers. According to the interventionist discourse, great powers will be more reluctant to deploy their troops abroad after the establishment of the ICC, as they would assume the risk of politicised prosecutions against their service members (and even policy-makers).

The fifth chapter addresses the sovereigntist discourse. Sovereigntism bears similarities to the legalistic discourse in as much as it equates order with the rule of law. Yet according to sovereigntists, legal institutions have to be embedded in constitutional structures, which the international society of states is largely lacking. For this reason, sovereigntists consider the domestic level of states as the only viable and legitimate venue for the enforcement of human rights. They emphasise that courts are only able to guarantee due process if they are incorporated into the constitutional structures and democratic checks and balances within a state. For sovereigntists, international legal institutions do not refer to the international society of states as a collective. Rather, they rest upon the consent of single states. Viewed from this perspective, advocates of sovereigntism also criticise the universal aspirations of the ICC, as it claims to have jurisdiction over citizens of non-party states.

The progressivist discourse (Chapter 6), represents the most difficult case in the framework of the analysis. It played only a marginal role in the context of the debates about the ICC. Whilst both interventionists and sovereigntists did not oppose the idea of an international criminal court as such and mainly challenged the institutional design of the Court as envisaged by legalists, progressivists questioned the usefulness of the ICC *per se*. According to them, we face a trade-off between the prosecution of offences against international humanitarian and human rights law on the one hand and the demand for democratisation on the other: if authoritarian leaders assume that they will face trial for their crimes, they will try to remain in power for as long as possible and even risk the continuation of armed conflict in order to evade prosecution. Yet due to the fact that progressivist voices were rare within the debate about the ICC it was difficult to find appropriate empirical evidence about the basic features of the progressivist discourse from the initial data set. Additional data collected from debates about the relevance of international organisations with respect to the domestic democratisation of states complements the data set (Chapter 6 includes a detailed discussion of the collection of additional data). Progressivists emphasise the framework of domestic politics as the appropriate venue for the enforcement of human rights. At the same time, they consider the international level as crucial for human rights issues. However, they perceive international society as an 'invitation-only club' access to which should depend on the domestic human rights record of states. Moreover, progressivists draw upon the hypothesis of 'democratic peace', that is, the idea that democracies do not fight each other. In short, for advocates of progressivism, international order and peace are mainly derivative of the domestic structure of states.

The conclusion summarises the findings and discusses them with reference to several questions: first, what conclusions can we draw from the US stance on the ICC? And second, how can we explain the fact that the UK and France shifted their positions on the Court in 1997 and 1998, respectively? Moreover, the conclusion will discuss what consequences emerge from the fact that different actors in international relations have different conceptions of international order and the role that sovereignty and human rights are supposed to play within that order? In short: how does this affect the concept of international society?

As a caveat before moving on to the next chapter, it should be explained why the book focuses on the *transatlantic* debate over the ICC. Arguably, the establishment of the ICC was accompanied by international negotiations in which almost all states participated. The LMG consisted of far more states than the EU member states. It is not the intention of the book to belittle the efforts of non-European LMG states and of NGOs that supported their position. Moreover, the US is not the only state to oppose the institutional design of the ICC. China, India and a number of Middle Eastern states voiced equally strong concerns and have not ratified the ICC statute, though for different reasons than the US (cf. McGoldrick, 2004: 437ff.; Roach 2005). Yet the transatlantic conflict over the ICC developed into the most visible debate concerning the

Court. The topic of the ICC became a preferred venue for the EU's construction of its external identity and its demarcation against the US (cf. Scheipers and Sicurelli, 2007). Most importantly, the transatlantic debate over the ICC is a puzzling case: while the 'West' is usually seen as a region with a shared normative foundation, underpinned by joint institutions like NATO and the OECD, the case of the ICC illustrates that even under these circumstances, norm contestation remains possible.

Notes

1   Justice Robert H. Jackson: Opening Statement for the Prosecution. Second Day, Wednesday, 11/21/1945, Part 04, in: *Trial of the Major War Criminals before the International Military Tribunal. Volume II. Proceedings: 11/14/1945–11/30/1945.* Nuremberg: IMT, 1947. pp. 98–102.
2   David J. Scheffer, 'U.S. policy and the proposed Permanent International Criminal Court. Speech at Carter Center', Atlanta, GA (13 November 1997).
3   This asymmetric situation gave rise to the charge of 'victor's justice' against the Nuremberg Trials and its sponsors. Cf. Economides (2001: 113).
4   It should be noted that non-governmental organisations (NGOs) also played an important role during the institutionalisation process of the ICC. See also Chapter 3 on the influence of NGOs on the creation of the ICC.
5   Rome Statute of the International Criminal Court, Art. 17 (a); U.N. Doc. A/CONF.183/9.
6   The UK and France were initially reluctant towards an independent ICC, but eventually came to support the LMG, so that a widely shared consensus in favour of a strong and independent Court emerged among the European countries (Fehl, 2004).
7   President Clinton had signed the Rome Statute in the very last minute on 31 December 2000, although it was clear that the Statute would not gain the support of the US Congress and thus would not be ratified in the near future (Weller, 2002).
8   In November 2006, President Bush issued a waiver for the ESF restrictions for some Latin American and African countries, since the effects of both the ASPA and the Nethercutt Amendment were perceived as detrimental to US national interest. In addition, Congress adopted the 'John Warner National Defense Authorization Act for Fiscal Year 2007', according to which parts of the restrictions included in the ASPA will be lifted for all states. Cf. Mark Mazzetti, 'U.S. Cuts in Africa Aid Said to Hurt War on Terror', *New York Times* (23 July 2006).
9   This explanation is in line with Martti Koskenniemi's assessment of the US profession of international lawyers after 1960. According to Koskenniemi (2002: 474ff.), they overwhelmingly endorsed Carl Schmitt's and Hans Morgenthau's perspective on international law, i.e. a deformalised notion of international law, in which the law is supposed to serve and to justify the ends of political decision-makers. Peter Maguire uses the term 'strategic legalism' (2000: 9).
10 Even if the rule of non-intervention is not always respected, intervention is usually justified as an exceptional case, which in turn reaffirms the rule of non-

intervention (Weber, 1995).

11   War crimes historically belong to the law of armed conflict (the 1899–1907 Hague Conventions I-IV, the 1949 Geneva Conventions I-IV and the 1977 Additional Protocols I and II). Since 1945, however, the law of armed conflict has been increasingly influenced by human rights values (Cassese, 2005: 404).

12   See, among others, Lyons and Mayall (2003), Jacobson (2001), Krasner (1999) and Henkin (1995). This view is also prominent in the English School approach to the configuration of sovereignty and human rights, at least as far as the pluralist and the world society strand of the English School are concerned. For the pluralist perspective, see Jackson (2000, Mayall (2000) and Bull (1995). For the world society perspective, see, for instance, Linklater (1998).

13   An exception to this is Mervyn Frost, who argues that sovereignty and human rights are equally constitutional, so that none prevails over the other (1996).

14   Regarding the notion of 'sovereigntism', see Spiro (2000).

15   Although 'rhetorical' and 'discursive' approaches differ concerning their conception of actor rationality, the rule of consistency seems to travel well between the two approaches. See also the Conclusion.

16   The major challenge to this consistency was the UK's and France's initial reluctance to endorse legalistic positions. Yet observers reported that at the Rome Conference 'Europe, minus France, was united within the Like-Minded Group … France joined with it voting for the statute after obtaining a final concession on the scope of the court's jurisdiction' (Benedetti and Washburn, 1999: 31).

2 The configuration of sovereignty and human rights

The transatlantic debate over the ICC is located at the interface of sovereignty and human rights. Regarding the latter, the ICC mainly targets political and civil rights, but leaves aside questions of economic, social and cultural rights.[1] Additionally, in the context of political and civil rights, the provisions included in the Rome Statute target the most 'urgent rights' (Rawls, 1999: 79): the prohibition of genocide, of crimes against humanity (such as the persecution and displacement of ethnic or political groups, disappearances and arbitrary detentions, torture and rape) and of war crimes (aimed at the protection of civilians in armed conflicts and at the proper treatment of combatants and prisoners of war).

Despite the limited range of rights that the ICC Statute addresses, the Court arguably represents the most ambitious project concerning the enforcement of human rights in recent years, as it aspires to a global reach and includes enforcement mechanisms. At the same time, the establishment of the ICC touches upon the question of state sovereignty, since it affects the relation of states to their citizens with respect to the prosecution of offences against international criminal law (Broomhall, 2003; Economides, 2001; Fehl, 2004).[2] Whilst there were some attempts to prosecute genocide and crimes against humanity on the basis of universal jurisdiction[3] before the entry into force of the ICC Statute in 2002, these were not widespread and rather reluctant. Investigations often proved to be too complex and costly, and sometimes politically inopportune (Broomhall, 2003: 118ff.; Moghalu, 2008: 90ff.). Temporary international criminal tribunals such as the international tribunals in Nuremberg and Tokyo after World War II and, more recently, the ICTY and ICTR have been more common, but they were spatially and temporally limited. In sum, before the establishment of the ICC, a large number of offences against international criminal law remained unpunished. Impunity for these crimes was the rule rather than the exception.

In contrast to the preceding attempts to prosecute genocide, crimes against humanity and war crimes, the ICC is a permanent international institution aiming at the regular enforcement of international justice with respect to the above-mentioned crimes. Its chief prosecutor is able to initiate investigations without prior state consent. Arguably, the complementarity principle[4] included in the ICC Statute gives priority to trials before domestic courts. However, these are under scrutiny by the ICC prosecutor, who can interfere if a state proves 'unable or unwilling' to properly exercise its criminal jurisdiction.[5] Hence, Marc Weller interprets the establishment of the ICC as an instance in which 'human rights and humanitarian law, in particular, had undermined state-centred thinking' (2002: 695). The ICC aspires to close the loopholes of impunity by compelling state parties to prosecute serious offences against international criminal law. Moreover, the establishment of the ICC has a great influence on domestic criminal law. As the principle of complementarity places a premium on prosecutions by national courts, state parties have to include elements of crime covered by the ICC Statute into their domestic criminal codes (Schabas, 2001: 19).

Large parts of the recent literature on human rights in international relations considers humanitarian intervention as the 'classic' case in which the configuration of sovereignty and human rights is at stake, as intervention directly contradicts the principle of non-intervention embodied in the notion of sovereignty (Wheeler, 2000). Yet the establishment of the ICC as an empirical case might provide different, if not deeper insights into the question of sovereignty and human rights for two reasons. First, the case of humanitarian intervention often captures instances of a broad international consensus, at least in cases of interventions that take place under a mandate of the UN Security Council. This often leads to overly optimistic and premature conclusions concerning the extent to which political actors agree upon the relevance of human rights on a global scale. Though scholars acknowledge that cases like the NATO intervention in Kosovo were indeed contested, the overall assessment is often that, at the beginning of the twenty-first century, we can observe a paradigm shift in international relations towards a world order that gives more significance to human rights and is more ready to enforce them through interventions than ever before (Wheeler, 2000; Bonacker and Brodocz, 2001). Yet this conclusion tends to obscure the extent to which issues of human rights and sovereignty are contested. In this respect, the ICC offers much more empirical evidence for ongoing contestation and debate. Secondly, the ICC case is more encompassing than cases of humanitarian intervention. It includes the establishment of a permanent legal institution for the enforcement of human rights, but the debates about the ICC also touched upon the question of humanitarian intervention: in the course of the Rome Statute's entry into force and while the Court took up its work, the US demanded an exemption from the Court's jurisdiction and made its support for the UN peacekeeping mission in Bosnia-Herzegovina dependent on this. Consequently, the debates about the ICC touched upon both the issue of humanitarian intervention and the relationship of states to international institutions, or rather, the transfer of sovereignty to the latter.

Sovereignty and human rights in International Relations theory

The English School approach to the normative foundations of international society provides a solid starting point for analysing the configuration of sovereignty and human rights. The following overview is not confined to the English School perspective, though it is structured according to the three traditions of *pluralism*, *world society* and *solidarism*, since virtually all theoretical contributions on the topic of sovereignty and human rights can be classified along their lines.

The debate about sovereignty and human rights is one of the core issues in English School theory. It is a debate about the foundations of international society (Buzan, 2004). Regarding the question of *which norms* form the fundament of international society and *how thick* the normative fundament of international society is, English School theory encompasses a range of quite varied answers. *Pluralists* privilege sovereignty as the most basic norm of international society. Sovereignty, they argue, allows for a maximum degree of difference while at the same time ensuring a more or less peaceful coexistence among states (Jackson, 2000; Mayall, 2000; Bull, 1995; cf. Buzan, 2004).[6] Due to the lack of a global consensus about the meaning of human rights efforts to implement human rights globally could undermine international order. Human rights are too 'thick', i.e. too substantial and advanced a norm to ground a pluralist international society in them. Sovereignty, in contrast, is regarded as a 'thin' norm, the lowest common denominator of international society.

Scholars of *world society* acknowledge the tension between the international society based on state sovereignty on the one hand, and the world society of individuals who bear human rights on the other. World society is identified with the realm of human rights because the latter are interpreted as inherently universal and cosmopolitan values (Caney, 2006; Luban, 1980). Universality and cosmopolitanism, world society scholars argue, contradict the principle of sovereignty, which divides the world into particularistic entities – territorial states. However, rather than decrying calls for the global enforcement of human rights as undermining state sovereignty, proponents of world society hold that state sovereignty represents an impediment to the realisation of a more just world order (Jacobson, 2001; Linklater, 1998; Allott, 1990; cf. Buzan, 2004: 27ff.; Diez and Whitman, 2002: 48f.; Bull, 1995: 90). This perspective is echoed in accounts of the emergence of a 'global civil society' (Lipschutz, 1996) or a 'world culture' (Boli and Thomas, 1997). Civil society actors and transnational networks are considered as the bearers of a cosmopolitan awareness and universal norms.[7] Moreover, the organisational structure of transnational networks is interpreted as defying the traditional model of sovereign politics: whereas the sovereign state is characterised by the hierarchical organisation of political authority within a given territory, non-governmental organisations (NGOs) are coordinated through network structures and their activities often cut across state borders (Gordenker and Weiss, 1996; Clark,

1995; Rosenau, 1990).

Finally, *solidarists* try to overcome the dichotomy between international society and world society by arguing that both realms in fact invoke each other: shared normative orientations at the level of civil society underpin the existence of the international society of states. Conversely, the framework of order provided by the international society allows for a greater convergence on normative questions on a global scale (Reus-Smit, 2001, 1999; Armstrong, 1999; Barkin, 1998; Vincent, 1986; cf. Buzan, 2004: 30). The basic solidarist argument is that in recent decades, the recognition of a state's sovereignty has become increasingly conditional on its adherence to human rights norms and that this development should be welcomed. According to Nicholas Wheeler, the policy of humanitarian intervention that developed during the 1990s is in line with an essentially 'solidarist claim: states that massively violate human rights should forfeit their right to be treated as legitimate sovereigns, thereby morally entitling other states to use force to stop the oppression' (Wheeler, 2000: 12f.).

The transatlantic conflict over the ICC has been analysed through the lens of the English School conceptualisations of sovereignty and human rights. Jason Ralph shows how the US position on the ICC and the European reactions to it can be understood with reference to the concepts of pluralism, solidarism and world society (Ralph, 2007; 2005). He argues that the US opposes the ICC because it wants to uphold a pluralist international society in which states are the main actors, whereas the ICC is constitutive of a 'world society' that is to a certain extent independent from the society of states. While such an approach highlights the degree to which the transatlantic conflict over the ICC involved a clash between different visions of world order, it is at the same time prone to force English School theoretical positions on an empirical debate that took place outside of the realm of IR theory. The second danger of such a deductive approach is to project too much coherence onto the positions of the national actors involved in the transatlantic debate over the ICC, in particular the US. Several observers have pointed out that the US position on the ICC during and after the Rome negotiations seemed incoherent and derived from several sources. Broomhall, for instance, argues that 'objections from the conservative wing of the Congress typically express themselves in "sovereignty"-based arguments', whereas 'leading military and State Department decision-makers are concerned that the U.S. ability to project force abroad will be constrained by possible ICC investigations into the actions of U.S. personnel' (2003: 165f.). Ralph is aware of the two different strands within the US position, yet he holds that the second is of minor importance: 'The argument that the ICC prevented the United States form committing troops to UN missions was an excuse rather than a justification. … The United States is on stronger, although still contested ground when it argues that is has the *right* to decide which laws govern its citizens' (Ralph, 2007: 120f.; original emphasis). However, 'interest'-based arguments about the role of great powers reflect as much a particular vision of international order as sovereignty-based arguments, although a different one. Neglecting one of the argumentative strands not only constrains our understanding of the US position on the ICC, it also does not fully capture the dynamic of the transatlantic conflict over the Court.

Re-reading the sovereignty and human rights debate

The fact that both the pluralist and the world society perspective on sovereignty and human rights assume an antithetic relationship between the two principles is reminiscent of what Richard Ashley wrote about the tendency of IR literature to establish dichotomies in the form of 'an absolute difference' (1988: 257) between two principles, thereby obscuring the constructedness of these dichotomies. Thinking of international relations in terms of dichotomies provides for order and thus 'opposes the realm of reasoned understanding against a realm of anarchical, threatening Otherness' (George, 1994: 202).

A first step in questioning the fixed dichotomies incorporated into IR theory is to acknowledge that within the framework of dichotomies, the alleged absolute difference obscures the inherent relationship between both parts of the dichotomy. Even if sovereignty and human rights are depicted as antithetic principles, this establishes a certain nexus between the two concepts. Their meaning is derived from this opposition, which in turn creates an implicit relationship of mutual constitution between sovereignty and human rights. Cynthia Weber addresses this problem with respect to the relationship between sovereignty and intervention and shows that they operate as 'conceptual opposites' (1995: 21), with the meaning of one being fixed with reference to the other and vice versa. The same applies to sovereignty and human rights. Consequently, even if pluralists and world society scholars emphasise the 'absolute difference' between sovereignty and human rights, this dichotomy establishes a relationship of mutual constitution between the two concepts, though this is not made explicit in either theoretical perspective. Solidarism, by contrast, claims that sovereignty and human rights are mutually constitutive. Its explicit objective is to overcome the view that sovereignty and human rights form 'two separate regimes, that stand in a zero-sum relationship' (Reus-Smit, 2001: 519).

According to Ashley, a second typical feature of fixed dichotomies in IR theory is their hierarchical structure. Two concepts are not only depicted as antithetic, but the relationship between them is determined by the prevalence of one concept. The paradigmatic case that Ashley refers to is the juxtaposition of sovereignty and anarchy, which he regards as a dogmatic assumption of IR literature. He argues that 'the theoretical discourse of the anarchy problematique … turns on a simple and hierarchical opposition: a dichotomy of *sovereignty* versus *anarchy*, where the former term is privileged as a higher reality, a regulative ideal, and the latter term is understood only in a derivative and negative way, as a failure to live up to this ideal and as something that endangers this ideal' (1988: 230).

The same structure applies to the configuration of sovereignty and human rights as constituted by the theoretical approaches discussed above. Pluralists interpret sovereignty as the prevailing concept. However, from this perspective, it becomes evident that the world society paradigm and the solidarist paradigm are rather similar with respect to the question of prevalence. The world society perspective maintains that due to structural changes in world politics that took place during the second half of the twentieth century, sovereignty lost parts of its significance as a guiding principle in international relations, whereas human rights acquired greater relevance. Thus, the world society perspective clearly privileges human rights over sovereignty. Solidarists argue that at some point within the second half of the twentieth century, the sovereignty of a state became increasingly dependent on its adherence to human rights standards. That is, although solidarists generally start from the assumption that sovereignty and human rights are *mutually* constitutive, viewed from the perspective of historical developments, they hold that human rights nowadays represent the primary concept. In the given historical situation, sovereignty is attributed a merely derivative status. Hence the predominance that solidarists attach to human rights *vis-à-vis* sovereignty eventually brings them close to the world society approach.[8]

The difference between the pluralist approach on the one hand and the world society and solidarist approach on the other concerning the question of which concept prevails in the configuration of sovereignty and human rights is linked to the problem of which concept is assumed to have a fixed meaning. Pluralists evidently consider the meaning of sovereignty to be fixed, but hold that the meaning of human rights is contested and unstable – this is exactly why Bull rejects human rights as a normative fundament of international society (cf. Wheeler and Dunne, 1996). According to Bull, 'there is no agreement as to what human rights or in what hierarchy of priorities they should be arranged' (1995: 85). In contrast, his definition of sovereignty is rather clear-cut:

> The *starting point of international relations* is the existence of states, or independent political communities each of which possesses a government and asserts *sovereignty* in relation to a particular portion of the earth's surface and a particular segment of the human population. ... The sovereignty of states, both internal and external, may be said to exist both at a normative level and at a factual level. (Bull, 1995: 8; emphasis added)

World society scholars and solidarists, by contrast, regard the meaning of human rights as unproblematic, but argue that the concept of sovereignty is contested.[9] Consider, for instance, the representation of human rights as an apparently unproblematic and uncontested concept as it appears in Reus-Smit (quoting Vincent):

Human rights, John Vincent argues, are the rights that everyone has, and everyone equally, by virtue of their very humanity. In holding such rights, all humans are entitled to make claims against other individuals, national communities, and humanity as a whole for the respect and satisfaction of certain civil and political freedoms and social and economic needs. At times these rights have been grounded in reason, need, custom and contract, but *in all cases they have been seen as universal and inalienable*. (Reus-Smit, 2001: 521; emphasis added)

As regards sovereignty, on the other hand, Reus-Smit holds that 'sovereignty should be viewed as a dependent or secondary principle – a historically contingent prescription about the distribution of power and authority that needs to be grounded in more fundamental existential values' (2001: 528).

Adopting such hierarchical dichotomies seems problematic because they tend to obscure the complexity of either sovereignty or human rights by assuming that the meaning of either concept is fixed. In doing so, they restrict the scope of possible perspectives on political conflicts over sovereignty and human rights. In contrast, the core claim of this book is that both sovereignty and human rights are contested concepts. In short, the aim is to show that several options to link the two concepts exist.

Sovereignty and human rights as contested concepts

The notion of 'essentially contested concepts' was initially coined by W. B. Gallie (1956) and was subsequently further elaborated by William Connolly (1983). Connolly refers to the term 'contested concepts' as follows (quoting Gallie):

When the concept involved is *appraisive* in that the state of affairs it describes is a valued achievement, when the practice described is *internally complex* in that its characterization involves reference to several dimensions, and when the agreed and contested rules of application are relatively *open*, enabling parties to interpret even those shared rules differently as new and unforeseen situations arise, then the concept in question is an essentially contested concept. Such concepts essentially involve endless disputes about their proper uses on the part of their users. (Connolly, 1983: 10)

According to Connolly, contested concepts typically involve some kind of value judgment, that is, these concepts are never neutral. Definitional struggles necessarily involve a normative point of view. 'Normative point of view', in this context, does not only refer to moral reasoning in the narrow sense, but also to features such as purpose, interest or standard (*ibid.*). Relations and links between concepts and hierarchies among them are established with reference to this normative framework. Both the definition of concepts and the normative framework involved in them are institutionalised by means of convention. These conventions enable actors to communicate. They may be altered, but alterations of the conventions need justifications (*ibid.*). Connolly argues that contestations about the legitimate use of concepts are an intrinsic part of politics, as they provide the space for political interaction (*ibid.*).

According to Jens Bartelson, while the concept of sovereignty is 'essentially uncontested as the foundation of modern political discourse, it is essentially contested as to its meaning within the same discourse' (1995: 14; cf. Kratochwil, 1995). Arguably, human rights qualify as a contested concept as well, as they involve appraisive statements and are internally complex. In fact, the numerous debates about human rights – both in scientific and political contexts – should leave no doubt about their contestability.

Considering both sovereignty and human rights as contested concepts, however, is not to say that the meaning of both concepts is completely arbitrary. Rather, both concepts comprise a typical ambivalence. As will be elaborated below, in the case of sovereignty, the typical ambivalence is the tension between the aspects of symmetry and asymmetry incorporated in the concept, whereas the concept of human rights oscillates between a claim to their enforcement on the supra-state level on the one hand and the idea that the domestic framework of states represents the appropriate venue for their enforcement on the other. The ambivalences embodied by both concepts structure the field of contestation. Taken together, these two ambivalences open up the field for competing discourses, with each discourse integrating sovereignty and human rights in a different way.

Sovereignty: symmetry and asymmetry

IR scholarship over the past two decades has acknowledged the contested and ambivalent character of the concept of sovereignty as the basic principle of international order. Yet the content and the nature of its ambivalence have been depicted in different ways. Scholars have paid much attention to the dual nature of sovereignty as establishing the domestic realm of states and at the same time the realm of international relations, i.e. the *internal* and *external* dimensions of sovereignty (cf. Bull, 1995: 8; Hinsley, 1986: 158; Walker, 1993: 169ff.). It has been argued that sovereignty plays a constitutive role for both the modern state and the structure of international relations. In this vein, Anthony Giddens holds that the concept of sovereignty 'simultaneously provides an ordering principle for what is "internal" to states and what is "external" to them' (1985: 281). The principle of sovereignty establishes both the basic units of international relations – states – and the nature of the system itself, i.e. the terms of interaction between states as independent and self-governing actors (Ruggie, 1986; Kratochwil, 1986). Similarly, R.B.J. Walker contends that 'sovereignty is an expression of a politics that works both inside states and outside states, indeed as a principle that tells us why we must put up with a politics that is radically split between statist political communities and relations between such communities' (2000: 28). Hence, sovereignty fulfils a demarcating function and organises our knowledge of what qualifies as 'inside' and 'outside' (Bartelson, 1995; cf. also Ashley, 1988).

Apart from constituting the main units of the international order, sovereignty also prescribes a certain relationship between these units, in particular the claim to sovereign equality of all states. This claim aims at preventing the establishment of a superior power – a world government, thus making anarchy the defining feature of international relations. Anarchy, in this context, has to be distinguished from chaos: whereas the former allows for features of order in the form of common rules and institutions, but without a central authority, the latter marks the breakdown of order (cf. Holsti, 1996: 7). Moreover, the claim to sovereign equality of all states opens up the possibility of the emergence of international society, since a society not only relies upon common rules and institutions, but also upon a shared identity. Barry Buzan points out that the principle of sovereign equality provides for a basic degree of shared identity amongst the members of international society, as they thereby recognise each other as belonging to the same type of entity, i.e. sovereign states (1993: 345).

Benedict Kingsbury argues that the preoccupation with sovereign equality within the discipline of international law prevents scholars from explicitly addressing inequality in the international legal order (1998: 599). According to him, sovereignty and inequality are conceptual opposites that find themselves in a 'relationship of mutual containment' (ibid.: 602). Thus, he reaffirms the equation of sovereignty with sovereign equality. Gerry Simpson pushes this line of thought further by arguing that the concept of sovereignty *itself* has always provided for and sanctioned certain degrees of asymmetry within the international legal order, and continues to do so. According to him, sovereignty entails three different aspects of equality, only one of which reflects a truly symmetrical order between states: 'formal equality', i.e. the idea that states are to be treated equally before international judicial bodies (2004: 42ff.). In contrast, 'legislative equality' and 'existential equality' are mere aspirations of the concept of sovereignty in which symmetry never prevailed empirically. 'Legislative equality' denotes the equal ability of states to influence decision-making processes in international bodies and the process of international law-making, be it via the development of customary law or via treaty-making (ibid: 48ff.). However, from the Congress of Vienna to the establishment of the UN Security Council, the international order was always characterised by 'legalised hegemony', i.e. by legally sanctioned privileges for great powers (ibid: 52). Finally, 'existential equality arises out of a recognition by the international community that an entity is entitled to sovereign statehood and that equality is the immediate product of fully recognised sovereignty' (ibid.: 53). As with legislative equality, this aspect of sovereignty empirically never provided for symmetry between states. Rather, there is an extensive tradition of thought that distinguishes between an inner circle of fully legitimate states and a periphery of so-called 'outlaw' or 'rogue states', thereby establishing an asymmetric structure. Peripheral states are not considered fully legitimate members of the international society, which can result in a suspension of the rule of non-intervention towards them or in their exclusion from international bodies.

Yet even if great powers enjoy a special status within the framework of 'legalised hegemony', they cannot stretch their asymmetrical privileges too far. Theoretically, Bull argues, as outstanding actors within the international order, great powers also have the greatest interest in maintaining the existing order: 'any international order must have its custodians and guarantors, whose stake in order will be greater than that of other states'[10] Viewed from this perspective, great powers are expected to act upon not only their single-minded 'raison d'état', but also upon the 'raison de système', to use Adam Watson's expression (Buzan, 1993: 346).

The raison de système, however, implies the enforcement and reaffirmation of the basic features of international order, the core principle of which is sovereignty. Hence, although the claim to sovereign equality of all states does not eliminate de facto power inequalities between states (cf. Camilleri and Falk, 1992: 33), it transforms them: great powers are expected to contribute to the reinforcement of the principle of the sovereignty. Therefore they cannot use their capabilities in an unrestricted way.[11] For this reason, great powers are to a certain extent bound by the 'fiction' of the sovereign equality of all states, for if they destroyed this fiction, they would undermine the fundament of international order as such (Badie, 2002: 93; Krisch, 2003a: 139f.). At the same time, the principle of sovereignty protects less powerful states against elimination (Buzan, 1993: 347). In fact, in the second half of the twentieth century, the claim to external sovereignty safeguarded the existence of so-called 'failed states' or 'quasi-states', as Jackson puts it (1990).

In sum, the concept of sovereignty oscillates between the claim to the sovereign equality of all states, i.e. a perfectly symmetrical international order, and legally formalised asymmetries, which grant privileges to great powers and exclude 'deviant' peripheral states from international society.

Human rights: enforcement on the supra-state level or within the domestic framework of states

The idea of the universality of human rights emerged from two traditions of thought: first, the tradition of natural law holds that human rights are universal. For this tradition, the claim to universality is grounded in the authority of God and his role as the creator of humankind. Second, the idea of the universality of human rights is rooted in the tradition of the Enlightenment. In contrast to the earlier natural law tradition, however, human rights are not grounded in the role of God as the creator of humankind, but rather in the universality of human reason. Jürgen Habermas's approach to human rights stands in this tradition. Habermas considers freedom rights and political participation rights as equally fundamental (1994). He claims that human rights and popular sovereignty are mutually constitutive, as codified law derives its legitimacy from the fact that all members of the political community have been involved in its codification. The polity is at the same time author and subject of the law. Whilst this account of human rights is well suited for the realm of the nation state, it encounters difficulties when it is applied to the global level, as the latter largely lacks the institutional structures necessary for democratic self-legislation. Habermas tries to solve this problem by pointing out that in the international realm; 'humanity or, rather, an alleged republic of citizens of the world' (ibid: 139; translation S. Sch.) could figure as a point of reference for the universal validity of human rights (cf. also Lohmann, 1999).

Communitarian thinkers like Alasdair MacIntyre radically take issue with this claim: MacIntyre rejects the idea of universal human rights by arguing that there is no universal rationality, but rather a variety of context-dependent rationalities (1985). He draws the conclusion that rights always refer to and acquire their validity from the particular and limited polities in which they emerged. Most theoretical approaches to human rights, however, refrain from such a radical relativism. They try to encompass both universality and particularity as central features of human rights. John Rawls, for instance, holds that only negative freedom rights, which he refers to as 'urgent rights' (1999: 79), are universal in reach and validity. Similarly, moderate communitarians and liberals like Michael Walzer (2000) and Michael Ignatieff (2003) suggest that universal validity only applies to freedom rights, but not to political participation rights. The latter are subject to realisation within the boundaries of particular political communities. Moreover, the global human rights regime, Ignatieff argues, should focus more on the prevention of the worst violations of human rights and less on debates about universality and relativism of rights (*ibid.*), thereby echoing Judith Shklar's demand to 'concentrate on damage control' (1998: 9).

Instead of dividing the content of human rights into universal and particularistic aspects, Thorsten Bonacker and André Brodocz (2001) argue that the tension between universality and particularity is an inherent and irresolvable feature of human rights. Drawing upon the work of Hannah Arendt (1986), they explain that human rights were initially linked to the particularity of states, which ensured their enforcement within their own borders (cf. also Frost, 1996; 2000). But since human rights were regarded as the ultimate foundation of the validity of domestic law as such, they already transcended the realm of the particular states and pointed towards universality – just to avoid the infinite regress concerning the question of the foundations of the validity of law. Bonacker and Brodocz hold that this ambiguity persists even if human rights nowadays are claimed to be detached from states and to reside in a global realm: the requirement of interpretation and institutionalisation within a particular political community will always counter the claim to universal validity.

Bonacker and Brodocz arguably have a point in holding that the attempt to perceive specific aspects of human rights as inherently universal, whilst regarding others as particular in nature, is doomed to fail for logical reasons: even if positive participation rights are considered to be realisable only in a particular context, this implies that every human being should be part of a particular political community in order to be able to enjoy these rights, i.e. it implies the universal right to citizenship. Yet the empirical investigation revealed that actors in political debates circumvent this paradox of human rights. They refer to the ambivalence of universality and particularity, but they translate it into less abstract categories. The most significant question with respect to human rights in political debates is to what kind of political community do they refer? On the one hand, human rights may be understood to refer to the entire humanity, i.e. to an imagined community of all human beings. According to this view, human rights reside in the global realm and should accordingly be enforced by supra-state institutions. On the other hand, human rights can be interpreted as evolving from concrete and limited polities, i.e. nation-states. This interpretation stresses the link between human rights, democratic self-government and constitutional structures and consequently regards the domestic level of states as the most appropriate venue for the institutionalisation of human rights.

The discursive formation of sovereignty and human rights

Sovereignty and human rights are not only contested concepts entailing specific ambivalences. As mentioned earlier, they are also mutually constitutive concepts, the meaning of which emerges from their reference to each other and is embedded in larger systems of signification to which I will refer as *discourses*. The combination of the ambivalences embodied in the dimension of sovereignty on the one hand and the dimension of human rights on the other opens up a four-field matrix encompassing four possible discourses. Each discourse constitutes the configuration of sovereignty and human rights in a specific way. These four competing discourses form the *discursive formation* of sovereignty and human rights. The scheme shown in Figure 2.1 visualises the discursive formation of sovereignty and human rights.

A discourse is a limited amount of texts and verbal utterances that are linked to each other by way of making reference to particular objects and by the rules according to which they constitute these objects (Fairclough, 1995a, b; Morrow, 1994). Discourses define '*subjects authorized to speak and to act*', '*knowledgeable practices* by these subjects towards the objects which the discourse defines' and, finally, objects of knowledge and action (Milliken, 1999: 229; original emphasis). In this sense, discourses are *productive* of the things they define. However, this is not to say that a reality external to discourses does not exist: '[o]bjects of knowledge might be said to exist independently of language, but when they enter in any meaningful way into human, social life, they enter not as name-

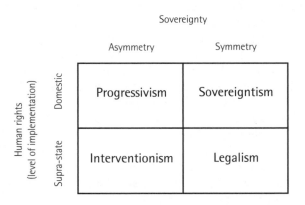

Figure 2.1 The discursive formation of sovereignty and human rights

and shapeless objectivity, but as "something": they are necessarily categorized and conceptualized' (Wæver, 2004: 198).

The poststructuralist perspective on discourses can be demarcated against two other approaches. First, it differs from *cognitive approaches* insofar as discourses are not understood as revealing something about the intentions or mental states of actors. Actors are able to deploy discourses strategically; however, they are not able to dispose of discursive means freely. Rather, they become entangled in the already-existing structures of meaning (Wæver, 2004; Diez, 1999). Secondly, it differs from a *historical sociological* perspective, as 'the notion of *context* drops out as a category explaining the meaning of what has been said and done with words' (Bartelson, 1995: 70; emphasis added).[12] Reducing the meaning of statements to the context in which they occur would imply that the 'context' is available as a non-discursive entity that is meaningful in itself. Moreover, such a reduction would mean that – at least in a specific context – the meaning of statements is stable and uncontested. The perspective of poststructuralism, by contrast, holds that the ultimate closure of meaning is impossible. Discourses are dynamic in that the meaning of statements is only partially and temporarily fixed (Laclau and Zac, 1994). Discourses are a structure of meaning, but a very unstable one. Having rejected context as a possible source of meaning, Bartelson concludes that 'discourse is autonomous and has primacy, but is not itself foundational; its autonomy and primacy does not reside in any magical or metaphysical ability to produce physical reality, but in its ability to organize knowledge systematically, so that some things become intelligible, and others not' (1995: 71). This is not to say that discourses are hermetically sealed against non-discursive influences, however; the latter only have an impact if they are mediated by discursive means (Diez, 1999).

By defining legitimate ways of referring to certain objects and by excluding others (options of reference as well as objects), discourses are vested with power – definitional power (*ibid.*). This definitional power of discourses proves effective by way of disciplining actors' knowledge and assessment of themselves and their environment. Discourses determine legitimate ways of referring to empirical phenomena and thus provide a 'regime of truth' (Milliken, 1999: 229). Arguably, this structural form of power is not existent apart from via human agency. But unlike material power resources, it is not at the deliberate disposal of actors; rather, it 'empowers' or 'disempowers' actors by way of defining roles and identities they might perform (Guzzini, 1993: 472).

In the case of contested concepts, this definitional power does not remain unchallenged in as much as different discourses claim to constitute the same object. The meaning of the notion 'democracy', for instance, differs when it occurs in the discourse of liberalism from its usage in the discourse of republicanism. A group of discourses that refer to allegedly identical objects, but constitute these according to different rules, is a discursive formation (Diez, 1999: 45). The relationship between different discourses belonging to such a formation is twofold: on the one hand, they compete with each other and contradict each other by way of the different rules according to which they constitute their objects. On the other, since the fixation of meaning is always only partial and unstable, different discourses belonging to one discursive formation may have interfaces and even overlapping sections. According to Roxanne Doty, the 'exterior limits [of a discourse] are constituted by other discourses that are themselves also open, inherently unstable, and always in the process of being articulated. This understanding of discourse implies an overlapping quality to different discourses' (1996: 6).

The four-field matrix displayed in Table 2.1 encompasses the discursive formation of sovereignty and human rights. The four fields labelled 'progressivism', 'sovereigntism', 'interventionism' and 'legalism' represent the four available discourses within this discursive formation. The analysis of the empirical data indicated that these four options exhaust the discursive formation of human rights and sovereignty – at least with respect to the transatlantic conflict over the ICC in the analysed period (1996–2005): all analysed statements fit into one of the four discourses. The four discourses represent articulations of competing visions of international order for which the configuration of sovereignty and human rights is of central importance. These competing discourses form the basis of the transatlantic debate about the ICC. Thus, the cleavages in the conflict about the ICC were not between advocates of sovereignty on the one hand and proponents of human rights on the other. Rather they were between different discourses that all claim to integrate sovereignty and human rights in a specific way. Due to the complex nature of discourses as structures of meaning, however, it is not possible to trace a deterministic kind of causality between discourses on the one hand and policy decisions on the other. Rather, discourses have a non-deterministic impact on the level of policy decisions in that they provide both a pattern of perception and a normative orientation for what may qualify as legitimate political action (cf. Yee, 1996).

The legalistic discourse developed into the common discourse of advocates of a strong and independent ICC and thus increasingly guided and unified the argumentative strategies of the European states under consideration. It combines an emphasis on the sovereign equality of all states, i.e. the aspect of symmetry, with the claim that human rights should be enforced on the supra-state level. The term legalism is intended to reflect the central role that this discourse accords to international law as a source of international order (Shklar, 1986). It is important to note, however, that this does not imply that legalism is a 'specialist' discourse in which only lawyers engage or that all lawyers take a legalistic stance. Neither is this to say that international law does not play a role in the other three discourses. The notion of legalism is merely intended to reflect the idea that in this discourse international law is regarded as the most important source of a peaceful and sustainable international order. As will be demonstrated in more detail in the following chapter, it exerted the greatest influence on the establishment of the ICC and on its institutional design. According to legalism, a symmetrical relationship between the constitutive units of world politics is the only feasible fundament of international order. If powerful states such as the US were granted exemptions from the ICC, this would send out dangerous signals to other states and potentially undermine the relevance of international law as such. Advocates of legalism stress the idea of the sovereign equality of all states as a precondition for a peaceful and secure global order. Arguably, they do not deny power inequalities between states; they simply hold that if these inequalities would be taken into consideration too overtly, international law would lose its legitimacy and would give way to the principle of 'might is right'. Regarding human rights, legalists hold that supra-state institutions represent the appropriate venue for their enforcement. According to them, the central point of reference for human rights is the international society of states and/or the world society of individuals (this ambiguity will be discussed in more detail in Chapter 3) rather than domestic political communities.

The empirical chapters will provide evidence that the legalistic discourse eventually gained a hegemonic position in the debate about the ICC. In a neo-Gramscian context, the notion of hegemony refers to 'areas of relative stability, moments when a mainstream has consolidated or is only marginally threatened by critique' (Koskenniemi, 2004: 202; cf. Torfing, 1999: 101ff.). As we will see, several aspects support the assumption that the legalistic discourse in fact gained a hegemonic position: first, it eventually served as a unifying basis for a group of states that pushed, in conjunction with NGOs, for a strong Court. Secondly, some of the most important features and claims of the legalistic discourse were codified in the Rome Statute of the ICC, thereby transforming them into legal provisions, which in turn established the 'terms of trade' for possible challenges of the Court.[13] Finally, the legalistic discourse provided some groups of US media commentators with a discursive fundament from which they challenged the US government's position on the Court.

As will be shown in the following chapters, the remaining three discourses are 'antagonistic forces' challenging the emerging hegemony of legalism. They were mainly brought into play by US diplomats and commentators opposing the ICC in its final shape, though some European media commentators also aligned themselves with these discourses. The interventionist discourse envisages the supra-state enforcement of human rights, but unlike legalism, combines this feature with an asymmetric notion of sovereignty. The term 'interventionism' is borrowed from H. W. Brands (1998a, b), who holds that interventionism is deeply rooted in the history of US foreign policy. According to him, it captures the idea that military interventions abroad are vital for both the maintenance of international order and the pursuit of US national interest. Although the interventionist discourse is not entirely congruent with Brands's notion of interventionism, the basic idea is similar. According to advocates of interventionism, the sovereignty of a state should be regarded as being conditional upon its ability and willingness to enforce and guarantee human rights standards within its borders. They argue that if a state does not abide by human rights standards, the international society, represented by its most powerful states, is entitled to intervene in order to stop the violation of human rights. Consequently, power inequalities between states are extremely significant within the discourse of interventionism, as interventionists argue that powerful states carry a higher burden when it comes to the enforcement of human rights on a global scale. Opponents of the ICC frequently articulated their reservations about the Court within the framework of the interventionist discourse. They argued that the ICC could eventually develop into an impediment to the enforcement of human rights as its establishment would threaten powerful states with prosecutions of their citizens, thereby discouraging them from participating in humanitarian interventions.

The sovereigntist discourse combines the feature of symmetry regarding the dimension of sovereignty with the assumption that the domestic realm of states is the best venue for the enforcement of human rights. At first glance, the term 'sovereigntism' might seem somewhat misleading, as this discourse is not entirely based upon the concept of sovereignty, thereby excluding human rights. Yet the label is useful because it is already established in the literature. Spiro, for instance, refers to advocates of ideas that are essential to this discourse as 'the new sovereigntists' (2000). Within this discourse, human rights and sovereignty are connected by the constitution of a state, which is interpreted to guarantee human rights on the one hand, and to serve as a fundament for sovereignty on the other. The constitution of a state is particularly relevant in the context of the sovereigntist discourse, as it is perceived as both the ultimate normative fundament of state sovereignty and as the only entity that is able to constrain the exercise of a state's sovereignty prerogatives. Sovereignty is understood as 'constitutional sovereignty'.[14] Sovereigntists are not hostile to international law *per se*; however, they hold that in order to be valid, international legal provisions need the explicit consent of those states that are supposed to be bound by them. Though there were some sovereigntist voices in Europe, the sovereigntist discourse was most prominent in the US. US opponents of the Court frequently argued that the ICC Statute ignores the requirement of state consent by illegitimately targeting non-party states. This gave rise to heated debates, as advocates of the Court stressed that it actually targets individuals, not states.

Finally, the progressivist discourse claims that human rights should be implemented on the domestic level of states and combines this claim with the idea that international order is asymmetric. The notion of progressivism is usually linked to Woodrow Wilson. The progressivist discourse is not coextensive with the ideas of what has been labelled 'the progressive movement' in American history, which itself represents a rather fuzzy and incoherent concept (cf. Rodgers, 1982). However, the progressivist discourse shares with the historical concept the preoccupation with democratisation as a way of international reform and the emphasis on popular sovereignty (cf. Franceschet, 2000). According to the progressivist discourse, human rights should be implemented on the domestic level of states. In contrast to the sovereigntist discourse, however, the progressivist discourse regards human rights as a feature of civic culture rather than as a vital part of the constitution. In line with this focus on civil society, the progressivist discourse espouses the notion of popular sovereignty, meaning that the ultimate source of sovereignty is the people. At the same time, this notion of sovereignty implies asymmetry: states in which popular sovereignty is institutionalised qualify as belonging to the righteous 'club' of democracies, whereas others are excluded. Thus, although the progressivist discourse does not favour the enforcement of human rights on the supra-state level, it regards international bodies as an appropriate means to promote democracy and human rights. Yet according to progressivists, international organisations are not supposed to interfere directly with the domestic structures or politics of states, but to reward democratisation by mechanisms of inclusion and exclusion. As will be elaborated in more detail in Chapter 6, the progressivist discourse only played a marginal role in the debates about the ICC.

As this short overview of the four discourses indicates, neither of these discourses fully matches the three approaches to the problem of sovereignty and human rights –pluralism, solidarism and world society – outlined at the beginning of this chapter. As the following chapters will show in more detail, both legalism and interventionism accept the world society idea that individuals and their rights play a role in international relations, yet they do not envisage that this may cause an erosion of state sovereignty. Moreover, although both discourses highlight the importance of human rights in international relations, they do not simply conclude that sovereignty has become 'conditional' on compliance with human rights standards, as solidarists argue. Rather, they construct the notion of sovereignty in different ways: as 'new sovereignty' in the case of legalism and as 'conditional sovereignty' in the case of interventionism. And even the interventionist notion of 'conditional sovereignty' is not equivalent to the usage of the term in the solidarist paradigm: the interventionist notion of 'conditional sovereignty' implies a gap in the roles of great powers and outlaw states that the solidarist paradigm does not capture. Similarly, the sovereigntist discourse shares various traits with the pluralist paradigm – most importantly the idea that international relations are a realm of normative pluralism that is best accommodated by upholding a traditional notion of sovereignty. Yet the sovereigntist discourse proves to be richer than the pluralist paradigm in that it emphasises the idea of sovereignty as constitutional sovereignty, for instance. Finally, progressivism at first glance seems to allude to solidarist claims by stressing that a state's democratic and human rights credentials should have an impact on its recognition in the international realm. However, whilst solidarism aims to integrate world society and international society, in the progressivist discourse the individual is first and foremost a citizen of a specific state and not a member of world society.

In sum, this book aims to show that sovereignty and human rights play a central role in political debates, although the way in which they are referred to and linked in these debates differs from the theoretical approaches to sovereignty and human rights. This is not to say that the theoretical approaches are *per se* 'wrong'. On the contrary, they are a useful starting point for analysing the relevance of sovereignty and human rights in political debates and have sometimes – most probably through the involvement of international lawyers in the negotiation processes – influenced these debates. Yet these theoretical approaches cannot be 'forced' on the empirical discourses, which tend to be less abstract, richer in detail and, perhaps most importantly, feature as a political battlefield. Taking a more inductive approach and analysing abstract principles like sovereignty and human rights 'in action', i.e. in empirical political debates, is important for two reasons: first, it allows us to explore how reference to these principles impact on the outcome of political conflicts. Secondly, it enables us to feed empirical findings back into the theoretical debate by discussing, for instance, how the political debates about sovereignty and human rights affect our understanding of the international society as an anarchical society.[15]

Methodological approach

Identification and demarcation of the different discourses

Large parts of the methodological literature on discourse analysis emphasise the close links between discourse analysis and grounded theory (cf. Meyer, 2001). Grounded theory is rooted in the works of Barney Glaser and Anselm Strauss, who claim that empirical phenomena can – and should – be approached without any theoretical bias on the part of the researcher, thereby opting for an inductive research strategy (1967). According to Glaser and Strauss, theory is supposed to emerge directly from the collection and analysis of empirical data, but should not be 'forced' upon the data, as this would lead to biased and false conclusions. Whilst this objective seems valuable, it is hard to see how it could be achieved within the framework of this study. Given that both sovereignty and human rights are by their very nature highly theoretical concepts, it is questionable to what extent it is possible to avoid a theoretical bias in conducting empirical research on these concepts. Consequently, a purely inductive strategy does not seem feasible. Instead of claiming not to be biased theoretically, it is more reasonable to make theoretical biases explicit. Therefore, the first step of this research was to derive preliminary criteria for the distinction of the four discourses from the theoretical literature on sovereignty and human rights.

The conceptualisation of sovereignty and human rights within the framework of IR and political theory discourses deviates from the way in which policy makers, international lawyers and media commentators (see next section for the selection of discursive arenas) construct them. Therefore, the theoretically derived preliminary criteria had to be amended and adapted in a second step in order to bridge the gap between scientific and political conceptualisations of sovereignty and human rights. In sum, the research process consisted in moving constantly back and forth between theory and empirical data. The aim was to avoid both the pitfalls of working with an implicit theoretical bias on the one hand and to 'force' theory upon empirical data without the possibility of adjusting the former to the latter on the other.[16]

The ambivalences in the concepts of sovereignty and human rights thus derived, i.e. symmetry versus asymmetry and supra-state versus domestic enforcement, served as the core criteria for the classification of texts and statements. In particular, the following set of questions guided the analysis of texts and statements and provided the basis for the summary representations of the different discourses included in the empirical chapters:

- How is time constructed in the statement? (Conservative or progressive? Reformist or revolutionary?)
- What qualifies as a source of international order according to the text?
- How are the basic features of international order depicted?
- What qualifies as the basic units, i.e. as the ontological references of the statement? (States or individuals? Single or collective?)
- How is the notion of interest constructed and to which entities does it refer?
- What notion of sovereignty emerges from the statement?
- What entity is regarded as the major point of reference of human rights? (International society? World society? Nation-states?)

Arguably, most of the analysed statements only provided answers to some of the questions specified above. However, in sum, it was possible to trace clusters of specific answers that permitted the establishment of the central features of the four discourses and to categorise the statements accordingly. There were, however, cases in which one text belonged to more than one discourse. In these cases, the statements and texts in question were assigned to two or three discourses at the same time.

The discursive arenas

Statements and texts were drawn from three different discursive arenas, i.e. political and professional locations from which statements are made and texts are produced: the discursive arena of *diplomacy*, the arena of *legal experts* and finally the discursive arena of the *media*. These discursive arenas cut across the boundaries between the international and the domestic realms. While the discursive arena of diplomacy is mainly international, the media report on international events and frame them for domestic publics.[17] The arena of legal expert is transnational; it is a specialist arena that cuts across state boundaries. Data from the discursive arena of diplomacy consists in, first, the official records of the 1998 Rome Conference. Additionally, debates in the UN Security Council, the General Assembly and the General Assembly's Sixth (Legal) Committee were taken into account. Arguably, the discursive arena of diplomacy is difficult to investigate, since large parts of the negotiations consist of 'private diplomacy' (cf. Kirsch and Holmes 1999; Parsons 1993). Nevertheless, the negotiations on the ICC were the most important venue in which diplomats explained and justified their countries' position on the Court.

There are obviously many links between the discursive arena of diplomacy and that of legal experts. Outstanding international lawyers often participate in both the discursive arena of diplomacy – as delegation members – and the arena of scientific legal expertise. In order to capture the academic legal debates, the data set includes publications from several major European and US law journals (for a complete list of considered journals see the Appendix). The place of publication of the journals (the US, Britain, France and Germany) turned out to be of minor importance, as the discursive arena of legal experts features a high degree of transnationalisation.

Finally, data were collected from the discursive arena of the media. The relevance of media debates for foreign policy has a long-standing tradition in political science.[18] Moreover, the investigation of media texts is firmly established in approaches to discourse analysis (Fairclough, 1995 a, b). The media has increasingly become the main arena of political discourses aimed at domestic publics. This is in particular true if international events are not or at least not mainly debated in domestic political arenas such as national parliaments.

The selection of statements and texts

As the study focuses on the transatlantic debate about the ICC, the selection of the US as one of the countries under consideration does not require any further explanation. With respect to the European side of the debate, the UK, France and Germany seemed to be the most appropriate choices, for several reasons: first, all three countries are considered major players within Europe. Secondly, all three countries played a crucial role in the debates about the ICC in the UN Security Council – France and the UK as permanent members, of course, but also Germany as a non-permanent member in 2003 and 2004. At the same time, the three European countries represent a certain variation in terms of their overall relationship to the US: whereas France and Germany often tend to form an alliance against certain features of US foreign policy – most recently with respect to the Iraq war – Britain frequently emphasises its 'special relationship' to the US.

The time span for the collection of data is January 1996 until April 2005. Owing to the scarcity of recorded material in the discursive arena of diplomacy, all official statements by the four countries during that time were collected. The same applies to the arena of legal experts, where every article specifically addressing the topic of the ICC was included in the data set. Since the ICC was rarely debated in the arena of legal experts and the media before the Rome Conference, data collection in these two arenas starts only in 1998.

The selection of texts for the discursive arena of the media was more difficult to handle. The collection of data was limited to six short phases chosen with reference to political events in the process of the establishment of the ICC (for a complete list of considered phases see the Appendix). LexisNexis was used as a database for the media coverage of the ICC in all four countries.[19]

The data set was further limited by applying the following criteria. Only op-ed articles and comments were included. The aim was to collect a maximum of fifteen articles per country for each time span. In the event that the number of results was still too high after having considered all selection criteria mentioned above, results were reduced by random selection (e.g. selecting every other or every third article).[20]

The strategies for analysing texts and statements

The analysis of the empirical data was not based on the detailed operational procedures that one frequently finds in the methodological literature on discourse analysis (cf. among others Fairclough, 2003; the contributions in Wodak and Meyer, 2001 and Milliken, 1999). These operational procedures are often derived from linguistics and are concerned with the microstructures of texts, i.e. sequences, grammar, metaphors, etc. Arguably, they have the advantage of offering a formalised procedure for investigating large amounts of text. But they also distract from the macro level of the meaning of certain statements (Wæver, 2004). As the objective of this study is to reveal structures of meaning that together form encompassing visions of international order, a micro-level access to texts would have been of little use. The aim was thus to concentrate on the elaboration of characteristic features of the discourses and the discursive formation as a whole on the basis of a non-formalised interpretation of collected texts and statements.

Notes

1   For an overview of different fields of human rights, see Donnelly (2002) and Beetham (1999), for a debate about the importance of specific groups of rights see among others Nussbaum (2000), Shue (1996) and Cranston (1973).
2   According to Kenneth Abbott and Duncan Snidal (2000: 437), international legal arrangements entail high sovereignty costs for states if they impinge on the relations between a state and its citizens, which is clearly the case with respect to the ICC.
3   Universal jurisdiction means that perpetrators could be prosecuted by national courts regardless of their own nationality, the nationality of the victims and the territory on which the offence took place.
4   The complementarity principle incorporated in the ICC Statute grants priority to the jurisdiction of national courts over that of the ICC. That is, 'a case is to be declared inadmissible to the ICC if it is being investigated or prosecuted (or has been investigated) by national authorities, unless the State in question is unable or unwilling genuinely to carry out the investigation or prosecution' (Cassese, 2005: 457).
5   Rome Statute of the International Criminal Court, Art. 17, U.N. Doc. A/CONF.183/9.
6   See also Terry Nardin's account of international society, according to which it has to be understood as 'an association of independent and diverse political communities, each devoted to its own ends and its own conception of the good, often related to one another by nothing more than the fragile ties of a common tradition of diplomacy' (1983:19).
7   See, among others, Heins (2002a, b), Risse (2002), Risse and Sikkink (1999), Keck and Sikkink (1998), Sikkink (1993), Falk (1995) and Rosenau (1995).
8   Moreover, the criticism that their assessment of the historical development of sovereignty in the twentieth century is inaccurate applies to both the world society and the solidarist doctrine. Both world society scholars and solidarists argue that due to changes in political structures and/or practices, the concept of sovereignty either lost part of its significance or became increasingly dependent on human rights and frequently refer to the new situation as a 'post-Westphalian' order (Linklater, 1998). This indication of a historical break from a presumably Westphalian to a post-Westphalian order implies that there was once a 'golden era' of sovereignty, in which states in fact did not face any limits concerning the exercise of power on their own territory and over their own populations. However, Stephen Krasner (1993, 1999) has shown that historically sovereignty always faced challenges, be it in the form of intervention or in the form of competing principles. The increasing relevance of human rights during the twentieth century notwithstanding, sovereignty has always been challenged by universal political norms such as religious tolerance or minority rights. Moreover, Chris Brown draws our attention to the fact that until the first half of the twentieth century, international relations were governed by two different sets of norms, one of which characterised the

European, Westphalian order, whereas the other applied to the non-European realm. Within the latter, the norms of sovereignty and non-intervention did not apply, as its members were not deemed members of the international society (2002: 141; cf. Keene, 2002: 60ff.).

9   This holds at least true for the solidarist perspective. World society scholars rather assume that the meaning of both concepts is fixed. With changes in the political and societal structures, they argue, the significance of sovereignty decreases.

10 This theoretical claim of course raises the question to what extent great powers have in fact historically lived up to their roles as guarantors and custodians of international order. Bull himself admits that great powers 'frequently behave in such a way as to promote disorder rather than order' (1995: 201).

11 This begs the question to what extent great powers can legalise their special status. Bull argues that 'great powers cannot formalise and make explicit the full extent of their special position', since this would 'engender more antagonism than the international order could support' (1995: 221). Simpson, on the contrary, persuasively shows how the privileged status of great powers did indeed become formalised within the framework of international law and international bodies (2004: 91ff.). Yet it is plausible to assume that even 'legalised hegemony' is only possible within certain boundaries in order to not unravel the international order.

12 Cf. Weber (1995) and Bonacker and Brodocz (2001), and Chalaby (1996) and Meyer (2001) for the opposite argument.

13 When the Bush administration, for instance, demanded an exemption from the ICC's jurisdiction in the UN Security Council, the ICC Statute provided the legal basis to which any exemption had to refer to in order to be legally binding.

14 I borrowed this term from Hideaki Shinoda (2000), though the way in which I use it is not entirely similar to Shinoda's understanding. See Chapter 5, 'The constitution as a benchmark and constraint of sovereignty'.

15 See the Conclusion.

16 This research strategy has been labelled 'abductive approach'. See Wodak (2001: 70); cf. also Reichertz (2003), Meyer (2001) and Lueger (2001: 363ff.).

17 Debates over the ICC in domestic parliaments started only after the Rome Conference and usually followed international debates rather than setting the international agenda. An exception in this respect was the adoption of the ASPA in the US Congress, which fed back into the international debate. However, in Germany, France and the UK national parliaments primarily became involved with the ICC in the process of adopting implementing legislation as required in the ICC Statute. Given this constellation, data from domestic parliamentary debates were not included in the data set.

18 See, among others Robinson (2000), Bennett and Paletz (1994), Bennett (1994), Zaller (1994) and Hallin (1986).

19 LexisNexis is an archive with a search engine that encompasses a range of different national newspapers, meaning that I did not have to decide which newspapers to take into account before searching, but could select articles from all sorts of newspapers from every country. The search term was in every case 'International Criminal Court' (in French and German 'Cour pénale internationale' and 'International★ Strafgerichtshof★', respectively).

20 Random selection was applied only in two instances: in the cases of the US and the UK media coverage of the entry into force of the Rome Statute (30 June – 2 July 2002). Given the fact that the entry into force of the Rome Statute was the most outstanding event in the process of the establishment of the ICC, it comes as no surprise that it attracted extensive media attention. This applied in particular to the US media coverage,

as the US government opposed the Court and regarded it as a potential threat to its foreign policy. The total number of US newspaper articles after applying all selection criteria was 42. Therefore only every third article was included in the data set. In the case of the UK, the increased media coverage was not caused by a major contestation of the issue of the ICC. Rather, it reflected the lively debate in the US. However, with 28 articles after the selection procedure, it proved less lively than in the US case and allowed for retaining every other article for analysis.

3 The legalistic discourse

Almost all officials of the European states under consideration, the majority of legal experts and a large proportion of media commentators, both in Europe and the US, eventually engaged in the legalistic discourse. Legalism can be considered as taking a hegemonic position in the debates that surrounded the creation of the ICC and exerted a strong influence on the institutional design of the Court. NGOs had a vital impact on the rise of the legalistic discourse and on the consolidation of its hegemonic position.

At the initial stages of the negotiations, there had been considerable differences between the positions of Germany, France and the UK. The German delegation was determined to argue for a strong and independent Court during the negotiations and represented one of the leading members of the LMG (Broomhall, 2003; Weller, 2002). Both France and the UK were initially reluctant about an independent Court, but joined the Like-Minded Group shortly before the Rome Conference.[1] The statements made by their delegations, however, partly still echoed their initial concerns. France in particular continued to take a rather restrictive position with respect to the prosecution of war crimes. It argued in favour of a seven-year opt-out provision for the prosecution of war crimes (Economides, 2001: 120).[2]

The fact that these three European states started out from different and even partially contradictory positions triggers the question of why the legalistic discourse provided the possibility of integration and even convergence on some points, so that it was eventually perceived as a more or less unified European standpoint on the issue of the ICC. Three aspects account for this: first, the legalistic discourse as such maintains high degrees of instability when it comes to the meaning of signifiers. The establishment of the ICC and its impact on state sovereignty, for instance, can be assessed in different ways. On the one hand, the Court can be interpreted as an expression of sovereignty – states exert their sovereignty prerogatives by voluntarily joining the Rome Statute. On the other hand, the ICC Statute might be seen as an intrusion into state sovereignty, as it sets out clear rules for coping with infringements of international criminal law and thereby binds states to its provisions. In the first case, sovereignty is understood as a legal principle that can be adjusted to changing political circumstances; in the second, the notion of sovereignty relates to a rather static idea of independence of states from any higher authority. In fact, both meanings of sovereignty come up within the framework of the legalistic discourse, but the tension between them never becomes explicit. This is what Ernesto Laclau labelled 'the intrinsic ambiguities of the hegemonic project itself' (1990: 28).

The European states under consideration had also different positions on specific aspects of the negotiations. The debate over the ICC's jurisdiction bears witness to this. In the run-up to the Rome Conference, the unifying slogan among members of the LMG and NGOs was 'inherent jurisdiction' (Glasius, 2005: 63). At the Rome Conference itself, however, this term turned out to be vague, with different delegations attaching different meanings to it. For the German delegation (and a number of NGOs), 'inherent jurisdiction' was synonymous with 'universal jurisdiction', meaning that the chief prosecutor would be able to investigate situations regardless of whether any of the affected states (the state on the territory of which the situation occurred, the state of nationality of the suspect, the state of nationality of the victim(s) and the state of custody of the suspect) were party to the Rome Statute. In contrast, France was initially in favour of a consent regime whereby all affected states had to express their consent before the Court could start investigations (Hall, 1998a: 131). The unifying effect of notions as vague as 'inherent jurisdiction' once again underscores the close connection between ambiguity and hegemony.

Second, the strong involvement of NGOs in the negotiations of the ICC Statute had a unifying effect on the members of the LMG and helped to shape the legalistic discourse. A coalition of NGOs pushing for the establishment of the ICC (Coalition for the ICC; CICC) had formed in 1995 and had reached a membership of over 800 organisations by the time of the Rome Conference (Glasius, 2005: 26ff.). NGOs were particularly effective in providing diplomatic delegations in Rome with information on other delegations' positions and lobbying them informally (*ibid.*: 37). They extracted 'virtual votes' on particular issues from the negotiations, thereby rendering majority positions visible (*ibid.*: 53). Their strategy was to focus on and to reinforce those positions on which a consensus seemed most likely.

Third, the involvement of all three states in the EU, the fact of European integration and the binding and supporting policy framework which it provides must not be ignored. Apparently, an intersection between discursive features belonging to the realm of European integration on the one hand and to the institutionalisation of the ICC on the other emerged, since the Court developed into one of the most prestigious and ambitious projects of EU external policy (cf. Scheipers and Sicurelli, 2007; Smith, 2003: 197).

Even though the success of the legalistic discourse was partly built upon the ambiguous nature of some of its core concepts, its content is not completely arbitrary. If this were the case, the discourse would lose its constitutive qualities. Rather, the legalistic discourse is characterised by three core elements that form a common point of reference for all of its advocates and demarcate the boundaries of the discourse: first, the perception of the temporal dimension in terms of *progress*; second, the idea that order emerges from *law*; and third, *symmetry* as the structural feature of order. Beyond these three common denominators, the legalistic discourse subdivides into two branches according to the basic ontological units privileged by each subdivision, i.e. states or individuals. Although this bifurcation impacts on the notion of interest, the concept of sovereignty and on the perception of human rights, the three common features provide a unifying basis for the legalistic discourse and allow for a precise distinction from the other discourses.

Table 3.1 summarises the most central features of the legalistic discourse.

Construction of time	Sources of order	Features of order	Ontology/ basic units	Notion of interest refers to	Notion of sovereignty	Human rights refer to
			States	Community of all states	New sovereignty	Consensus of states
			or:	or:	or:	or:
Progress	Law	Symmetry		Community of all	Erosion of	Collective conscience of
			Individuals	individuals	sovereignty	humanity

Table 3.1 Basic features of the legalistic discourse

The underlying narrative of legalism: a progressive world order based on law

Progress

One of the major features of the legalistic discourse is its emphasis on progress. It follows the well-known theory of history as envisaged by Enlightenment philosophy.[3] Just as the latter, the legalistic discourse conceives of progress as rationalisation, legalisation and professionalisation. Its proponents interpret the establishment of the ICC as a major step in this direction. Consider for instance a comment published in *Le Figaro* after the Rome Statute came into effect in 2002: 'Whatever its detractors might say, the ICC represents a *significant advance of international law*, a *major leap forward* in the evolution of a universal conscience and a *historical progress* towards respecting the dignity of individuals and peoples.'[4]

One year later, on the occasion of the inauguration of the chief prosecutor of the ICC, Steve Crawshaw, London director of Human Rights Watch, wrote in the *Observer*: 'The inauguration in the Hague tomorrow of the first chief prosecutor of the International Criminal Court marks a remarkable moment in history. Dictators and tyrants around the world can be brought to book, by a single court. It is an astonishing achievement – and one that seemed, until just a few years ago, unimaginable.'[5]

It is not only media commentators who interpret the establishment of the ICC as an instance of historical progress towards a more just world order, but also diplomats who negotiated its Statute at the Rome Conference. Hans-Peter Kaul, head of the German delegation, stressed that progress is the ultimate benchmark against which all proposals for the definition of crimes have to be assessed. In justifying his delegation's stance on the question of whether the ICC should have jurisdiction over international crimes committed in internal armed conflicts he argued that 'any other proposal would be a *retrogression* in the development of international humanitarian law.'[6]

Although the emphasis on progress is one of the most consensual aspects of the legalistic discourse, there is a slight disaccord over the question of whether the envisaged progress constitutes a revolutionary or an evolutionary development. Antonio Cassese, for instance, legal expert and participant in the Rome Conference, depicts the progressive development as a revolutionary one:

> In the case of the International Criminal Court (ICC), whose Statute was adopted in Rome on 17 July 1998, however, one should be mindful of the fact that firstly, this is a *revolutionary institution* that intrudes into state sovereignty by subjecting states' nationals to an international jurisdiction. Consequently, if and when it becomes an operational and effective judicial mechanism, the ICC could mark a real *turning point* in the world community. (Cassese, 1999: 145; emphasis added).

The same applies to a comment published in the *St. Louis Post-Dispatch*, which is representative of legalistic contributions within the US media coverage of the ICC: 'When the Rome Conference agreed on a charter for an international criminal court, after a month of tense debate, attention focused on the compromises and the politics. But what happened in Rome last week was more important than the details. I think it will be seen as a *turn in the road of history*.'[7]

In contrast, in the discursive arena of diplomacy, most actors depicted progress as evolutionary. Dominique de Villepin, former French ambassador to the UN Security Council, in a debate on the rule of law in 2003 described the establishment of the ICC as one step in the broader development of international law that had been preceded by the establishment of the ICTY and the ICTR.

> The second challenge is to ensure that justice and the values of peace prevail wherever crime and arbitrary acts have sown terror and hatred. This is what led the Security Council to create the international criminal tribunals. In the ongoing, difficult quest to achieve a balance, the International Criminal Court represents a *major stride forward*.[8]

The fact that diplomats tend to conceive of progress in terms of evolution, whereas media commentators who align themselves with the legalistic discourse regard the ICC as a revolutionary institution comes as no surprise given the different professional backgrounds of both discursive arenas: diplomacy represents a traditional institution that is linked to continuity, whereas the media functions according to a logic of subversive newness. However, as already indicated above, such contradictory interpretations did not lead to major tensions or conflicts amongst proponents of legalism. Rather, they were absorbed by adherence to the more general notion of progress.

Besides the nature of the progressive development, the legalistic discourse indicates the ultimate aim or *telos* of progress. It depicts the ICC as part of a broader *mission civilisatrice*. In this sense, Günther Pleuger, German ambassador to the UN Security Council, argued that 'the International Criminal Court is an important step towards *global civilization*'.[9] In contrast to the civilising mission that eighteenth- and nineteenth-century colonialists pursued, which was firmly grounded in the idea of Europe's cultural superiority *vis-à-vis* the non-European realm and aimed at the cultural assimilation of colonial societies (Gong, 1984: 40; cf. Keene, 2002), the *mission civilisatrice* included in the legalistic discourse focuses on the adherence to human rights standards. Whereas colonialist discourses tend to justify the use of military force in order to impose the envisaged standards of civilisation (Gong, 1984: 42f.), the advocates of legalism emphasise non-coercive measures and instruments such as negotiations and multilateral treaties.[10] Finally, the legalistic discourse differs from eighteenth- and nineteenth-century colonialism with regards to its focus on symmetry: although legalists consider themselves to be the vanguard with respect to the institutionalisation of human rights on a global scale, they stress the reciprocal relationship among all states regardless of their size, power and cultural tradition.[11] Moreover, they perceive symmetry as the precondition for a peaceful international order. In short, whereas the nineteenth-century discourse of colonialism relied on exclusive identities, i.e. European vs. non-European, the legalistic discourse is based upon inclusive identities: its point of reference consists of the international community of all states or, rather, the world society of individuals, which are bound together by shared norms and values, particularly human rights. In order to participate, actors have to align themselves with these norms and abide by them, but they are not permanently excluded by way of their inherent characteristics.[12]

Order means law

The ultimate *telos* of historic progress according to legalism lies in the establishment of a peaceful global order by means of the law.[13] As one commentator in the French newspaper *Sud Ouest* put it:

> The ICC constitutes nothing less than historical progress. For the first time, the international community establishes a legal instrument in order to punish

persons who have committed crimes against universal values ... The Dutch minister of justice is entirely right to say that it was time to *replace the right of the most powerful with the power of law*.[14]

The equation 'law leads to order and peace', which emerges from the above quotation is also prominent among diplomats and legal experts, if they engaged in the legalistic discourse.[15] It could not be more explicit than in the following quotation from an article by two legal experts: 'Though large parts of the Statute of the International Criminal Court represent the outcome of a compromise, it epitomises significant progress concerning efforts to institutionalise the rule of law as an essential precondition for a peaceful order in international relations' (Blanke and Molitor, 2001: 169).

The discursive arena of diplomacy echoes this perspective. François Alabrune, French ambassador to the Sixth Committee (Legal) of the UN General Assembly, argued

that the International Criminal Court should be established as soon as possible in order to guarantee effective respect for international humanitarian law and human rights. The Court would be an instrument for dealing with and preventing the worst crimes affecting the international community and would *strengthen the primacy of international law, thus contributing to the reign of peace in the world*.[16]

The tacit assumption, which becomes evident in the wording 'dealing with and preventing' hints at the concrete functions that the ICC is intended to fulfil according to the legalistic point of view: to reconcile societies that have disintegrated owing to civil war and/or to deter potential perpetrators from violating humanitarian and human rights law. On the occasion of the adoption of UN Security Council resolution 1593 (2005; referring the situation in Darfur, Sudan, to the ICC) Sir Emyr Jones Parry, British ambassador to the UN Security Council, said: 'Tonight, by this vote, the Security Council has acted to ensure accountability for the grave crimes committed in Darfur, and I hope to send a *salutary warning to anyone intending to commit any further such atrocities*.'[17] In the same vein, Günther Pleuger said in a 2004 Security Council meeting on the topic of the protection of civilians in armed conflicts: 'First, let us put an end to impunity. Impunity is one of the worst root causes of the violation of the integrity of civilians. ... If we do not end impunity for the violations of international humanitarian law, there will be no *deterrent* for the perpetrators of acts of violence and aggression.'[18]

Whilst both Parry and Pleuger stressed the deterrence function, Michel Duclos, French ambassador to the UN Security Council, put the emphasis on 'what a great contribution the ICC can make, not only in the area of justice, but in bringing about *reconciliation* and dealing in depth with the wounds of a society that has been traumatized by a particularly horrendous conflict'.[19]

Depoliticisation

Whether its proponents emphasise the deterrent or the reconciliatory function of the ICC, the legalistic discourse contrasts power politics with the law and privileges the latter over the former as the fundament of global order. However, the legalistic preference for the law over power politics should not distract from the fact that legalism is as much a *political* discourse as the interventionism, sovereigntism and progressivism. In the political battle over the institutional solutions for a legitimate world order, it assigns primacy to international law.

At a very early stage of the negotiations, Rolf Welberts, German delegate to the UN General Assembly's Sixth Committee, emphasised the need for the Court to be shielded from power political considerations – in particular the UN Security Council: '[T]he court must be independent of political power. While the Security Council might be in a position to refer situations or cases to the court, it should not be able to control access to it.'[20] Legalism aims at a *depoliticisation* of international criminal law. One legal expert expressed this idea as follows:

> Indeed, some international criminal law has been included within general international law at least since the Nuremberg trials. Subsequently, this area of international law was little used; only recently has this changed. New developments suggest that there has been major movement toward the active and effective application of this law. Many believe that this progress heralds a breakthrough in the achievement of rights protected by international criminal law. ... One might hope that the recent developments favour a more active and *apolitical approach* to these crimes, yet it is not clear that a significant change has occurred. (Charney, 1999: 452–3; emphasis added)

The tension between power politics and the law as major alternative sources of international order became particularly evident on the occasion of the adoption of UN Security Council resolution 1422 in June 2002. This resolution provided an exemption for citizens of states not party to the ICC and was widely criticised both by the media and by legal experts as preparing the ground for inequality and discrimination amongst both states and their citizens before international criminal law (cf. Alvarez, 2003: 886). Commentators blamed the US, which demanded this exemption and made their approval of a renewal of the UN peacekeeping mandate for Bosnia-Herzegovina dependent on the adoption of resolution 1422, of preferring a power political approach to international order. They depicted Europe, on the other hand, as opting for the allegedly more reasonable, more just and more successful way of furthering international law. Kenneth Roth, executive director of Human Rights Watch, made this view explicit in a comment published in the *Financial Times*:

> The real reason behind Washington's blackmail is the most troubling. An increasingly influential faction in the Bush administration believes that US military

and economic power is so dominant that the US is not longer served by international law. … No effective global system can rest solely on *coercion*. Global order depends on *most governments abiding voluntarily by shared norms*, leaving a more violent and inhumane world. Europe must stand up to this superpower folly.[21]

Roth equates power politics with coercion and contrasts it with multilateral consensus and norm compliance that he regards as the only possible fundament of a peaceful world order.

From the legalistic perspective, the most disturbing and irritating feature of the US stance towards the ICC and the request for exemption is that, by arguing that the UN Security Council should exempt US citizens from the ICC jurisdiction in order to comply with its task of maintaining peace and security, the US undermines the legalistic equation that the promotion of international justice leads to peace: 'How can the world superpower … claim to *dissociate justice from peace?*', as one French commentator put it.[22]

An exception to the legalistic claim for the independence of the ICC from the Security Council emerged with respect to the crime of aggression. In this case, it was the Non-Aligned Movement (NAM) that pushed for keeping the ICC's jurisdiction independent from the Security Council. In contrast, the P5 states initially insisted that aggression should only be included in the list of crimes if the Security Council were to determine whether an act of aggression had occurred before the ICC could proceed with the prosecution of individuals (von Hebel and Robinson, 1999: 82, cf. Arsanjani, 1999: 29ff.). Both in the PrepComs and in Rome the German delegation made efforts to broker a compromise between these two positions by suggesting a narrow definition of aggression and by ensuring that the Security Council's role with respect to aggression would be reflected in the Statute. Britain's and France's position on the crime of aggression moved into the direction of this proposal. At the Rome Conference, however, the NAM's resistance to Security Council involvement hardened, whereas the US had apparently grown increasingly concerned over the inclusion of aggression in the ICC Statute (Hall, 1998b: 551). In the end, aggression was included in the Rome Statute, but its definition was left open to subsequent negotiations.[23]

Independence of the ICC and professionalism

From a legalistic perspective, the major means to reach a depoliticised approach to international criminal law is guaranteeing the independence of the ICC and its prosecutor. In this respect, it is crucial that the prosecutor is able to start investigations *proprio motu*, i.e. on his or her own initiative. The independence of the prosecutor was also 'the single biggest issue on the agenda of the CICC and many of its constituent organisations' (Glasius, 2005: 50). NGOs played a vital role in rallying support for this option among state representatives and in reinforcing the central relevance of this issue.

Hans-Peter Kaul expressed the idea that a high degree of independence of the prosecutor would imply a depoliticisation of the prosecutions before the Court:

> Mr. Kaul (Germany) said Germany believed that in order to ensure the *independence of the Prosecutor* it was vital to give him or her the power to initiate investigations *ex officio*, since otherwise prosecutions could only be brought if a State party or the Security Council referred a situation to the Court. Giving the Prosecutor the power to act *proprio motu* would have the advantage of *depoliticizing the process of initiating investigations*.[24]

Given that France joined the LMG rather late on and French diplomats only reluctantly engaged in the legalistic discourse, the French delegation was initially worried about investing the prosecutor with such overwhelming authority concerning the initiation of investigations. It requested further checks and balances, but refrained from keeping the decision to investigate under the control of either state parties or the UN Security Council. The proposal to make prosecutions dependent upon the approval of a pre-trial chamber consisting of three judges (Art. 15 (3) of the Rome Statute), promoted by the French delegation, was a compromise between the more demanding (Germany) and the more reluctant proponents (France) of the legalistic discourse: 'Regarding matters taken up on the Court's own initiative, he, Marc Pavrin de Brichambant, could accept the idea of a decision taken by common agreement between the Prosecutor and the Pre-Trial Chamber … For the Prosecutor to take such a decision in isolation would not respect the necessary institutional balance.'[25]

In contrast, during the Rome Conference the UK and Germany emphasised the *professionalism* of the ICC prosecutor and the judges as providing an 'internal' control mechanism, as it were. According to Sir Franklin Berman, member of the British delegation to the Rome Conference, the professionalism of the ICC staff implies impartiality of the Court and is thus intended to prevent the risk of politically motivated prosecutions:[26]

> The first [vital task in the establishment of the ICC] was a need for an electoral system that would ensure that judges and the Prosecutor had the necessary rigorous *impartiality* and *judicial skills*, without which no country would feel that the checks and balances in the Statute could be relied upon in practice, and the International Criminal Court would not command the necessary *authority*.[27]

Eventually, even France came to endorse the idea that professionalism lies at the core of a successful performance of the ICC. In this vein, Michel Duclos argued in an UN Security Council meeting in 2003 that 'the Court's *professionalism* will be judged on the facts. The recognized quality and competence of the Court's members ensures without doubt the *credibility* of that international body. That credibility provides the best safeguard against any possible suspicion of a politically motivated Court.'[28]

Not only diplomats stressed the importance of the professionalism of the future ICC prosecutor and judges; legal experts also considered this a major point:

> One of the keys to its [the ICC's] success, it is submitted, lies in the choice and election of *highly professional and absolutely independent* persons for the positions of Prosecutor and Judges. The election of persons of *great competence* and *integrity* may ensure that the ICC will become an *efficient body*, capable of administering international criminal justice in such a manner as to attract the trust and respect of states, while fully realising the demands of justice. (Cassese, 1999: 171; emphasis added)

In short, professionalism and legal expertise are regarded as providing for impartiality, authority, credibility and efficiency, and thus for the success of the ICC as such. However, some legal experts are quite aware that the complete prevention of political entanglements is a mere illusion:

> Only this last possibility [the initiation of prosecutions *ex officio*], which surprisingly was not included in the draft of the International Law Commission, would release the Court at least *de jure* from the exertion of *political influence* as to the question of when and who is supposed to be prosecuted. Vesting the prosecutor with the competence to investigate and prosecute *ex officio* would also represent a major progress compared with former international criminal tribunals, as with respect to the latter, it was the Security Council which decided on the admissibility of offences. On the other hand, one should not ignore that the election of the Chief Prosecutor thereby acquires an eminent *political importance*. (Zimmermann, 1998: 92; emphasis added)

The ICC, states and individuals

The legalistic discourse sets out a certain background of unquestioned assumptions and at the same time promotes specific instruments and measures that are regarded to be the most appropriate means to reach the objective of a just and peaceful world order. In doing so, it simultaneously constitutes its main units of reference – the ICC as a supra-state institution, states and individuals – and the relations among them in a particular way. Students of International Relations frequently describe the project of the ICC as one that puts individuals to the fore of international law, thereby cutting across state borders and decreasing the significance of the state system as such (Economides, 2001: 127; cf. Armstrong, 1999: 554). This account of the Court, however, is too simple and does not capture the main features of the ICC accurately. First, despite the importance of NGOs for the establishment of the ICC (cf. Glasius, 2005; Deitelhoff, 2007), the central role of states in this process cannot be denied. Second, and even more importantly, the performance of the ICC will essentially depend on the cooperation and the enforcement capacities of states (Broomhall, 2003: 151ff.). The Court will only be able to perform successfully if state actors arrest and extradite suspects to the ICC and cooperate with the Court in the collection of evidence for prosecutions.

Though the relationship between the ICC, states and individuals is far more complicated than simply interpreting the Court as an outcome of an increasing move towards cosmopolitanism on a global scale, parts of the legalistic discourse cling to this idea as well. Yet there are also proponents of legalism who regard the project of the ICC as one that has been primarily initiated and carried out by states. As will be shown below, the legalistic discourse comprises two branches of argumentation that differ with respect to the question of which entity lies at the core of the institutionalisation of the ICC – individuals or states. With reference to the English School theory, the former will be labelled the world society-oriented subdivision and the latter the international society-oriented strand of legalism.

International society

The international society-oriented branch of the legalistic discourse embraces the idea that states form the most central point of reference for the establishment of the ICC. According to its advocates, one central feature that specifies the relationship between states and the ICC is that the legitimacy of the ICC as a supra-state institution is derived from the community of states that deliberately decided to confer parts of their criminal jurisdiction upon the Court. This idea served as a justification for the proposal to provide the ICC with universal jurisdiction, which was favoured by the German delegation during the Rome negotiations:

> Under current international law, all States might exercise universal criminal jurisdiction concerning acts of genocide, crimes against humanity and war crimes, regardless of the nationality of the offender, the nationality of the victims, and the place where the crime had been committed. ... It meant that each State could bring to justice individuals who had committed, for example, acts of genocide in third States, even if the offender and the victim were not nationals of the prosecuting State. *The Court would be acting on behalf of the international community as a whole.* ... Thus the application of the principle of universal jurisdiction by the Court would not violate the sovereignty of third states not party to the Statute.[29]

According to this point of view, international society emerges as a structure that comprises more than just the sum of the states that belong to it; rather, it is prior to the single state. Moreover, it shapes and is shaped by the framework of international law. The legitimacy of the ICC is thus derived from a collective body of states.

The jurisdictional regime was one of the issues on which the European states under consideration initially disagreed. The German delegation was eventually unsuccessful with its attempt to grant the ICC universal jurisdiction. The UK had put forward a proposal according to which the consent of the state on the territory of which the crime occurred and the custodial state of the suspect were necessary for the exercise of jurisdiction.[30] France opposed universal jurisdiction, but changed its position on the issue of jurisdiction several times: during the PrepCom negotiations, the French delegation proposed that the consent of the territorial state, the custodial state, the state of nationality of the accused and the state of nationality of the victim should be required as a precondition for the ICC's jurisdiction (Hall, 1998a: 131). At the Rome Conference, it supported the British proposal but promoted a specific consent regime for war crimes: since war crimes could be 'isolated acts', the Rome Statute should allow for some 'flexibility': 'There could be a system requiring consent by the State of nationality of the perpetrator, so that the Court could exercise its jurisdiction.'[31] This proposal came close to US claims for a jurisdictional regime based on the consent of the state of nationality of the accused for all three core crimes. In the end, jurisdiction was based on the consent of *either* the territorial state *or* the state of nationality of the accused and France's concerns were accommodated with a one-off seven-year opt-out provision for war crimes. France was one of only two states making use of this provision upon ratification of the Rome Statute.[32]

There are several reasons for the disunity on the preconditions for the ICC's jurisdiction: first, in this case the ambiguity of core concepts of the emerging legalistic discourse turned out to be a liability rather than an asset: 'What bedeviled the negotiations was the expression "inherent jurisdiction", which meant automatic jurisdiction for some, but nothing less than universal jurisdiction for others' (Glasius, 2005: 74). Second, NGOs that often reinforced an emerging consensus at the Rome Conference by publishing 'virtual votes' on certain issues found it difficult to monitor majority positions on this issue, since there were several ways to approach the problem of preconditions for jurisdiction, i.e. state consent regimes or opt-in/opt-out solutions (*ibid.*: 74). Third, the stalemate on the issue caused the chairman of the negotiations, Philippe Kirsch, to convene the permanent five members of the Security Council shortly before the end of the Rome Conference for negotiations behind closed doors. The result was a 'temporary joint approach by the permanent five members of the Security Council' (Kaul, 1998: 55), who came up with a compromise proposal that was more restrictive than many LMG states had wished. Although this proposal was subsequently further amended during the official negotiations, many delegates and observers were disappointed by 'the reversion, accepted by the chair, to old-fashioned diplomatic methods which were out of character with the rest of the negotiations' (Glasius, 2005: 75). Others, however, pointed out that this move was necessary in order prevent an overall failure of the Rome Conference (Kirsch and Holmes, 1999: 9ff.).[33]

Although the German delegation was not successful in its attempt to place the ICC on the fundament of universal jurisdiction, the reasoning behind universal jurisdiction played a crucial role in the debate between supporters of the ICC and US officials opposing the eventual institutional design of the Court. One of the main points of US legal experts and advisors aiming to justify the US position was that the Rome Statute illegitimately imposes treaty obligations on non-party states because according to Articles 15, 53 and 58 of the Statute, citizens of non-party states could be brought to trial before the ICC in the event that they were suspected to have committed genocide, war crimes or crimes against humanity in the territory of a state which had ratified the Rome Statute (Broomhall, 2003: 164). US officials and some legal experts argued that this would contradict the provisions of the 1969 Vienna Convention on the Law of Treaties.[34] Against this challenge, German legal experts reiterated the claim of German negotiators, advancing the argument that universal jurisdiction – at least with respect to genocide – forms a part of established international law:

> Yet, changes that have taken place since 1948 prove that is by now a firmly established standard of customary international law that in accordance with the principle of universal jurisdiction, *every* state is entitled to try genocide in its own national courts, irrespective of the question of where, by whom and against who it has been committed. If this is the case, however, several states can also transfer their national penal power to an international body, which would also be vested with universal jurisdiction regardless of the approval of one or more affected states. (Zimmermann, 1998: 86f.)

Some commentators even expressed the hope that although the ICC itself does not have universal jurisdiction, the complementarity principle included in the Rome Statute will encourage states to exercise universal jurisdiction over international crimes. In Louise Arbour's words: 'The express preference for domestic prosecutions in the Rome Statute will invariably lead to an increase in national prosecutions for war crimes in all cases where a state has an interest in avoiding the scrutiny of the international forum, and it may lead to an increase in the exercise of universal jurisdiction by states' (Arbour, 2003: 587).

Even though the ICC does not have universal jurisdiction, the legalistic discourse emphasises that the ICC can impose obligations on states. This becomes clear from a remark made by the British chief negotiator to the Rome Conference, Sir Franklin Berman:

> Another issue of great importance was the obligation of States to cooperate with the Court. That was not simply a matter of surrendering indicted defendants or of the proper operation of the complementarity mechanisms. At least as important was cooperation over the provision of evidence for the prosecutions before the Court, including, of course, evidence that might be needed by the defendant himself.[35]

The reason for these obligations is not simply grounded in the fact that the ICC represents a supra-state institution and is thus able to exercise power over states. Rather, the international society-oriented subdivision of the legalistic discourse holds that the Court acts for the community of states as a whole and pursues its collective interest, which is deemed superior to the single state and its special interest:

This particular structure can also be applied to crimes of such a nature insofar as the ICC could be regarded as *protecting the interests of all states parties*. Only the ICC itself, and *not individual states* therefore, will be able to decide on whether certain crimes can be prosecuted. The ICC could be regarded as *defending the interests of the community of states parties*. Unlike the horizontal relations in extradition and judicial assistance, *the relation between the ICC and states parties is a vertical one*. (Hafner *et al.*, 1999: 112; emphasis added)

In this sense, the supra-state level is regarded as superior to the state level only insofar as the former is rooted in the community of all states as opposed to the individual state. This construction provides the supra-state level and its institutions with the legitimacy and weight required to impose binding obligations on single states. According to the logic of the legalistic discourse, international society is not simply based upon shared norms and values among states. Rather it is grounded in the perception of a common good and a collective interest which transcends the narrow notion of the national interest of individual states.

World society

The second subdivision of the legalistic discourse depicts individuals as the basic units of international relations and as the major point of reference for the establishment of the ICC. Generally, there are two different roles that individuals might play according to this strand of the legalistic discourse: first, individuals are depicted as bearers of a common interest and second, as potential perpetrators of crimes against international criminal law.

In the case of the first role, proponents of the world society strand of legalism hold that the rationale behind the ICC's establishment is that it is supposed to serve the interest and the common good of all human beings:

By acknowledging the concept of humanity, international law in fact makes reference to the *common interests of all human beings*, to the *universal common good*, and it seems obvious that the Statute of the International Criminal Court to a certain extent bears witness to the existence of a more solidary international community. (Carrillo-Salcedo, 1999: 24; emphasis added)

This world society-oriented approach to the establishment of the ICC implies at the same time a certain role for states. According to Carrillo-Salcedo, the Rome Statute expresses a certain degree of mistrust *vis-à-vis* states as well as it presents the Court as an institution intended to exert control over states with respect to the fulfilment of jurisdictional obligations.

While it acknowledges the eminent role of states, the three options to initiate an investigation [i.e. by state parties, by the UN Security Council and by the prosecutor *ex officio*] envisaged in the Statute express a certain distrust towards them, as it aims at compensating their shortcomings – a latent mechanism of accusation that reveals a lot about the spirit of this agreement: it puts states under control and in some sense under suspicion. (*ibid.*)

The world society-oriented subdivision of the legalistic discourse also stresses the importance of holding accountable individual perpetrators of crimes against humanitarian and human rights law. In this context, perpetrators are portrayed as individuals detached from states and official positions that they might hold within the framework of states. The fact that the Rome Statute in Article 27 itself rules out claims to immunity before the ICC can be regarded as an expression of this idea (cf. Broomhall, 2003: 136ff.). The discursive arena of legal experts is especially focused on the role of individuals as potential perpetrators. Referring to the topic of progress, legal experts evaluate the establishment of individual accountability within the framework of the ICC as a positive development in international law: 'The Statute reinforces the principle of individual criminal responsibility according to which grave violations of international law can be prosecuted. It is especially this fact that makes clear that there are *obligations of the individual vis-à-vis the international community as a whole*' (Blanke and Molitor, 2001: 169; emphasis added).

Thus, the legalistic discourse interprets the ICC as an institution that provides a direct link between the level of individuals and the supra-state level. It transcends the notion of the individual in its primary role as a citizen of a nation state, moving towards a cosmopolitan interpretation of the individual. In any event, the discursive construction of individuals, in particular in the world society branch of legalism, establishes a mutual relationship with respective rights and obligations between the individual as a single human being on the one hand and the 'international community' on the other.

However, in the discursive arena of diplomats there is evidence that some transitions exist between the world society and the international society-oriented branch of the legalistic discourse: Consider, for instance, Sir Jeremy Greenstock's comments at a UN Security Council meeting in 2000:

[C]areful consideration of the needs of ordinary people has to be at the heart of all our conflict prevention strategies. We have to remember that civilians, so often the *tragic victims of conflict*, are *individuals with the same rights as the rest of us*, but caught up in adverse and specific circumstances. Their particular protection needs, whether they be children, women or other more vulnerable groups, must be properly identified and met. For their sake above all, the international legal framework needs to be upheld, and the Rome Statute of the International Criminal Court and the Ottawa Convention on anti-personnel mines must be signed and ratified by all of us. ... This concept of *security for individuals* should guide us in our work. It will play an intrinsic part in the *wider goal of security for States. When individuals are protected and their human, economic, social, political and cultural rights are upheld, international stability is consolidated.*[36]

Greenstock's remarks imply that the protection and security of individuals constitute a precondition for 'the wider goal of security for States'. Instead of omitting the state as an intermediary instance between individuals and supra-state institutions, he constructs the state level as a mediating instance between the two levels, thereby providing the possibility of unifying both the world society and the international society-oriented branches of the legalistic discourse.

Sovereignty and human rights

New sovereignty and the erosion of sovereignty

In accordance with the two subdivisions of the legalistic discourse, namely the international society-oriented branch and the world society-oriented branch, two different notions of sovereignty emerge. The international society-oriented proponents of the legalistic discourse generally hold that the ICC does not intrude into state sovereignty, and some have even argued that it would strengthen and further it. Most advocates of the international society-oriented subdivision of legalism opt for an understanding of sovereignty in the sense of 'new sovereignty' (Chayes and Chayes, 1995: 27).[37] According to them, as a result of globalisation and increasing international and transnational interdependence (cf. Scholte, 2000; Keohane and Nye, 2001), the notion of sovereignty has profoundly changed: instead of independence or autonomy of states, sovereignty nowadays consists in the exercise of influence within international regimes and institutions – one of which is the ICC. In this vein, Edzard Schmidt-Jortzig argued that 'in an interdependent, globalized world, States must accept the Court's jurisdiction over the three core crimes; *sovereignty would be better served by cooperation than by futile attempts to stand alone*'.[38]

The world society oriented-subdivision of the legalistic discourse, on the other hand, construes the ICC not as a reaffirmation of sovereignty, but as an intrusion into it. However, given that its advocates regard sovereignty as an impediment to a more cosmopolitan world order, they do not deplore this development. Overcoming sovereignty is viewed as a major achievement in moving towards a more just world order: 'Institutionalising the rule of law on an international scale is the only source of legitimacy which can serve as a constraint to the sovereignty of states and the right of the powerful, that is, the "state of nature" among states.'[39] This idea was prominent in the discursive arena of the media as well as among parts of the legal expert arena:

> Evidently, the establishment of the ICC entails an unprecedented encroachment upon state sovereignty: suffice it to point out the fact that the Statute is the only conventional measure in the field of international humanitarian and human rights law with a general scope that envisages a jurisdictional mechanism leading to binding decisions. (Condorelli, 1999: 8)

According to the world society-oriented subdivision of legalism, states and state sovereignty simply have not proven useful when it comes to the protection of individuals and their rights. The idea of overcoming the 'state of nature among states' hints at the social contract that Thomas Hobbes confines to societies constituted *within* states. In contrast to Hobbes, proponents of the world society strand hold that this social contract could be at some point extended *beyond* state borders and could become global in reach. Ironically, whilst Hobbes regarded the – national – social contract as the basis of the establishment of a sovereign authority, the world society-oriented branch of legalism holds that concluding a cosmopolitan social contract requires the abolition of the principle of sovereignty.

Symmetry

Apart from the features of progress and order based on law, there is a further common feature that both the international society- and the world society-oriented branch of legalism endorse: the idea of *symmetry* is depicted as the core of the concept of sovereignty as well as being central to the vision of a cosmopolitan world order. Although this idea is implicit in most statements belonging to the legalistic discourse, it is made increasingly explicit after the US took up a more openly hostile stance towards the ICC. Whilst the Clinton administration aimed at 'negotiating a fix' with the Assembly of State Parties to the ICC concerning the exemption of US citizens from the jurisdiction of the Court, after the election of George W. Bush and the entry into force of the ICC Statute in 2002, US resistance became more resolute. Besides taking domestic measures against the ICC, the US government pressed for a UN Security Council resolution ruling out the extradition of non-party citizens to the ICC for a one-year period. Although resolution 1422 was eventually adopted unanimously by the UN Security Council, most European commentators were highly critical of it. In particular, they criticised the asymmetry that this resolution implies. Asymmetry, as becomes evident from the following quotation from the *Hamburger Abendblatt*, is equated with power politics as the foundation of international relations:

> The decision of the UN Security Council leads to a dead end. As long as the United States of America claim to defend human rights and freedom, the values of civilisation and the rule of law, and wage war for them, especially the US has to put its citizens under the scrutiny of an independent court – in case they violate relevant norms. ... The US' *special role* emanating from Bush's blackmail concerning the renewal of the mandate for Bosnia-Herzegovina will backfire on the International Criminal Court. ... Thus, *the right of the powerful outplays the rule of law* – a vicious compromise, which cannot serve as the basis for security policy.[40]

Moreover, according to the legalistic discourse, asymmetry decreases the degree of global order and jeopardises security, as Steve Crawshaw and Richard Dicker, both leading executives of Human Rights Watch, emphasise: 'The ICC's supporters have understood what the US administration seems so reluctant to grasp: when America places itself above the law, it send a danger-ous signal.'[41] Generally, proponents of the legalistic discourse equate the rule of law with equality, even though they often do not specify among which units equality is supposed to be established – states or individuals.

In fact, a close reading of texts and utterances belonging to the framework of the legalistic discourse reveals that the object of reference for structural sym-metry differs, depending on the orientation: the international society-oriented subdivision tends to interpret symmetry as the sovereign equality of states, whereas the world society-oriented strand of legalism is inclined to under-stand symmetry as the equality of individuals before the law. With regard to the former, the role of the UN Security Council has great significance, first because the Security Council has a limited membership; and second because only the permanent five members hold a veto. Proponents of legalism evaluate both aspects as undermining the sovereign equality of all states:

> Such an exertion of influence [by the UN Security Council] requires a justifica-tion that is in accordance with a strict rule, since it generally could undermine the independence of the Court and therefore its recognition. Moreover, one must take into consideration the principle of the *sovereign equality of all states*, which could be violated in case of an intrusion into the (delegated) jurisdiction of state parties. (Heselhaus, 2002: 926; emphasis added)

Sovereign equality in this sense also implies that all states are considered equal (at least in a legal sense), regardless of their actual size or power, which is one of the major cleavages between the legalistic discourse and the interventionist discourse.[42]

The world society-oriented strand of the legalistic discourse, in contrast, fo-cuses on the equality of individuals before the law when it refers to symmetry. It comes as no surprise that this point of view is especially prominent among NGO representatives, whose perspective on international relations tends to transcend the statist framework (cf. Glasius, 2005, Heins, 2002b). Steve Crawshaw from Human Rights Watch, for instance, argued that 'American contempt for the court – and its determination to bring the court's supporters to heel – sends a disastrous message worldwide. It suggests that there is one standard of justice for *Americans* and another for *anybody else*.'[43] The left-liberal media in particular supports and amplifies this attitude: 'Human rights or-ganisations were right to condemn in advance such exemptions as a violation of the principle of the *equality of all before the law*.'[44]

Human rights

Both strands of the legalistic discourse depict the supra-state level as the most relevant point of reference for human rights. However, depending on the re-spective alignment of the two branches, they come to this conclusion in dif-ferent ways. Whereas the international society strand of legalism regards the consensus principle as the most important point of reference for human rights – meaning consensus among states – the world society-oriented subdivision argues that human rights refer to the collective conscience of all individuals, thereby approaching the natural law tradition in a Lauterpachtian sense.

According to the consensus principle, provisions of international law are valid because a majority of states agreed to them and the remaining minority of non-consenting states has to abide by them as well. This interpretation of international law refrains from alluding to the natural law tradition, but nonetheless grants legal provisions a high degree of validity and independence *vis-à-vis* states. The validity of international law is not directly dependent upon the approval of all states at any time (cf. Bull, 1995: 148). According to this perspective, a state has to comply with international law even if it did not approve of a particular rule (but a majority of other states did) or if the compliance with a rule contradicts its immediate interest at a certain point of time (but it did approve it in former times). By focusing on the majority of states in order to assess the validity and binding effects of a legal provision, the international society strand of legalism reaches a quasi-universal fundament for human rights without making reference to the natural law tradition. Jean-Marc de la Sablière, French ambassador to the UN Security Council, expressed this direct link between majority and universality in one of his public statements: 'That Court is the instrument par excellence of the primacy of law and justice. *More than half of the United Nations Member States* are parties to its Statute. It should become *universal*. That is our hope and that idea is inherent in its conception.'[45] The interpretation of the Rome Statute as a universally binding legal code also becomes evident in a comment by a legal expert, who criticised US opposition to the ICC and argued that the Statute cannot be amended because of the reservations of one single state:

> The international community of states would regard it as a major retrogression if the scope of application of one of the most important agreements in the history of international law was retrospectively constrained because of the *special interests* of one single state, the standpoint of which is incomprehensible for the *overwhelming majority of states*. (Stahn, 2000: 658; emphasis added)

The idea that support of a majority of states is a sound foundation of international law was reinforced by the activities of NGOs at the Rome Conference, who published 'virtual votes' on contested issues (Glasius, 2005: 59). The underlying idea was that majority positions could claim more legitimacy than minority opinions. Moreover, this majoritarian approach to international negotiations was in line with the concept of the equality of states: 'it counteracted the customary tendency of negotiators of concentrating on "powerful states"' (*ibid.*).

The world society subdivision of legalism, in contrast, deduces the validity and obligatory character of the ICC Statute from the collective 'conscience of humanity'.[46] Irrespective of this difference, its proponents also opted for the implementation of human rights on the global level:

> These provisions and the values that they stand for express to a certain extent an ideology that envisages the international community mainly *as a single collective of human beings*, the global character of which consequently requires a multilateral approach to international law. ... This progressive claim implied in the notion of international community, which is inherent in contemporary practice and doctrine explains why *relativism indisputably loses its significance*. This development goes along with the appearance of notions of *binding rules and erga omnes obligations in contemporary international law*. (Carrillo-Salcedo, 1999: 25; emphasis added)

However, the international society-inspired reading and the world society interpretation concerning the validity of human rights do not contradict each other; rather, one could understand them as two aspects that are both of equal importance and perhaps even converge. This is reminiscent of the question that divided the legal scholars Alfred Verdross and Hersch Lauterpacht during the interwar period: while the former considered the existence of a global community of human beings as a precondition for a cosmopolitan international law, the latter held that a cosmopolitanisation of international law would give rise to the emergence of such a community (Koskenniemi, 2002: 365f.). One legal expert seems to agree with Lauterpacht in arguing that the effect of the ICC Statute might well reach beyond what is normally expected of multilateral treaties:

> According to its legal form, the ICC Statute is first and foremost a multilateral treaty like any other, which has to overcome the high hurdle of 60 ratifications in order to enter into force. Once this happened, however, it seems likely that the Statute of Rome will represent a further piece in the mosaic of norms which shape *the identity of the international community as the subject of international law* and which may be perceived as partial elements of an international constitutional order. (Stahn, 1998: 590f.; emphasis added)

Irrespective of the differences between the international society-oriented and the world society-oriented subdivisions of the legalistic discourse, one might come to the conclusion that whichever strand dominates the debate, the institutionalisation of the ICC could eventually epitomise a rapprochement of both aspects – the international society of states and the world society of individuals, as both attitudes exerted influence on the final shape of the Court. In the words of one legal expert: 'The creation of this universal Court, which does not judge states but individuals, squarely reaffirms the notion of a genuinely international public order, *neither merely transnational, nor merely inter-state*' (Weckel, 1998: 986; emphasis added).

Conclusion

The emergence of the legalistic discourse in the framework of the negotiations over the ICC was characterised by subdivisions and the initial ambiguity of some of its basic concepts. While this ambiguity was arguably an asset in that it broadened the spectrum of potential proponents, it sometimes turned out to be a liability. The clearest example in this respect was the initial use of the concept of 'inherent jurisdiction', the ambiguity of which proved divisive during the Rome Conference.

Yet despite these ambiguities and subdivisions, legalism can be regarded as a clearly demarcated discourse. One of the features common to both its strands is the underlying narrative of progress: proponents of legalism generally hold that the ICC represents one step within a broader development that leads from an international order based on power politics towards an international order based on law. In addition, proponents of legalism hold that progress towards an international order based on law also implies a depoliticisation of international law on the one hand and a professionalisation of international legal institutions on the other.

When it comes to the question of which ontology forms the foundation of the legalistic discourse, the divide within the legalistic discourse reveals itself. Generally, one strand of legalism follows the ontology of international society and regards states as the basic units of international relations. The second subdivision of legalism, in contrast, aligns itself with the paradigm of world society, meaning that it considers individuals as the most important entities. This, however, does not create serious tensions or conflicts within the discourse, since the binding features of progress, order as law and symmetry are fundamental enough to bridge both alignments.

The division of the legalistic discourse also affects the conception of the notion of interest: whilst the international society-oriented branch of legalism links the notion of interest to the international community of all states, the world society perspective of this discourse refers to individuals as the bearers of a global common interest. One option to unify the different notions of interest is conceiving of interest as a nested concept, with the collective interest of individuals as the foundation for the collective interest of states.

The divide within the legalistic discourse also accounts for the varying notions of sovereignty and the different points of reference for the validity of human rights. The international society subdivision interprets sovereignty in terms of 'new sovereignty', meaning that as a result of globalisation, states exert their sovereignty through cooperation with other states and through participation in international regimes and organisations rather than by insisting on autonomy and independence. The point of reference for human rights is the consensus of the majority of all states, which in turn leads to a quasi-universal status of human rights.

The world society subdivision of legalism, on the other hand, stresses the erosion of sovereignty: according to this view, the ICC was established in order to protect individuals and is able to exert a certain pressure on states with respect to their compliance with humanitarian and human rights law, thereby eroding state sovereignty. Human rights refer to the idea of the collective conscience of humankind. Just as in the case of the international society strand of legalism, the supra-state level is considered the appropriate venue for the enforcement of human rights, as the notion of common conscience is related to the cosmopolitan community of individuals which are neither separated by their citizenship nor by their cultural affiliation.

Notes

1. Britain joined the LMG after Labour came to power in 1997; France did so on the last session of the Preparatory Committee in March 1998. See also Chapter 7, 'International society: hegemony and anarchy'.
2. This opt-out provision (Art. 124 Rome Statute) rules that state parties to the ICC can make a request to be exempted from the Court's jurisdiction over war crimes for a period of seven years starting from the entry into force of the Rome Statute.
3. These aspects of Enlightenment philosophy are certainly themselves contested concepts. For the relevant debates on Enlightenment political thought, its roots and the respective debates, see, among others, Koselleck (1992) and Skinner (1978). For a contemporary reading of Enlightenment thought, see, for instance, Rengger (1995).
4. Terry Olson, 'Une défense de la Cour pénale internationale', *Le Figaro* (19 July 2002); emphasis added. All translations from French or German are the author's.
5. Steve Crawshaw, 'Why the US Needs this Court: America's Rejection of the International Criminal Court is a Threat to its own Security', *Observer* (15 June 2003).
6. Hans-Peter Kaul, DipCon 3rd meeting (17 June 1998); U.N. Doc. A/CONF.183/C.1/SR.3, Vol. II, p. 146; emphasis added.
7. Anthony Lewis, 'U.S. Denied its Heritage in Failing to Embrace World Court', *St. Louis Post-Dispatch* (21 July 1998); emphasis added.
8. Dominique de Villepin, UN SC meeting 'Justice and the rule of law: the United Nations role' (24 September 2003); U.N. Doc. S/PV.4833, p. 7.
9. Günther Pleuger, UN SC meeting 'Justice and the rule of law: the United Nations role' (24 September 2003); U.N. Doc. S/PV.4833, p. 16; emphasis added.
10. Of course, some legalists consider humanitarian intervention; that is, the imposition of human rights standards by military means, as legitimate. But this constellation already belongs to possible transitions between legalism and interventionism.
11. See 'Symmetry', below.
12. For a detailed discussion of the concept of inclusive and exclusive identities, see Rumelili (2004: 36ff.). According to Rumelili, exclusive identities rest upon the construction of inherent characteristics, whereas inclusive identities are defined by acquired ones. Edward Keene, in contrast, does not take into consideration the distinction between inclusive and exclusive identities (2002: 120ff.). According to him the major difference between the colonialist idea of civilisation and contemporary *missions civilisatrices* is that the distinction between civilised and non-civilised does not necessarily parallel the geographical categories of European–non-European anymore.
13. As will become apparent from some of the statements and comments quoted below, advocates of legalism often use the terms 'law' and 'justice' interchangeably.
14. Paul Meunier, 'La Cour sans les grands', *Sud Ouest* (2 July 2002); emphasis added.
15. In fact, the legalistic emphasis on the international law as the foundation of a peaceful international order seems to tie in with the debate among international lawyers on the emergence of an international (or global) constitutional order (cf. Breau, 2008).

16 François Alabrune, Meeting of the Sixth Committee (Legal) of the UN General Assembly (12 December 2000); U.N. Doc. A/C.6/55/SR.9, p. 3; emphasis added.

17 Sir Emyr Jones Parry, UN SC meeting 'Sudan' (31 March 2005); U.N. Doc. S/PV.5158, p. 7; emphasis added.

18 Günther Pleuger, UN SC meeting 'Civilians in armed conflict' (14 December 2004); U.N. Doc. S/PV.5100, p. 18; emphasis added.

19 Michel Duclos, UN SC meeting 'Civilians in armed conflict' (9 December 2003); U.N. Doc. S/PV.4877, p. 20; emphasis added.

20 Rolf Welberts, Meeting of the Sixth Committee of the UN General Assembly (1 November 1996); U.N. Doc. A/C.6/51/SR.29, pp. 11–12.

21 Kenneth Roth, 'Human rights, American Wrongs: Europe Must Resist the US Obduracy that Is Threatening to Undermine the International Criminal Court', *Financial Times* (1 July 2002); emphasis added.

22 'L'amérique, la justice et la paix', *Les Echos* (2 July 2002) – emphasis added.

23 The ICC Assembly of State Parties decided in 2002 to set up a Special Working Group for the Crime of Aggression. The legal provisions concerning the crime of aggression will be discussed in the first review conference in 2009. For a discussion of the post-Rome negotiations on the crime of aggression, see, e.g., Kress (2007), McDougall (2007) and Schuster (2003).

24 Hans-Peter Kaul, DipCon 10th meeting (22 June 1998); U.N. Doc. A/CONF.183/C.1/SR.10, p. 204; emphasis added.

25 Marc Perrin de Brichambaut, DipCon 8th meeting (22 June 1998); U.N. Doc. A/CONF.183/C.1/SR.8, p. 189.

26 The legalistic argument about professionalism constitutes the counterpart to the interventionist fear of politically motivated prosecutions. See also Chapter 4.

27 Sir Franklin Berman, DipCon 6th plenary meeting (17 June 1998); U.N. Doc. A/CONF.183/SR.6, Vol. II, p. 9; emphasis added.

28 Michel Duclos, UN SC meeting 'United Nations peacekeeping' (12 June 2003); U.N. Doc. S/PV.4772, p. 24; emphasis added.

29 Hans-Peter Kaul, DipCon 7th meeting (18 July 1998); U.N. Doc. A/CONF.183/C.1/SR.7, Vol. II, p. 184; emphasis added.

30 Bureau Proposal, U.N. Doc. A/CONF.183/C.1/L.59 (Article 7, Option 2), pp. 9–10.

31 Marc Perrin de Brichambaut, DipCon 8th meeting (19 June 1998); U.N. Doc. A/CONF.183/C.1/SR.8, p. 190.

32 The other state was Colombia.

33 There were two issues on which members of the LMG could not reach agreement in Rome. Yet in both cases the cleavage lines reflected to a large extent a North–South divide rather than an intra-European one. First, the crime of aggression was included into the Rome Statute, but its definition was left open for future negotiations in the ICC's Assembly of State Parties. European states insisted that the UN Security Council should determine whether an act of aggression had occurred, whereas many developing states demanded that the Security Council should not be involved in that decision (Politi, 1999: 828). In this case, the position of the European states under consideration was opposed to both the US, who was against including the crime of aggression into the ICC Statute (see Chapter 4 below) and to the position of developing states. Secondly, several states from the developing world (in particular India), insisted that the ICC Statute should include nuclear weapons in the list of prohibited weapons. They argued that prohibiting biological and chemical weapons but omitting nuclear weapons would target developing states in particular, who could not afford nuclear weapons (Kirsch and Holmes, 1999: 7).

34 See also Chapter 5 on this point.
35 Sir Franklin Berman, DipCon 6th plenary meeting (17 June 1998); U.N. Doc. A/CONF.183/SR.6, Vol. II, p. 98.
36 Sir Jeremy Greenstock, UN SC meeting 'Prevention of armed conflicts' (20 July 2000); U.N. Doc. S/PV.4174, p. 7; emphasis added.
37 Cf. also the notion of 'pooled sovereignty' coined by Keohane and Hoffmann (1990: 10).
38 Edzard Schmidt-Jortzig, DipCon 4th plenary meeting (16 June 1998); U.N. Doc. A/CONF.183/SR.4, Vol. II, p. 83; emphasis added.
39 Christian Semler, 'Wider die Logik der Erpresser', *tageszeitung* (5 July 2002).
40 Franz-Josef Hutsch, 'Recht des Stärkeren statt Stärke des Rechts', *Hamburger Abendblatt* (15 July 2002).
41 Steve Crawshaw and Richard Dicker, 'Britain's Flawed Position on the Global Court', *Financial Times* (22 June 2004).
42 See also Chapter 4.
43 Steve Crawshaw, 'Why the US Needs this Court: America's Rejection of the International Criminal Court is a Threat to its Own Security', *Observer* (15 June 2003); emphasis added.
44 Bernd Pickert, 'Für Darfur reicht der Fortschritt nicht. Sicherheitsrat bricht US-Widerstand gegen Strafgerichtshof', *tageszeitung* (1 April 2005); emphasis added.
45 Jean-Marc de la Sablière, UN SC meeting 'Justice and the rule of law: the United Nations role' (6 October 2004); U.N. Doc. S/PV.5052, pp. 20–1 – emphasis added.
46 Rome Statute of the International Criminal Court, Preamble; U.N. Doc. A/CONF.183/9.

4 The interventionist discourse

The interventionist discourse denies that international law is an appropriate instrument to change the established international order. According to the interventionist perspective, international law is generally subordinate to politics. Thus, it may merely serve the purpose of maintaining the status quo in international relations. This is not to say that interventionists dismiss the significance of human rights as a central part of international law. Rather, they hold that legal bodies like the ICC do not further the global compliance with human rights provisions. Interventionists privilege political action culminating in military intervention over legal institutions as the preferred way to enforce human rights. Viewed from this perspective, the ICC is not only considered inappropriate for the protection of human rights but is seen as being downright detrimental to that purpose, since it exposes peacekeeping troops to the jurisdiction of the Court, thereby deterring potential contributors from participating in humanitarian interventions. Moreover, interventionists maintain that legalistic projects such as the ICC potentially undermine the existing international order by trying to bind major powers legally. This is problematic given the interventionist belief that, due to their superior military capabilities, great powers play a crucial role in safeguarding the international order.

Table 4.1 displays the most central features of the interventionist discourse.

Construction of time	Sources of order	Features of order	Ontology/ basic units	Notion of interest refers to	Notion of sovereignty	Human rights refer to
Continuity	Power politics	Asymmetry	States	Overlap between international society and great powers	Conditional sovereignty	International society/ customary law

Table 4.1 Basic features of the interventionist discourse

The interventionist discourse is one of the discourses that informed US opposition to the ICC. Its main proponents are US diplomats, legal experts aiming at corroborating the US opposition to the ICC from a theoretical standpoint, and parts of the US media. However, the interventionist discourse is not entirely confined to US political actors and commentators. Some European diplomats also aligned themselves with the interventionist perspective – in particular during the early stages of negotiations about the ICC. This applies especially to political actors from France and the UK, both of which traditionally engaged in military interventions abroad. For instance, the French proposal of a seven-year opt-out provision for war crimes, which was eventually included in the Rome Statute, echoes an interventionist perspective.[1] However, as soon as the French concerns were accommodated at the Rome Conference and their proposals were incorporated in the ICC Statute, they dropped all claims inspired by interventionism.[2] Nevertheless, some voices from the European media continued to echo interventionist ideas.

The narrative of interventionism: power politics provide for international order

A conservative approach to international law

One of the most contentious issues concerning the establishment of the ICC was the extent to which various proposals made at the Rome Conference as well as the final version of the ICC Statute were in accordance with existing provisions of international law. Whereas the legalistic discourse espouses a perspective of change and progress with regard to legal provisions, interventionism emphasises continuity, thereby taking a rather conservative stance on international law. One of the often-repeated interventionist arguments against particular proposals made at the Rome Conference as well as against the final Rome Statute was that they contradicted established provisions of customary international law.[3] This points to the fact that legalists and interventionists had a different understanding of what they intended to achieve at the Rome Conference. Whilst the latter aimed at codifying existing customary law, they charged the former of attempting to engage in a law-making effort. Consider in this respect the following assessment by a US legal expert: 'As a matter of international law, the ICC Treaty breaks new ground in how the international community comes to agree upon what is or is not international law. *Far from taking a customary law approach, this Treaty attempts to legislate international law*' (McNerney, 2001: 181; emphasis added).

David Scheffer, US chief negotiator at the Rome Conference, reiterated the idea that customary law should be the ultimate benchmark for the codification of crimes within the Rome Statute in an article published in the *American Journal of International Law*. He argued that the negotiation process was seriously hampered by the fact that the participants of the Rome Conference held different views of the purpose of the negotiations:

The U.S. delegation actively participated in drafting the definitions of war crimes at the Preparatory Committee and later in Rome. Throughout the process, we were determined to include *only those war crimes that qualified as such under customary international law*. This objective required intensive negotiations with other delegations, some of which wanted to stretch the list of war crimes into actions that, while reprehensible, *were not customary international law at the end of the twentieth century*. (Scheffer, 1999: 14; emphasis added)

In short, interventionists insisted that the Rome Conference was intended to codify customary law rather than introducing major changes to the already existing provisions of humanitarian and human rights law. However, once it became evident that the ICC Statute would in some instances reach beyond the framework of customary law,[4] proponents of interventionism challenged its legitimacy on the grounds of what they perceived as amendments to the applicable rules of humanitarian and human rights law.

Order is based on power politics

The reason why interventionists treat the idea of a further development of international law with great reserve is their conception of the relationship between international order, politics and law. Unlike legalists, interventionists do not believe that international order can be mainly based on international law. Rather, the law is considered to be subordinate to politics – it cannot create order, it can merely justify and help maintaining order that has been provided by power politics beforehand. This is not to say, however, that interventionists are generally hostile to international law. Rather, they hold that a flexible approach to international law that properly reflects the outstanding role of great powers, either through formal rules or through informal practices, is indispensable for a peaceful and sustainable international order.

According to the interventionist discourse, the law cannot be the prime foundation of international order. It is simply not equipped to deal with situations in which order is at risk, for instance, a protracted civil war spilling over into neighbouring states and threatening to destabilise entire regions. The law can only be applied once order has been established. This idea is even prominent amongst European liberals such as Ian Buruma, who wrote in a comment for the *Guardian*:

Alas, our peaceful Europe is not well equipped to deal with gangsters – before they come to court. Against a Milošević it proved to be useless. Only American power saved millions of Bosnian lives. ... As long as this contradiction persists, we cannot expect the Americans to be keen on our European civilising mission. There is only one way out of this dilemma, which is to rebuild European military power. We cannot match the US, but we can share more of its burden. If we want the Americans to sign up to the ICC, we too must do the dirty work, and take risk of being held accountable.[5]

If the subordinate role of international law and its institutions is not taken into consideration and legal provisions are understood in terms of unconditionally valid rules, the result may be detrimental to the maintenance of international order, interventionists argue. If international law becomes overloaded with ambitions, it could even endanger the international order – especially if it targets major guarantors of this order and small states (or even so-called 'rogue states') indiscriminately (cf. Scharf, 1999). This concern became particularly evident with respect to the attempt to codify aggression as one of the core crimes of the ICC, as one legal expert explains:

> The worry of Washington is that the category of aggression may be misused by some states to discourage the necessary deployment of military forces in peace enforcement, peacekeeping, freedom of navigation and anti-terrorist exercises. … *It often takes armies* – and in turn a supportive electorate, willing to mobilise its armed forces – *in order to stop genocide*. … Unfounded accusations of aggression in an international juridical forum may also contribute to an electorate's view that troops should be kept at home. (Wedgwood 1999: 105; emphasis added)

From an interventionist perspective, democratic states are subject to particular constraints concerning the use of military force, in particular regarding the support of domestic constituencies (cf. Merom, 2003). Consequently, democratic states are more vulnerable to prosecutions of their military personnel or policy makers by a highly visible supra-state court: trials of their citizens before the ICC could attract a high degree of media attention and could subsequently diminish the legitimacy of military operations in the eyes of domestic and international publics.

In addition, the crime of aggression plays an important role in the interventionist discourse because it is closely related to the responsibilities of the UN Security Council. Advocates of interventionism hold that it is the prerogative of the UN Security Council to determine when an instance of aggression occurred and to decide upon appropriate measures. Consequently, they interpret the proposal to include aggression in the ICC's jurisdiction as an attempt to challenge the role of the Security Council and to destabilise the UN system as such. Eric Rosand, legal adviser and US delegate to the Sixth Committee (Legal) of the UN General Assembly, mentioned the perceived challenge to Security Council responsibilities that would result from inclusion of the crime of aggression into the ICC Statute as one of the major reasons for US opposition to the Court: 'Moreover, despite the Security Council's role under the Charter of the United Nations, the Rome Statute suggested that the Assembly of State Parties was competent to define instances of aggression.'[6]

The interventionist concern about the ICC's potential to diminish the role of the Security Council does not only concern the crime of aggression, but to a broader range of issues, for instance, the referral mechanisms that would trigger the investigation of a case by the ICC: according to a proposal by the US delegation in Rome, these should have been restricted to referral by the UN

Security Council and state parties. The general conception underlying these reservations about a Court independent from the Security Council reflects the idea that the latter should be able to fulfil its function of 'maintain[ing] or restor[ing] international peace and security'[7] – in other words, international order – unhindered by the Court. As an institution based on power politics and reflecting the distribution of power in international relations, advocates of interventionism consider the Security Council to be better suited to deal with questions of international order than the ICC as a genuinely legal institution. As one US delegate to the Rome Conference put it:

> The Court must be part of the international order, in which the Security Council, with its responsibility for maintaining international peace and security, must play an important role, inter alia regarding its trigger mechanism. ... The powers of the Council under Chapter VII of the Charter of the United Nations would be absolutely essential to the working of the Court.[8]

In this context, for interventionists, the most favourable arrangement for the ICC would have consisted of a structure comparable to that of the two international criminal tribunals for Yugoslavia and Rwanda (ICTY and ICTR), as these were established by the UN Security Council, which defined its jurisdictional competences.[9] US Ambassador James Cunningham's statement before the UN Security Council can be regarded as exemplary in this respect:

> The United States yields to no country in its historical leadership in the struggle for international justice and accountability for war crimes. After all, the United States was the first country to codify the laws of war and international humanitarian law. It was also an original participant in the creation of every successful international effort to date to adjudicate allegations of war crimes and crimes against humanity. It has been, and will continue to be a strong supporter of the tribunals established under the aegis of the Council. *But, unlike the ICC, those tribunals are accountable to the Security Council.*[10]

The ICC as a politicised institution: the potential of politically motivated prosecutions

In contrast to the legalistic discourse, the interventionist discourse is built upon the assumption that it is difficult to keep the realms of politics and law separate. As a consequence, legal procedures and institutions could easily become interwoven with political questions. The objective of the advocates of interventionism is not to separate politics neatly from law. Rather, they assert that both realms will always overlap and intersect to a certain extent. This becomes evident in the interventionist expectation that the ICC could be used as a forum for politically motivated prosecutions, especially against powerful states like the US. However, viewed from an interventionist perspective, this prospect does not discredit international law or courts as such; rather, interventionists suggest that the most important task is to maintain the *primacy of politics* in this amalgamation of law and politics. Interventionists cannot accept the legalistic idea of professionalism as offering a sufficient safeguard against the risk of politically motivated prosecutions, as this option represents a genuinely legal-professional measure, but not a political one. Instead, they opt for making prosecutions dependent upon a political institution like the UN Security Council: 'Clearly, however, a Government which could file a complaint with the court against an individual was not only as political as the Council, but possibly even more so. On the other hand, because of its overall composition and responsibilities, the Security Council transcends the individual political views and agendas of its members.'[11]

It was not only US diplomats who promoted this view. The French delegation also shared the US preoccupation when the Rome Conference began, as becomes evident from the following quotation from Hubert Védrine:

> Coordination between the Security Council and the Court was necessary. … France believed that the Court must not become a political arena where frivolous complaints were brought with the sole aim of challenging decisions of the Council or the foreign policies of the all-too-few countries that agreed to take the risk of peacekeeping operations. … The Court would lose strength and credibility if it were not part of the international institutional system that already existed.[12]

Whereas France abandoned its objections to the independence of the prosecutor,[13] US diplomats maintained their concern about the risk of politically motivated prosecutions and repeatedly stated that it was the major reason for the US opposition to the Court. Consider, for instance, the following statement by US delegate Eric Rosand to the Sixth Committee of the General Assembly in 2004: 'First, it [the US] remained deeply concerned about the danger of politically motivated prosecutions: nothing about the structure of the International Criminal Court provided any guarantee against that eventuality.'[14]

The US media, as far as they aligned themselves with the interventionist discourse, echoed this view and considered the US decision to oppose the ICC as being entirely justified against this background: 'Joining the International Criminal Court would put U.S. troops and elected leaders in jeopardy of being prosecuted for political reasons, and that is a risk that both President Bush and Congress rightly refused to take.'[15]

In the comment quoted above, international law and its institutions are depicted as potential weapons of the weak against powerful states. This idea is particularly prominent amongst some US defence policy experts and advisers and is frequently referred to as 'lawfare'. This concept found its way into the US 2005 National Defense Strategy, which includes the following statement: 'Our strength as a nation state will continue to be challenged by those who employ *a strategy of the weak using international fora, judicial processes,* and terrorism.'[16] Parts of the US media amplified this concern and specify that the ICC represents the most prominent and exemplary of such 'international fora':

'The sad truth is that our enemies know we're a law-abiding people, and that this at times can make us vulnerable. Better to admit it than pretend every well-intentioned prosecutor at the International Criminal Court has all the relevant information.'[17]

According to the interventionist perspective, power politics permeate legal institutions to such an extent that the only countermeasure lies in binding the law to political institutions – even though this might sound somewhat paradoxical. However, in order to ensure that the existing international order is not undermined, the law should be controlled by political institutions that reflect the established balance of power. This is why the US opted so vociferously for a subordination of the ICC to the UN Security Council.

The ontological underpinnings of interventionism: states, individuals and the supra-state level

One of the most central features of the interventionist discourse is the extent to which it demands that the supra-state level should reflect the power asymmetries of the international system. Moreover, in contrast to the legalistic discourse, it largely neglects individuals as possible points of reference for supra-state institutions. The interventionist discourse is opposed to a cosmopolitanisation of the international order. To some degree, its proponents regard the state level as constitutive for both the individual and the supra-state level: they refer to individuals first and foremost as citizens of particular states. In addition, according to interventionism, the supra-state level is in large part influenced by the power inequalities displayed on the state level, as international organisations and institutions are mainly created, maintained and implemented by great powers.

This is not to say that interventionism does not maintain the idea of an international society of states as an important point of reference for the concept of human rights. On the contrary, advocates of interventionism embrace international society, not only in the thin, pluralist sense, but rather in the thick sense of an international society of states that is unified to a certain extent by shared norms and values. Yet the interventionist perception of international society differs from the legalistic discourse: whereas the latter rests on the claim to symmetry among states and the primacy of the community of states *vis-à-vis* the single state, interventionism sees great powers as the most important elements of international society. This is due to the interventionist claim that powerful states in particular uphold the norms and values of international society. The role that interventionists ascribe to great powers is similar to Nicholas Wheeler's concept of vigilantes:[18] vigilantes 'claim to be enforcing agreed law on behalf of the community ... in the absence or breakdown of officially constituted legal bodies' (2001: 141). Neither do they need explicit entitlement from the international society for doing so, nor do they create new norms.[19] Rather, they postulate that their actions are legitimate because they are in accordance with established legal provisions and because they safeguard the order and the persistence of the international society as a whole.

The international society of states

According to interventionist discourse, international law depends on powerful states insofar as they are the only entities able to implement it. As international law lacks enforcement mechanisms of its own, it would remain completely ineffective if great powers did not put its provisions into force. This feature of the interventionist perspective is especially prominent among US diplomats who continued to point to the huge contributions on the part of the US concerning law enforcement. In this vein, David Scheffer stressed the US commitment to enforcing international criminal law before the Sixth Committee of the UN General Assembly:

> The Clinton Administration had a record that pointed towards that objective [putting an end to impunity], and had ensured *that United States support for the two existing international criminal tribunals for the former Yugoslavia and Rwanda was second to none.* Many other Governments had also made important contributions to the success of the tribunals. But not only did the United States provide both tribunals with significant financial resources, it also used its diplomatic resources, made in-kind contributions of personnel and equipment, offered the tribunals important information, and even brought United States military capabilities to bear to ensure that the tribunals were effective.[20]

The discursive arena of the media echoes the idea that the ICC relies upon the support of great powers in order to fulfil its function: 'Clearly the court needs support beyond Britain and countries such as San Marino, the Marshall Islands and Nauru. ... Such a body can be remotely successful in grappling with those responsible for man's apparent inhumanity to man only with the support of countries with an international muscle.'[21]

The assumption that international legal institutions largely depend on the enforcement capabilities of great powers once again emphasises the idea of a fundamental asymmetry among states. This idea gains particular significance in the debate about the two UN Security Council resolutions (1422 and 1487) granting US and other other non-party states exemption from ICC jurisdiction. Whereas legalists perceived these resolutions as a major defeat for the rule of law in international relations,[22] proponents of interventionism consider this exemption as entirely legitimate, given the vital role that the US plays in the enforcement of international law and the maintenance of global order. US ambassador to the UN Security Council James Cunningham could not be clearer with respect to this point:

> The provisions of this resolution are as relevant and necessary today as resolution 1422 (2002) was a year ago. We all know that United Nations operations are

important if the Council is to discharge its primary responsibility for maintaining or restoring international peace and security. We also know that it is not always easy to recruit contributors, and that it often takes courage on the part of political leaders to join military operations established or authorized by the Council. It is important that Member States not add concern about ICC jurisdiction to the difficulty of participating.[23]

Even parts of the European media aligned themselves with this view:

The choice for the United Nations now is between one *abstract notion of international law* and the very *real needs of international order*. The United States (and others) will not participate in peacekeeping missions if the price of being the Good Samaritan is the retention of a legal adviser never more than a few yards away. ... The result will be *a world of fewer policemen, but more lawyers*. It is hard to see how the many victims of political evil will benefit from that at all.[24]

The image of the lawyer and the policeman in the quote above reiterates the assumption that order is a prerequisite for justice. At the same time, it raises the question of why the policeman and the lawyer are juxtaposed to each other in this context, whereas in the domestic realm both are perceived of as vital parts of the same institutional setting. This is due to the limitations of the domestic analogy when applied to the international order: in the absence of a superior authority, there is no guarantee that policemen and lawyers are following the same objectives. The policemen mistrust the lawyers and there is no institutionalised possibility for arbitration or mediation between them.

Besides exemptions for powerful states, the interventionist discourse concentrates on the UN Security Council as the supra-state body that reflects the asymmetric relationship among states. At the beginning of the Rome Conference, the French delegation shared the US preoccupation that the establishment of the ICC could weaken the role of the UN Security Council and stressed the need for the smooth integration of the Court into the existing supra-state structure, whereby the latter is dominated first and foremost by the UN Security Council:

France would work constructively and pragmatically to make the court as universal as possible, emphasizing the concept of an international system forming a unified whole. *It was not in favour of adding mutually contradictory elements that might complicate organization and regulation throughout the world.* He [Hubert Védrine] was thinking in particular of the linkage between national courts and the Court and between the action of the Security Council and that of the Court.[25]

The emphasis that the interventionist discourse puts on the UN Security Council as the predominant organ of the supra-state level becomes even more evident in the following contribution from the US delegate to the Rome Conference, David Scheffer:

In view of the Security Council's responsibilities under the Charter for restoring and maintaining international peace and security, recognition of its role in the Statute was vital to the proper functioning of the Court, in accordance with the obligations of the Member States under the Charter. His delegation was willing to work with others to find a compromise with respect to the Council's proper role, but *the powers of the Council must not be rewritten.*[26]

In the same vein, Anne Patterson, US ambassador to the UN Security Council, justified the tacit approval of the US with respect to UN Security Council resolution 1593 (2005), which refers the situation in Darfur, Sudan, to the ICC. Since 2002, the region had been the venue of civil war and counterinsurgency measures supported by the Sudanese government, in the course of which offences occurred that fell under the ICC's jurisdiction. The EU and its member states had pushed for a referral of the situation in Darfur to the ICC for a long time. The US, however, due to its general opposition towards the ICC, was initially opposed to this possibility. By the end of March 2005, the US government eventually agreed not to obstruct the according resolution in the Security Council. In her statement on the US voting behaviour, however, Patterson reaffirmed that the US abstaining from the vote did not indicate a change in its genuine opposition to the ICC. She pointed out that the US tacit approval was due to the fact that resolution 1593 acknowledges the central role of the UN Security Council in initiating prosecutions by the Court:

> The United States is and will continue to be an important contributor to the peacekeeping and related humanitarian efforts in Sudan. The language providing for protection for the United States and other contributing States is precedent-setting, as it acknowledges the concerns of States not party to the Rome Statute and recognizes that persons from those States should not be vulnerable to investigation or prosecution by the ICC, absent consent by those States or a referral by the Security Council. ... The Council's action today plays an important role in that regard. *We expect that the Council will continue to exercise such oversight as investigations and prosecutions pursuant to the referral proceed.*[27]

Individuals as peacekeepers or victims

The fact that the interventionist discourse regards states – first and foremost great powers – as the most relevant entities in international relations does not imply that individual actors are completely ignored. However, proponents of interventionism derive the roles that individuals play from the state level, thereby reaffirming the primacy of states over individuals.

It comes as no surprise that advocates of interventionism view as suspect the existence of powerful individuals who by virtue of their office may challenge the authority of great powers – as is the case with the chief prosecutor of the ICC. Given the primary significance that interventionists ascribe to great powers, an individual actor who is to a certain degree decoupled from both the state level and from the UN Security Council appears illegitimate. Consider, for instance, the following remarks by a legal expert:

The inclusion of the independent prosecutor – independent in the sense of having authority to initiate investigations without a formal state complaint or Security Council referral – has been hailed by many states and commentators as a great achievement. It constitutes a dramatic step away from the ILC's original assessment that an independent prosecutor was not feasible 'at the present stage of development of the international system,' toward a vision of international law enforcement that enhances the power of individuals and demonstrates less solicitude for state sovereignty. ... Yet this independence comes at a price. Independence necessarily entails institutional autonomy and discretion, a result *potentially threatening to states*. (Danner, 2003: 515–16; emphasis added)

Since the office of the prosecutor and his or her independence and leverage to prosecute citizens of great powers and lesser states alike displays a certain neglect of the power asymmetries amongst states, interventionists consider him or her a potential 'threat'.

Whilst the existence of powerful individuals independent of great powers and the UN Security Council represents an illegitimate case, the role of individuals as peacekeepers is central to the interventionist discourse and is looked upon favourably. This depiction of individuals is especially prominent in the US media. It provided the interventionist discourse with additional appeal for the domestic public. One commentator from the *Salt Lake Tribune* offers an especially lively image: 'No doubt, the vision of some American peacekeeper, handcuffed and miserable, being tried and convicted by a judge from Iran or China or some other country with a questionable human rights record, is appalling.'[28] In the same vein, the *Tampa Tribune* writes: 'With some 200,000 U.S. troops deployed in various hot spots or potential hot spots around the world, the risk that Americans could be prosecuted for mistakes, or that they could be framed by clever adversaries, is real.'[29]

It is striking that within the framework of interventionism, peacekeepers are always depicted as citizens of a particular state,[30] though this is not inevitable: peacekeepers could also be depicted with reference to a cosmopolitan community of individuals or as enforcers of the supra-state level of UN Security Council resolutions. Yet the image of peacekeepers as citizens of a particular state stresses the importance of great powers as the actual enforcers of international order, even if particular military operations are mandated by the UN Security Council. Moreover, it also corresponds with the fact that in recent years, the US has increasingly deployed forces outside the framework of UN peacekeeping troops in the narrow sense and has sought to safeguard a high degree of operational discretion.[31] Nonetheless, according to interventionist media comments, the US is particularly exposed to international criminal law and its institutions because it is the state that has by far the highest number of troops overseas.

Within the framework of the interventionist discourse, 'innocent civilians'[32] who become the victims of crimes against humanitarian and human rights law constitute the counterpart of peacekeepers. The suffering of civilians and its amplification by the media represents a vital part of interventionism, since, unlike legalists, interventionists privilege political and military measures in order to enforce human rights over legal means. This, however, might be costly and has to be justified given the restrictions to the use of military force as laid down in the UN Charter. Images and reports of human suffering facilitate garnering support for a military intervention on part of the domestic constituency and potential allies alike.[33] Thus, in contrast to legalism, the interventionist discourse emphasises the role of the victim rather than that of the perpetrator – its basic rationale is saving the former rather than prosecuting the latter.

Unlike peacekeepers, though, victims are not referred to as citizens of a particular state. As advocates of interventionism maintain, just as states lose their sovereignty prerogatives in case they do not protect the basic rights of their citizens (see below), individuals affected by such atrocities lose their primordial link to the state in question. Consequently, in such cases the international society of states is in charge of safeguarding the life and well-being of these individuals and of re-establishing the rule of law. In the case of the breakdown of a state or the loss of sovereignty of a state due to its failure to guarantee human rights domestically, a direct link between individuals and the international society emerges. Yet this development does not occur by way of cosmopolitanisation, since the basic point of reference for the individual-as-victim is not the world society of individuals, but the international society of states.[34] Thus, although humanitarian intervention and the related discourse are often said to erode state sovereignty, this only holds true with respect to the states that become the targets of such an intervention. With regard to the international society of states as a whole, the opposite effect is more likely: as long as intervention is carried out by state actors, it reproduces the system of states rather than eroding it – though in an asymmetric form.

Conditional sovereignty and the enforcement of human rights

The conditionality of sovereignty

The core feature of the concept of sovereignty as promoted by the interventionist discourse is conditionality. In this perspective, sovereignty is not an a priori and unchangeable attribute of states. Rather, it depends on a state's capacity to fulfil vital functions of statehood and its adherence to legal standards. Ironically, the concept of conditional sovereignty originated in the post-Cold-War Europe. It was intended to provide a strategy of dealing with political units emerging from the former Soviet Union and Yugoslavia that aspired to statehood.[35] As such, the concept of conditional sovereignty mainly emerged from the discursive arena of legal experts:

> Conditional sovereignty may be applied to the accumulation of increased sovereign authority by the substate entity, or it may be applied as a set of standards to be achieved prior to the determination of the substate entity's final status. These

benchmarks vary depending on the characteristics of the conflict and generally include conditions such as protecting human and minority rights, halting terrorism, developing democratic institutions, instituting the rule of law, and promoting regional stability. (Williams and Pecci, 2004: 10)

However, the European concept of conditional sovereignty was subsequently taken up by US policy-makers and underwent significant modifications. Whereas the European interpretation of conditional sovereignty implies that this concept is designed for political units that have not yet achieved statehood but only aspire to it, and that the requirements which have to be met for that purpose are spelled out explicitly, advocates of interventionism abandon both limitations. According to them, conditional sovereignty applies to already existing states as well. Moreover, they do not specify the conditions that a state has to meet in order to avoid being deprived of its sovereignty prerogatives, but refer rather vaguely to a lack of governance capabilities, the occurrence of intolerable violence against a state's own population and conditions that entail a general risk for security and peace:

> One challenge to sovereignty arises when states have too little of it. Around the world, many governments lack the legitimacy and capacity to translate their nominal sovereignty into effective governance. ... In all of the situations I have just outlined – stopping genocide, fighting terrorism, and preventing the spread of weapons of mass destruction – the principle remains the same: With rights come obligations. *Sovereignty is not absolute. It is conditional.* When states violate minimum standards by committing, permitting, or threatening intolerable acts against their own people or other nations, *then some of the privileges of sovereignty are forfeited.*[36]

As becomes clear from the above quotation, interventionists tend to interpret grave violations of human rights as security threats and to equate them with terrorism or the proliferation of weapons of mass destruction. Thereby, the interventionist discourse refers to perpetrators of such atrocities within a securitisation framework.[37] The most important reason for the application of the securitisation framework probably lies in the history of humanitarian intervention since the establishment of the UN after World War II. According to the UN Charter and the restriction on the use of force that it includes, humanitarian interventions require the adoption of a resolution by the UN Security Council under Chapter VII of the UN Charter. It stipulates that the resort to military force is only legitimate in three situations, one of which is the need to 'maintain or restore international peace and security'.[38] Thus, the instrument of humanitarian intervention was traditionally bound to the existence of security threats, and the Security Council has reaffirmed this in several cases.[39] Yet even in the context of interventions without a mandate of the UN Security Council, involved states proved eager to stress that the principles of the UN Charter determined the purpose of the mission. Then US President Bill Clinton, for instance, emphasised that the NATO intervention in Kosovo 'helped vindicate the principles and purposes of the U.N. Charter' (quoted in Cassese, 1999: 793). An even more prominent – though also more contested – example of how the humanitarian and securitisation frameworks may overlap and intersect can be found in public justifications of the 2003 US-led intervention in Iraq.

Given the fact that the UN Security Council lacks enforcement capacities of its own and depends on states to fulfil mandated missions or to contribute to UN missions (or in some cases is even unable to mandate a mission owing to a veto); the difficult task for interventionists consists of reconciling the need to protect foreign populations with the national interest of potentially intervening forces.[40] Proponents of interventionism argue that if a state forfeits its sovereignty due to human rights violations, 'the responsibility to protect may devolve to the international community'.[41] However, as it is eventually up to *some* states to contribute to these efforts, humanitarian interventions are most likely when the interest of the international society as a whole and the national interest of states capable of carrying out such missions overlap to a certain extent. This implies that the decision to intervene is necessarily selective. As another member of the State Department policy planning staff put it:

> The tough question, of course, is deciding when to intervene. We are unlikely to come up with an ironclad, consistent rule to govern armed 'humanitarian intervention'. Our policy will inevitably remain *selective*, because our level of attention to different countries will vary, and because *the United States must balance its interest in preventing suffering with its pursuit of other important goals and commitments*. We cannot intervene everywhere.[42]

Consequently, the interventionist discourse is hostile to the codification of hard-and-fast rules to govern humanitarian intervention.[43] Even though interventionists claim that their efforts aim at enforcing established provisions of international law, a certain degree of vagueness and the need for interpretation suits them, as it leaves enough room for genuinely political decisions, thereby reaffirming the primacy of power politics *vis-à-vis* international law (cf. Alvarez, 2003; Vagts, 2001).

Asymmetry

The interventionist interpretation of the relationship among states as asymmetric complements the concept of conditional sovereignty. Both aspects are mutually constitutive: on the one hand, the fact that there are states that are so weak or so 'uncivilised' that they are not able to govern their own territory and population in a decent way necessitates the doctrine of conditional sovereignty. On the other hand, if sovereignty is conditional, there must be someone who is entitled to determine whether or not a certain state meets the requirements of full sovereignty. Formally, of course, interventionists ascribe this role to the UN Security Council; however, as already elaborated above, the Security

Council is an institution of the supra-state level that reflects the asymmetry of the state level. Moreover, as the cases of Kosovo and Iraq show, the decision about the sovereignty of a state might also be taken outside the framework of the UN Security Council.

Yet proponents of interventionism tend to emphasise that asymmetry is not brought about by powerful states that deliberately restrict the sovereignty prerogatives of weaker ones. Rather, they argue, it is the weakness of certain states and the security threat emanating from them that requires powerful states to fulfil their role as vigilantes. An observer of the Rome Conference quotes the following remark made by the US delegate David Scheffer in an informal discussion:

> The U.S. is not Andorra! ... the challenges of the post-Cold War world are so complex that, in some instances, the requirements of those few countries that are still in a position to actually do something by way of accomplishing various humane objectives simply have got to be accommodated. *And you can't approach this on the model of the equality of all states. You have to think in terms of the inequality of some states.*[44]

The interventionist demand for the exemption of powerful states from the ICC's jurisdiction is thus not grounded in the idea that powerful states are simply above the law, as some critics would have it. On the contrary, according to the interventionist discourse, citizens – especially, of course, senior officials and military personnel – of powerful states should be immune from the Court's jurisdiction because they *enforce* international law. As Robert Kagan wrote in a comment in the *Washington Post*:

> *Americans are hardly hostile to international law* – the United Nations was their idea. But the United States has a special problem, one that its European allies ought especially to appreciate. As the world's most powerful democratic power, *the United States is called upon – yes, called upon far more frequently than any other nation to dispatch its troops overseas for any number of purposes.* ... Unlike even the strongest European powers, which have trouble projecting military power anywhere at any time, which means the United States is always going to have far more soldiers vulnerable to some misguided ICC prosecutor than any other nation.[45]

Similarly, a legal expert stressed the outstanding international role of the US: 'The role of the United States in balance of power structures in Asia and Europe, and in support of transcontinental peacekeeping and peace enforcement operations, together with the deployment of 200,000 American troops abroad, may leave the United States in a *unique position* in regard to the Court' (Wedgwood 1999: 102; emphasis added).

The special position of the United States, however, implies an increased degree of vulnerability: 'The United States is a special case because, as the world superpower, we are also a special target.'[46] According to the interventionist discourse, a unique power position attracts the malevolence of less powerful actors. This assumption becomes evident in the following remarks by David Scheffer:

> The United States has special responsibilities and *special exposure to political con-troversy over our actions*. This factor cannot be taken lightly when issues of international peace and security are at stake. We are called upon to act, sometimes at great risk, far more than any other nation. This is a reality in the international system. (Scheffer, 1999: 12; emphasis added).

The assumption of the malevolence of lesser states ties in with the interventionist fear that the ICC could become a forum for politicised prosecutions. Some commentators refer to this malevolence as anti-Americanism: 'America in its unchallenged pre-eminence has responsibilities unlike any other nation now, or ever. And *anti-Americanism* permeates many foreign elites, who will shape the court's docket.'[47] This belief, however, is not confined to the US media. Some European commentators share this preoccupation. Consider, for instance, the following comment from the German newspaper *Welt am Sonntag*: 'Those who know the reality of *anti-Americanism* and of the marauding lawyers in this world and forget about romantic sentiment for a moment will recognise how many people are waiting for the opportunity to handcuff the Americans.'[48]

Human rights: how to enforce them?

A central assumption of the interventionist discourse is that human rights should be enforced at the supra-state level and that consequently state borders do not provide a shield against the prosecution of offences against humanitarian and human rights law. This idea, for instance, informs the US proposal to extend the definition of war crimes to domestic conflicts. Traditionally, internal armed conflicts have not been subject to international law, but were left to the operation of national criminal law (Cassese, 2005: 429).[49] The inclusion of internal armed conflict in the ICC Statute expresses the belief that war crimes occurring in intra-state conflicts should be a concern for the international community. US delegate David Scheffer depicts this as a success: 'A major achievement of Article 8 of the treaty is its application to war crimes committed during internal armed conflicts. The United States helped lead the effort to ensure that internal armed conflicts were covered by the Statute' (Scheffer, 1999: 16).

Whilst there is no conflict between the legalistic and the interventionist discourses concerning the claim that the main point of reference for the enforcement of human rights is the supra-state level, proponents of both discourses disagree with respect to the question of which supra-state entities are in charge of upholding them. As outlined above, in contrast to legalists, interventionists argue that human rights are first and foremost protected by political and military action by great powers and that legal institutions should play a secondary role. This idea is closely linked to the interventionist view on the sources of international law. For them, established customary law represents the basic point of reference for the negotiations of the Rome Statute. This implies that the entity to which the codification of legal rules refers is the international society of states rather than each and every single state. However, in contrast to the legalistic emphasis on the consensus principle as the foundation of the validity of legal rules, interventionists once more point out the role of great powers in this respect. The legal notion of custom is composed of two elements: 'State practice (*usus* or *diuturnitas*) and the corresponding views of States (*opinio juris* or *opinio necessitatis*)' (Cassese, 2005: 157). Customary law is viewed as a preferable source of international law for great powers because

> A hegemon confronts customary international law differently from other countries. In terms of the formation of customary law, such a power can by its abstention prevent the emerging rule from becoming part of custom. … Abstention by a hegemonic power does seem to be enough to keep it from being general. … If a custom has crystallized, the hegemon can disregard it more safely than a treaty rule and have its action hailed as creative. (Vagts, 2001: 887).

In short, customary law grants great powers a disproportionately large influence over its formation and is therefore more likely to reflect asymmetries in international relations than treaty law.[50] Yet whether this remains to be the case, in particular in the realm of international humanitarian law, is contested. The US government's response to the 2006 International Committee of the Red Cross (ICRC) Customary Law Study suggests that the ICRC had given too much weight to *opinio juris* and not enough to state practice.[51] In particular, it charges the ICRC Study of not sufficiently taking into consideration the practice of 'specially affected states'. According to the official US response to the ICRC Study, 'specially affected states' should be understood as states that 'have a distinctive history of participation' in armed conflict – a definition that points to states that have played the role of custodians of international order.

Conclusion

The interventionist discourse differs from the legalistic one with respect to the underlying narrative, the ontology and the configuration of sovereignty and human rights. One of its main tenets is that the international order is perceived as deriving from *power politics*, not from international law. According to the interventionist discourse, attempts to challenge or change the established international order via the law and legal institutions is downright dangerous because it entails a risk of destabilising international order. Proponents of interventionism therefore stress the requirement to subordinate international law to power politics in order to avoid possible contradictions between the two realms. They also privilege humanitarian intervention aimed at the protection of human rights over the legal prosecution of perpetrators of crimes against humanitarian and human rights law. Powerful states play the role of vigilantes enforcing established customary international law, but do not press for the codification of new legal provisions.

According to interventionism, states do share common values and thus form an international society in the English School sense of the term. Yet it is up to powerful actors to enforce these values on a global scale, which may lead to a certain tension between the interests of the international society as a whole, i.e. the maintenance of the existing international order, and the national interest of particular states, in particular those who are capable of undertaking stabilising functions.

Generally, interventionists argue that this tension is likely to be resolved in cases where the securitisation paradigm and the law enforcement paradigm overlap. The idea of such an overlap is linked to the concept of conditional sovereignty. This concept, in turn, is closely related to the idea of a fundamental asymmetry between states. On the one hand, some states forfeit their sovereignty prerogatives because they represent a risk to the international order and do not abide by the common norms of international society. On the other, great powers are in charge of the maintenance of the international order and the enforcement of these norms. Finally, this view ties in with the fact that customary law is the interventionists' preferred source of international law, since it grants great powers a disproportionate influence on the emergence of legal norms.

Notes

1 Initially, France also raised concerns over too extensive a definition of war crimes: '[The French delegation] had consistently maintained that only the most serious war crimes should continue to be included among crimes against the peace and security of mankind, provided that they were carefully defined – along the lines of the four Geneva Conventions of 1949, for instance. Conversely, his delegation was opposed to the inclusion of any reference to certain provisions of of Protocol I Additional to those Conventions or to the protection of the environment in times of armed conflict'; Damien Loras, Meeting of the Sixth Committee of the UN General Assembly (4 November 1996); U.N. Doc. A/C.6/51g/SR.31, p. 8.

2 It should be noted, however, that the French insistence on the seven-year opt-out provision for war crimes met with domestic opposition after France had ratified the Rome Statute. A majority of French MPs argued that the seven-year opt-out would be unnecessary, but President Chirac's position was unrelenting.

3 See also Vagts (2001) on great powers' preference for customary international law as opposed to treaty law.

4 For instance, the inclusion of 'gender crimes' such as systematic rape and forced pregnancy as a war crime was based on rather recent developments of case-law emerging from the ICTY and the ICTR (Bedont and Hall-Martinez, 1999: 70ff.).

5 Ian Buruma, 'Why We Must Share America's Dirty Work', *Guardian* (16 July 2002).

6 Eric Rosand, Meeting of the Sixth Committee of the UN General Assembly (30 November 2004); U.N. Doc. A/C.6/59/SR.27, p. 2.

7 Charter of the United Nations, Chapter VII, Art. 39.

8 Bill Richardson, DipCon 5th plenary meeting (17 June 1998); U.N. Doc. A/CONF.183/

SR.5, Vol. II, p. 95.

9   Arguably, the chief prosecutor of both tribunals enjoyed a rather high degree of independence as to her or his decisions to prosecute particular suspects, yet both tribunals were bound to the UN Security Council's leverage with respect to several crucial aspects: first, the Security Council defined the situations that the ICTY and the ICTR were entitled to address, meaning that it determined their temporal and territorial range of jurisdiction. Second, it had the final say about the content of the statutes of both tribunals and their amendments. Third, and perhaps most importantly, it appointed the chief prosecutor for both tribunals. Cf. Goldstone and Bass (2000).

10 James Cunningham, UN SC meeting 'United Nations peacekeeping' (12 June 2003); U.N. Doc. S/PV.4772, p. 23; emphasis added.

11 David Scheffer, Meeting of the Sixth Committee of the UN General Assembly (31 October 1996); U.N. Doc. A/C.6/51/SR28, 12.

12 Hubert Védrine, DipCon 6th plenary meeting (17 June 1998); U.N. Doc. A/CONF.183/SR.6, Vol. II, p. 101.

13 Crucial in this respect was the inclusion of a provision according to which the pre-trial chamber (consisting of three judges) is required to authorise investigations proposed by the prosecutor (Art. 15 (3) Rome Statute) (Broomhall, 2003: 79; Hall, 1998a: 132).

14 Eric Rosand, Sixth Committee of the General Assembly (30 November 2004); U.N. Doc. A/C.6/59/SR.27, p. 2.

15 'Joining International Court Would Be Grave Error for U.S.', Tampa Tribune (6 July 2002).

16 The National Defense Strategy of the United States of America (March 2005), p. 5; www.defenselink.mil/news/Mar2005/d20050318nds1.pdf (accessed August 2008); emphasis added.

17 'The Pentagon and "lawfare"', Washington Times (24 March 2005).

18 The concept of vigilantes is reminiscent of Bull's notion of 'custodians' of international order (1995: 221), yet the former is more specific as it entails a specific link to international law, whereas the latter merely indicates the general role of great powers in maintaining the international order.

19 Wheeler applies the concept of vigilantes to the NATO intervention in Kosovo and stresses that this intervention took place without a mandate of the UN Security Council. By way of contrast, he labels actors carrying out interventions mandated by the UN as 'posses': 'The idea of the posse is taken from the "wild west" and refers to a situation where the sheriff calls upon the assistance of a group of citizens to assist him with the task of law enforcement' (Wheeler, 2001: 141). Whilst Wheeler distinguishes between 'posses' and 'vigilantes' according to the nature of the mission in which they are involved, i.e. with or without Security Council mandate, I will set this distinction aside and use the term vigilantes for actors in both types of mission. This seems to be legitimate given the emphasis of the interventionist discourse on the role of great powers concerning the enforcement of international law and the fact that in its context, the UN Security Council is not depicted as a separate and independent entity, but as a further manifestation of the importance of great powers for the international order.

20 David Scheffer, Sixth Committee of the General Assembly (4 November 1998); U.N. Doc. A/C.6/53/SR.9, p. 8; emphasis added.

21 Michael Caplan, 'ICC Hopes to Give Peace a Chance', The Times (2 July 2002).

22 The legalistic consensus on the issue of exemptions through UN Security Council resolutions was slow to emerge. Whereas there was a unanimous vote on resolution 1422 (2002), Germany and France abstained from the vote for resolution 1487 (2003). The UK voted in favour. By 2004, however, it was clear that there would be no majority for

a renewal of resolution 1487.

23 James Cunningham, UN SC meeting 'United Nations peacekeeping' (12 June 2003); U.N. Doc. S/PV.4772, p. 23.

24 'Court Politics', *The Times* (2 July 2002); emphasis added.

25 Hubert Védrine, DipCon 6th plenary meeting (17 June 1998); U.N. Doc. A/CONF.183/SR.6, Vol. II, p. 101; emphasis added.

26 David Scheffer, DipCon 29th meeting (9 July 1998); U.N. Doc. A/CONF.183/C.1/SR.29, Vol. II, p. 297; emphasis added.

27 Anne W. Patterson, UN SC meeting 'Sudan' (31 March 2005); U.N. Doc. S/PV.5158, p. 3; emphasis added. Resolution 1593 was hailed as a 'breakthrough' in the transatlantic conflict over the ICC by some European observers. Yet operative paragraph 6 contains far-reaching exemptions for citizens of non-party states operating in Sudan. Robert Cryer explains that the US pressed for the inclusion of these exemptions in order to set 'a precedent for "immunity" from the ICC' (2006: 214).

28 Michael Nakoryakov, 'U.S. May Dislike World Court, but Staying Outside Won't Help', *Salt Lake Tribune* (14 July 2002).

29 'Joining the Court Would Be Grave Error for U.S.', *Tampa Tribune* (6 July 2002).

30 This not only holds true for US contributions to the interventionist discourse. Consider for instance a comment published in the German newspaper *Welt am Sonntag*: 'Apparently, the Federal Government would not mind if a German lieutenant and ten servicemen who are on duty in Bosnia were put on trial before the new International Criminal Court.' Herbert Kremp, 'Sonderrecht für die USA? Im Streit um den Internationalen Strafgerichtshof will Washington aus gutem Grund nicht einlenken', *Welt am Sonntag* (7 July 2002).

31 According to Thomas Weiss (1997), the US preference for military operations in the framework of coalition forces instead of contributing to UN forces can be regarded as a lesson learned from the case of Somalia.

32 David Scheffer, Sixth Committee of the General Assembly (4 November 1998); U.N. Doc. A/C.6/53/SR.9, p. 8.

33 On the politics of 'distant suffering', see Boltanski (1999).

34 This is not to say that the supra-state level represented by the UN Security Council and its mandate might not play a role as well, but the enforcement capabilities definitely rest with states.

35 'The element of conditional sovereignty originated in the European approach of earned recognition of the successor states of the former Soviet Union and the former Yugoslavia. In response to calls for international recognition by the republics of the Soviet Union and Yugoslavia, on December 16, 1991, the European Community Council of Foreign Ministers developed a policy of earned recognition. Under this approach, states seeking recognition by the European Community were required to meet a set of detailed criteria' (Williams and Pecci, 2004: 21). Obviously, the idea of conditional sovereignty has also intellectual roots in the nineteenth century 'standard of civilisation' (Gong, 1984).

36 Richard N. Haass, 'Sovereignty: Existing Rights, Evolving Responsibilities.' Remarks to the School of Foreign Service and the Mortara Center for International Studies, Georgetown University, Washington, DC (14 January 2003); emphasis added.

37 Securitisation refers to the depiction of specific actors or situations as an existential threat to the own political community (Wæver, 1995: 54ff.), whereby the term 'the own political community' can refer to the international society as such, as this example illustrates.

38 Charter of the United Nations, Chapter VII, Art. 39. The two other instances in which

the resort to force is admissible under international law are individual or collective self-defence (Art. 51 UN Charter) and the forcible protection of nationals abroad (also Art. 51 or by customary law unaffected by the UN Charter). Cf. Cassese (2005: 346f., 365ff.) and Brownlie (2003: 697ff.).

39 Cf. resolutions 836 and 844 (1993) with respect to Bosnia-Herzegovina, resolution 794 (1992) concerning Somalia, resolution 929 (1994) with regard to Rwanda and resolution 940 (1994) concerning Haiti. More recent are resolutions 1264 (1999, East Timor), 1497 and 1509 (2003, Liberia).

40 As mentioned above, media coverage of civilian suffering is a vital precondition for humanitarian intervention; however, it is not always sufficient, as is evident from cases like Rwanda in 1994 and Sudan in 2003.

41 Stewart Patrick, 'The Role of the U.S. Government in Humanitarian Intervention.' Remarks to the 43rd Annual International Affairs Symposium 'The Suffering of Strangers: Global Humanitarian Intervention in a Turbulent World', Lewis and Clarke College, Portland, Oregon (5 April 2004).

42 *Ibid.*; emphasis added.

43 The proposal to codify such rules is included, for instance, in the 2001 Report of the International Commission on Intervention and State Sovereignty 'The Responsibility to protect'; http://www.iciss.ca/pdf/Commission-Report.pdf; and in the 2004 Report of the Secretary-General's High-Level Panel on Threats, Challenges and Change 'A more secure world: Our shared responsibility', Part 3; www.un.org/secureworld/report2.pdf (accessed August 2008). Yet given the objections to the codification of such rules on the part of the adherents of the interventionist discourse, it is questionable to what extent this attempt will be successful.

44 David Scheffer, quoted in Weschler (2000: 102); emphasis added.

45 Robert Kagan, 'Europeans Courting International Disaster', *Washington Post* (30 June 2002).

46 'International Criminal Court. Bush Tries Shock Therapy on U.N.', *Herald Sun* (2 July 2002).

47 George F. Will, 'U.S. Isn't Wary Enough of New World Court', *Seattle Post-Intelligencer* (14 July 2002); emphasis added.

48 Herbert Kremp, 'Sonderrecht für die USA? Im Streit um den Internationalen Strafgerichtshof will Washington aus gutem Grund nicht einlenken', *Welt am Sonntag* (7 July 2002); emphasis added.

49 The 1977 Additional Protocol II to the Geneva Conventions was a first step in the direction of the codification of a legal framework for non-international armed conflict.

50 The degree of great power influence on customary law, however, is disputed. Cassese argues that it is 'at the least questionable whether States may object to the formation of a customary rule thereby remaining outside it. The international community is less anarchic and individualistic, and far more integrated than in the past. Consequently, community pressure on individual States, including Great Powers, is such that it proves difficult for a State to avoid being bound by a new general rule' (*ibid.*: 155).

51 Letter from John Bellinger and Jim Haynes to Jakob Kellenberger; www.defenselink. mil/home/pdf/Customary_International_Humanitiarian_Law.pdf (accessed August 2008).

5 The sovereigntist discourse

As with interventionism, the sovereigntist discourse is opposed to legalism and challenges the legitimacy of the ICC. However, whilst the main argument against the Court on the part of interventionists is that the Rome Statute exceeds the existing provisions of customary law, proponents of sovereigntism mainly charge the ICC with overriding state consent as the most central requirement for the validity and legitimacy of international legal institutions. More specifically, they disapprove of the reach of jurisdiction that the Rome Statute grants the ICC, as it does not exempt citizens of non-party states from prosecution by the Court. By ignoring the requirement of state consent, sovereigntists argue, the ICC also infringes upon symmetry as the basic feature of international order.

Table 5.1 summarises the most central features of the sovereigntist discourse:

Construction of time	Sources of order	Features of order	Ontology/ basic units	Notion of interest refers to	Notion of sovereignty	Human rights refer to
non-simultaneity	Rule of law/ co-existence	Symmetry	States	Single state	Constitutional sovereignty	Nation-state/ state consent

Table 5.1 Basic features of the sovereigntist discourse

The sovereigntist discourse, although different in content from interventionism, complemented the latter in that US opponents of the ICC drew upon it in order to justify US opposition to the Court. US diplomats engaged both in the interventionist and the sovereigntist discourse, often within the framework of one statement. At the domestic level, however, it is possible to discern different sources and/or alignments of both discourses: whilst the interventionist discourse was mainly prominent amongst Pentagon staffers and security experts, the sovereigntist discourse was rooted in the US Senate, with the Republican Senator Jesse Helms as one of its most popular proponents (cf. Broomhall 2003: 165f.). To make matters more complicated, there was crossover between these sources owing to personal links between actors. Observers hold, for instance, that William Cohen, Defense Secretary from 1997 to 2001, was influenced by Jesse Helms's position on the ICC (Scharf, 1999).

The sovereigntist discourse, however, was not entirely confined to US voices. In the early stages of the negotiations, French diplomats put forward sovereigntist arguments as well. At the Fourth PrepCom in 1997, for instance, France proposed that for a situation to be admissible to the ICC's jurisdiction, all 'interested states' had to give their consent: the state on whose territory the crimes were committed, the state of nationality of the perpetrator, the state of nationality of the victim and the custodial state (Hall, 1998a: 131). The final provision concerning the ICC's jurisdiction, however, is less restrictive and represents a middle ground between sovereigntist concerns on the one hand and claims for universal jurisdiction,[1] as put forward by Germany and South Korea,[2] on the other. Article 12 of the Rome Statute, eventually supported by the French delegation, stipulates that *either* the state on the territory of which the offence took place *or* the state of which the accused is a citizen have to accept the Court's jurisdiction.[3] Despite the fact that French diplomats refrained from sovereigntist statements once the French delegation joined the Like-Minded Group in Rome, some French legal experts and some media commentators continued to engage in the sovereigntist discourse.

The narrative of sovereigntism: coexistence and the constitutional order of states

A non-simultaneous approach to international law

The sovereigntist discourse resembles interventionism insofar as both reject the idea that international law is subject to development and progress, as legalists argue. There are, however, differences between sovereigntism and interventionism with regard to the way in which both construct the temporal dimension of international law. Whilst interventionists argue that established customary law is the ultimate benchmark for the codification of legal provisions and for the establishment of legal bodies such as the ICC, sovereigntists put the question of state consent to the fore. This becomes evident in the following contribution by David Scheffer, US chief negotiator at the Rome Conference, to a debate on the ICC's scope of jurisdiction:

> The universal jurisdiction proposal for the Court would represent an extraordinary principle, in conflict with certain fundamental principles of international law, and would undermine the Statute generally. The proposal by Germany and

the Republic of Korea would have the effect of *applying a treaty to a State without that State's consent* ... Even if a State was not a party, the Court would have jurisdiction to judge its official acts and imprison even its head of State. Such a situation could not be justified on the basis of existing law and the United States objected to it in principle.[4]

Hence, sovereigntists do not aim to preserve the specific contents of established customary law, but, rather more fundamentally, the way in which international law is made and applied. Moreover, they are suspicious of any attempt to transfer jurisdictional prerogatives from the state level to the supra-state level. Consider, for instance, the following remark by Bill Richardson, who was part of the US delegation to the Rome Conference:

To achieve the support of the international community, the court must *complement national jurisdictions* and *encourage national action* wherever possible. For that reason, it would be unwise to grant the Prosecutor the right to initiate investigations. That would overload the Court, causing confusion and controversy, and weaken rather than strengthen it. The Prosecutor should not be turned into a human rights ombudsman responding to complaints from any source. The proposal that the Prosecutor should have powers to initiate proceedings was *premature*.[5]

First and foremost, advocates of sovereigntism interpret any proposal that would diminish the central role of states as the basic actors in international relations as inappropriate. They frequently express the inappropriateness of such attempts in terms of a temporal misfit. However, whereas interventionists regard proposals such as universal jurisdiction as clearly 'immature' and utopian, sovereigntists hover between denouncing them as 'premature' on the one hand and as retrograde on the other. The second interpretation rests on the assumption that the ICC is inferior to domestic courts and their jurisdiction because it is not integrated into any constitutional structures. According to one media commentator, the ICC therefore represents a pre-modern institution: 'Although the ICC is supposed to advance the rule of law around the world, it is potentially – even inherently – inimical to the rule of law. And it is *retrograde – premodern*, actually – because it affronts the principle that every institution wielding power over others should be accountable to someone.'[6]

Yet the sovereigntist discourse does not endorse a completely conservative approach to international law as interventionists do. Rather, to the extent that sovereigntists link the validity of international legal provisions to the requirement of state consent, they envisage a non-simultaneous development of international law. Moderate sovereigntists suggest that international law should develop at different speeds. According to this perspective, there may be some states whose moral and legal convictions converge and could be codified as treaty law between those states. The important point for sovereigntists, however, is that such vanguard developments cannot be forced upon non-consenting states: different speeds of legal developments have to be tolerated.

Order emerges from the state and its constitution

Similar to advocates of legalism, sovereigntists assume that political order first and foremost emerges from the law. In contrast to the former, however, for sovereigntists 'the law' primarily means domestic law rather than international law. Sovereigntists are thus not generally adverse to the idea of enforcing human rights and fighting impunity. Yet they argue that a court at the supra-state level is the wrong venue for this purpose.

According to sovereigntists, order can be equated with the rule of law:

> The rule of law is indispensable to justice, freedom and economic development. Moreover, *the rule of law is indispensable to international peace and security abroad.* As a nation founded by law, the United States is the unflagging champion of the rule of law. ... For 200 years that has been our firm conviction and practice. And it will remain our first article of faith.[7]

From the sovereigntist point of view, the rule of law, in turn, involves certain political structures; more specifically, it has to be based on a constitution and to be accompanied by democratic representation and political accountability. Hence, for sovereigntists, the rule of law is necessarily confined to states and their domestic structures, since the international realm does not provide these structures. If there is order in international relations, it is mainly derived from the order provided on the state level. According to sovereigntism, international order comprises two elements: first, the foundation of international order consists of the norm of coexistence and non-intervention into the domestic realm of other states. Hence, sovereigntists regard both interventions by powerful states and the establishment of supra-state institutions that could interfere with the domestic realm of states without their prior consent as detrimental to the maintenance of the international order. Second, states can agree upon treaties that regulate matters of cooperation among them. Thus, in the context of the sovereigntist discourse, international law is primarily interpreted in the tradition of legal positivism (cf. Koskenniemi, 2002: 18ff.), i.e. as being based on the will of consenting states, and consequently as treaty law.

When it comes to the prosecution of offences against international criminal law, sovereigntists prefer the enforcement of such provisions in the domestic realm. As one US media commentator put it: 'American detachment from an international court grants the United States no license for war crimes. *The American political process and judicial system build in their own checks.*'[8] In the same vein, another media commentator emphasised that the US constitution represents the ultimate foundation of jurisdictional legitimacy, while at the same time providing the central point of reference and identification for potential defendants, namely US service personnel:

> Members of U.S. forces may well commit crimes abroad. When they do, however, it is the United States that should investigate any allegations and prosecute the accused according to U.S. laws, with full protection of the Constitution and its

Bill of Rights. Anything less would neither be fair nor just to those who have volunteered to defend that same Constitution.[9]

Given that sovereigntism draws upon legal positivism, it comes as no surprise that sovereigntists also criticise the definitions of crimes included in the ICC Statute. They argue that these definitions lack clarity and explicitness and are much too vague:

> The problem is not just that the ICC is 'above the law', but that *there is not much clear and pertinent law to be above*. The rule of law must involve a body of controlling precedents that give due notice of what behavior is required or proscribed. However, the ICC is both a roving prosecutor and a court. It will prosecute cases of torture, defined as 'any act by which severe pain and suffering, whether physical of mental, is intentionally inflicted'. It will prosecute the crimes of 'excessive' force and environmental harm.[10]

According to the sovereigntist discourse, if a single state can contribute to the maintenance of international order, this can only happen by way of providing a good example for others, but not by directly interfering with the domestic affairs of other states or by transferring sovereignty prerogatives to supra-state institutions. In this respect, US diplomats frequently point out the supposedly immaculate record of the US with regard to the domestic implementation of those laws that the ICC is intended to enforce:

> No nation devotes more resources to the training in, and compliance with, the law of armed conflict than the United States. In fact, a Department of Defense directive formally provides that all reportable incidents involving violations of the law of war committed by or against the United States or enemy persons be reported promptly, thoroughly investigated and, when appropriate, remedied by corrective action. The Department of Defense has formal procedures and responsibilities in place to ensure that all such violations of the law of war are prosecuted in appropriate cases. Commanding officers who receive an initial report of a possible war crime are required to request that a formal investigation be conducted. In addition, senior Department of Defense officials are required to provide for disposition of crimes cases under the Uniform Code of Military Justice in appropriate cases. *We hope that other countries will follow our example in that area* by training all their men and women in uniform in the legal obligations and by holding their soldiers accountable for violations of the laws of war.[11]

By stressing the exemplary way in which single states can potentially influence others to implement humanitarian and human rights law within their own borders, the sovereigntist discourse differs from the interventionist one: whilst the latter endorses intervention as an instrument that is in some circumstances necessary in order to safeguard the international order, the former rejects intervention as undermining the basic fundament of that order; namely non-intervention and coexistence (cf. Brands, 1998a, b).

Accountability within the framework of constitutional structures

As noted above, sovereigntists are deeply concerned about the delegation of jurisdiction from the state level to the supra-state level. Thus, it comes as no surprise that they criticise the ICC Statute for giving the chief prosecutor too much independence and discretion. Whilst proponents of the legalistic discourse argue that the chief prosecutor's professionalism will provide an effective shield against the abuse of his or her competences, professionalism is no remedy from the sovereigntist perspective. The only reliable safeguard against the misuse of official competences is embedding legal institutions and offices in constitutional structures. According to sovereigntists, however, such structures are not available at the supra-state level. Consequently, the central charge laid at the ICC is that the office of the prosecutor lacks *accountability*: 'America's constitutional democracy includes checks and balances – including elections – that circumscribe the courts' freedom. But *the ICC floats above accountability* to representative institutions.'[12]

A similar criticism can be found in an article published in the *Rocky Mountain News* on the occasion of the entry into force of the Rome Statute in 2002:

> If the Bush administration were to propose establishing a court in this land that would be hedged in by none of our checks and balances, walk over the free-speech guarantees of the First Amendment and not allow trial by jury, do you suppose that everyone would be shouting 'Glory, glory, hallelujah?' No, everyone would be aghast, and everyone ought to be similarly aghast at an International Criminal Court that has all those faults and others, to boot.[13]

The independence of the prosecutor is criticised by both sovereigntists and interventionists. Yet the background from which these charges emerge differs in both discourses. Interventionists regard the independence of the prosecutor as putting especially powerful states at risk. They assume that an independent prosecutor could be instrumentalised for politically motivated trials and that investigations could be triggered by anti-Americanism. In contrast, sovereigntists frame the criticism of the prosecutor's independence as a question of democratic legitimacy and accountability. They bolster US disapproval of the Court with reference to the US commitment to the rule of law rather than pointing to power-political concerns. This becomes evident from a statement of Eric Rosand, US ambassador to the UN General Assembly, on a draft resolution that was intended to outline the relationship between the ICC and the UN:

> Because of our long-standing concerns about the ICC, some of which were articulated today, the United States cannot join the consensus on the draft resolution under consideration. Nonetheless, I want to reiterate the commitment of the United States to accountability for war crimes, genocide, and the crimes against humanity. The United States has a record that is second to none in holding its

officials and citizens accountable for such crimes ... *Properly understood, therefore, our decision not to support the ICC reflects our commitment to the rule of law, not our opposition to it.*[14]

Given that the interventionist and the sovereigntist criticism of the independence of the ICC prosecutor emerge from different backgrounds, proponents of both discourses also envisage different remedies: interventionists would have preferred to make investigations by the ICC prosecutor dependent on the approval of the UN Security Council, whereas the sovereigntist proposal was to give the states involved the final say. This was the initial position of the French delegation: 'The Court would exercise its jurisdiction in respect of States parties. To enable it to act effectively, the State on whose territory the crimes were committed and the State of nationality of the perpetrators would have to be parties to the Statute.'[15] During the Rome negotiations, the US delegation, conversely, initially opted for the interventionist solution to grant the UN Security Council the final say about the start of investigations and only later, when it became clear that there was no majority for this solution, shifted to the sovereigntist claim for state consent (Weschler, 2000: 99). Thus, at least with respect to the issue of the independence of the prosecutor, the interventionist discourse was initially more relevant for the official political position of the US, whilst the sovereigntist discourse played a secondary role.

The ontological features of the sovereigntist discourse: the predominance of states

Sovereigntism privileges states as the most relevant entities in world politics *vis-à-vis* individuals and supra-state institutions. Both the sub-state and the supra-state level are merely derivative of and secondary to the state level. As already explained above, the privileged position of states in the context of the sovereigntist discourse rests upon the assumption that states are the ultimate source of order, which is understood in terms of domestic order and constitutional structures.

The single state as the point of reference

From a sovereigntist point of view, the ICC in its final shape represents an illegitimate institution, as it challenges the primacy of states in world politics. This idea is common to the discursive arenas of diplomacy, of the media and of legal experts in as much as they align themselves with the sovereigntist perspective. Proponents of sovereigntism interpret the fact that the ICC is supposed to complement the jurisdictional functions of states as an arrogation of power on the part of a supra-state institution. This could not be any clearer than in the following remark by James Cunningham, US ambassador to the UN Security Council, on the occasion of the renewal of resolution 1422 (1487) exempting US citizens from the jurisdiction of the ICC:

> As ambassador Negroponte explained last year, the power to deprive a citizen of his or her freedom is an awesome thing, *which the American people have entrusted to their Government under the rules of our democracy.* The International Criminal Court does not operate in the same democratic and constitutional context and therefore does not have the right to deprive Americans of their freedom.[16]

Surprisingly, however, parts of the sovereigntist legal experts target the complementarity principle of all features of the ICC with their criticism, though the principle of complementarity was designed to accommodate concerns about a supposed loss of states' jurisdictional prerogatives.[17] A French legal expert, for instance, dismissed the complementarity principle as falling short of safeguarding the competencies of states. He holds that instead of truly enlarging jurisdictional capacities, the ICC erodes the competencies of states:

> The preamble [of the ICC Statute] reaffirms the complementarity between the ICC and national criminal jurisdictions; that same preamble recalls a bit further on that 'it is the duty of every State to exercise its criminal jurisdiction over those responsible for international crimes'. ... As a result, and the text of the Convention confirms this, the ICC is not designed to intervene as long as the domestic jurisdictions perform their competences. Consequently, if the International Criminal Court only has jurisdiction if the domestic jurisdictions fail, *it reaffirms and protracts the breakdown of the states in question.* (Sur 1999: 42; emphasis added)

At the same time, sovereigntists assume that states and their competencies are also bypassed and undermined by actors from the sub-state level, first and foremost NGOs. Proponents of sovereigntism mainly challenge what they perceive as the lack of democratic legitimacy of these groups. Viewed from the sovereigntist perspective, the fact that NGOs have been involved in the establishment of the ICC, and not just states, increases the illegitimacy of the Court. States are thus exposed to pressure from both the sub-state and the supra-state level: 'And to institutionalize a weakening of national sovereignty in favour of unelected human rights groups on one end and unaccountable supranational courts and prosecutors on the other is fundamentally anti-democratic. To worry about such a trend is not to be pro-genocide.'[18]

Sovereigntists deny a direct, unmediated relationship between individuals and sub-state entities on the one hand and institutions on the supra-state level on the other. In sharp contrast to the legalistic discourse, they argue that there is no legal responsibility of an individual *vis-à-vis* the international society of states and/or the world society of individuals. They emphasise that the state is indispensable as a medium between the two planes, i.e. the sub-state and the supra-state level. The core argument of sovereigntists is that only states feature democratic and constitutional structures, whereas a direct link between the sub-state and the supra-state level is doomed to end up in an undemocratic mismatch between the originators of political institutions and those who are targeted by them. From a sovereigntist perspective, political legitimacy can only emerge from the immediate congruence between rulers and the ruled. Alluding to Abraham Lincoln's dictum, a media commentator declares that 'We believe in the United States of America as a nation that is strong, just, compassionate, humanitarian, cooperative with every good and admirable and peaceful interest – but always *independent and sovereign, with government, of, by and for our people*.'[19]

Yet according to the sovereigntist discourse, it is not only pressure on the part of the sub-state and the supra-state level that undermines the primacy of the state, but also the alleged superiority of the collective interest of the international society of states *vis-à-vis* the interest of the single state. In contrast to both the legalistic and the interventionist discourses, the notion of an international society of states is only of secondary significance within the framework of the sovereigntist discourse.

Sovereigntists do endorse the principles of coexistence and non-intervention as shared norms within the context of interstate relations that provide a normative fundament for a rudimentary international society. However, they reject the idea of a collective interest of the international society of states. For sovereigntists the notion of interest primarily refers to the interest of the single state. They are deeply suspicious of the assertion of a collective interest of the international society of states that may override the interest of the single state. According to them, such an assertion merely figures as a cloak for the specific interest of one state or a group of states which refer to the international society of states in order to gain greater legitimacy and support for their political preferences and projects. Hence, sovereigntists are also sceptical about multilateralism – at least if it is understood as a matter of principle. States may engage in multilateral actions, but only if these actions rest upon the proper interest of the sum of all states involved and not on the assumption of a superior collective interest. The following quote from an article published in the *Rocky Mountain News* on the occasion of the Rome Statute's entry into force seeks to justify US opposition to the Court with reference to US national interest, whereas it denounces claims to a collective interest of all states as hypocritical:

> The refrain of those insisting on American hand-holding with other nations on this court project is that we simply must be multilateralist, *as if multilateralism were an end in itself*. It isn't. *The point of multilateralism is to cooperate with others on matters in the mutual interest of all.* The point is not for the United States to engage in self-destructive acts because *a group of other nations sees some advantage for their interest* if we do so.[20]

Individuals as citizens of states

Sovereigntists interpret individuals first and foremost as citizens of states and reject the cosmopolitan idea that there are direct and unmediated links between the individual and the supra-state level. The role that the sovereigntist discourse attributes to individuals becomes especially evident in the debate about immunities. Article 27 of the Rome Statute stipulates that no immunities apply before the ICC: 'Immunities or special procedural rules which may attach to the official capacity of a person, whether under national or international law, shall not bar the Court from exercising its jurisdiction over such a person.'[21] Historically, immunities were a vital ingredient of state sovereignty. According to Antonio Cassese, immunities are 'the *natural legal consequence of the obligation to respect the sovereignty of other States*' (2005: 98). Immunities for heads of state and diplomats include both ceremonial and functional elements (Brownlie, 2003: 322). They facilitate diplomatic relations while at the same time demarcating symbolic boundaries of states and singling out their most powerful individuals. Immunities mark the symbolic fusion of a state with its political representatives. Viewed from this perspective, individuals acting as heads of state or senior officials may well play a role in international relations, but in that role, they are perceived as incorporating the state that they are representing (Cassese, 2005: 117). Moreover, immunities reaffirm the idea that the relationship between states should be based on symmetry, as no state is supposed to exercise jurisdictional authority over another (*ibid.*).

Given that the matter of immunities is a rather legal-theoretical one, it comes as no surprise that it was mainly debated within the arena of legal experts. As noted above, the ICC Statute clearly stipulates the suspension of immunities in trials before the Court itself. The question of whether this also applies to states acting at the request of the ICC, however, is more difficult. According to Article 98 (1) of the Statute,

> the Court may not proceed with a request for surrender or assistance which would require the requested State to act inconsistently with its obligations under international law with respect to the State or diplomatic immunity of a person or property of a third State, unless the Court can first obtain the cooperation of that third State for the waiver of the immunity.[22]

This means that immunities might still apply in cases in which the ICC requests a state to extradite the head of state or a senior official of a third state. Yet Broomhall argues that the limit to immunities stipulated by the Rome Statute is more encompassing than it may seem at first sight, at least with respect to representatives of state parties: if a state has ratified the ICC Statute, Broomhall suggests, it agrees to waiving the immunity of its officials with respect to cooperation requests by the ICC (2003: 145). The most contested question is then whether immunities apply if the third state in question is a non-party state. Some legalists argue that officials of non-parties cannot claim immunity before a court of a state party acting pursuant to a request from the ICC, as individual criminal responsibility applies irrespective of whether or not the state of nationality of the defendant has ratified the Rome Statute (cf. Cassese, 1999: 160). Sovereigntists, in contrast, challenge this possibility and hold that the immunities of non-party states are untouched: '[A] State Party that has present in its territory an alien who enjoys sovereign or diplomatic immunity under international law and against whom the ICC has issued an arrest warrant would honour such immunity to the extent that a third-State waiver were not obtained by the ICC' (Scheffer, 2005: 336f.). More generally, Ruth Wedgwood argues that

> the decision to remove a tyrant from office, and to strip him of ex officio immunity for the purpose of national trial, lies within the competence of local authorities and is a matter of the sovereign decision of that state. In that regard, national prosecution again may offer a safer course, compared to international prosecution. (Wedgwood, 2005: 787).

The provisions included in the Bilateral Immunity Agreements, however, exceeded this rather moderate sovereigntist claim. The BIAs immunise not only heads of states, diplomats or other persons acting in their official capacity on behalf of the US they shield *all* US citizens (i.e. businessmen, tourists and, crucially, members of Private Military Companies (PMCs)) staying in those states with which the US concluded a BIA from extradition to the ICC.[23]

The sovereigntist emphasis on the privileged relationship between states and individuals institutionalised within the framework of citizenship also emerges with respect to the question of the extent to which citizens of a state can in fact be assumed to be aware of the provisions of *international* criminal law. According to David Scheffer, citizens' effective notice of the elements of crime as laid down in the ICC Statute can only come about via the mediation of states. Individuals cannot be assumed to have knowledge about international criminal law if it is not incorporated in the domestic legislation of the state of which they are citizens. In a 2004 article, he claims that US citizens should not be prosecuted by the ICC for some time because even if the US government decided to ratify the Rome Statute, it would take years to actually implement that decision:

> A major objective of implementing legislation by States Parties is to ensure that domestic criminal codes are modernised to incorporate ICC crimes and, thus, greatly ensure the successful application of complementarity under the Statute. That exercise clearly puts nationals on effective notice of the criminality of the actions described in the Statute. Are we to assume now that all nationals of all non-Party states are on effective notice of the illegality of each and every ICC crime and the procedural consequences of the ICC of violations of the treaty law or customary international law that are associated with each such ICC crime, *even though their respective non-party governments may not have taken the actions (through treaty law or otherwise) internationally or domestically to confirm that illegality and put their nationals on notice of such criminal liability before the ICC*? (Scheffer, 2004: 3; emphasis added)

Constitutional sovereignty as the appropriate framework for the implementation of human rights

The constitution as a benchmark and constraint of sovereignty

The sovereigntist discourse links the notion of sovereignty to a rather 'traditional' understanding of the term. It equates it with the maintenance of jurisdictional competences of states and the independence of states from outside authorities. Sovereigntists thus differ from the legalistic understanding of sovereignty in terms of 'new sovereignty', meaning that at the beginning of the twenty-first century states exercise sovereignty mainly by exerting political influence within international institutions and regimes. The sovereigntist interpretation of sovereignty is also distinguished from the interventionist understanding, according to which sovereignty is conditional upon a state's adherence to certain international norms and codes of conduct, most prominently human rights.

In the context of the sovereigntist discourse, the jurisdictional competences of a state represent an indispensable element of its sovereignty. The most clear-cut statement in this respect comes from a French legal expert:

> To establish an exceptional jurisdiction does not only imply to sacrifice mechanisms for the enforcement of international order, to a greater extent, it also represents a deliberate self-constraint of states, their voluntary refusal to exercise their competences. It concerns ... competences that are intimately linked to their sovereignty; namely prosecution and punishment. (Sur 1999: 33)

Sur generally challenges the legitimacy of the ICC. From his point of view, the Court is an indication of the weakness of states, which deliberately refuse to exert their sovereignty prerogatives. Whilst this position is rather extreme within the framework of the sovereigntist discourse, the assertion that the prosecution of citizens of non-party states denotes an illegitimate intrusion into the sovereignty of the states in question is more widespread. This becomes apparent from a statement by Anne Patterson, US ambassador to the UN Security Council, in a Security Council debate in March 2005 on the question of whether the ICC should be concerned with the situation in Darfur, Sudan: 'The United States continues to fundamentally object to the view that the ICC should be able to exercise jurisdiction over the nationals, including government officials, of States not party to the Rome Statute. *That strikes at the essence of the nature of sovereignty.*'[24]

A further criticism made by advocates of sovereigntism concerns the extent to which the Rome Statute stipulates an obligation to cooperate with the ICC on the part of the state parties. Given the ICC's lack of enforcement capacities, it is obvious that it has to rely on the cooperation of state parties. Part 9 of the Rome Statute (Articles 86–102) stipulates that all state parties commit to cooperate with the requests of the ICC. This obligation to cooperate covers the arrest and surrender of suspects and the provision of evidence for trials before the ICC. The legal procedures involved may be governed by national legislation, although state parties have to ensure that their legislation does not conflict with the ICC requirements, i.e. they may have to adapt their national legislation (cf. Broomhall, 2003: 155). If a state party refuses to cooperate, the Court may refer this to the Assembly of States Parties of the ICC, which in turn could take measures against the non-compliant state. If the Security Council has referred a situation to the ICC (as was the case with Darfur, for example) instances of non-cooperation could also be dealt with by the Council itself, which could even authorise the use of force in support of the ICC. However, Broomhall suggests that severe measures against a non-cooperating state party will be probably rare in order to safeguard overall support for the Court (*ibid.*: 156f.). In sum, he holds that '[f]ar from subordinating sovereignty to a supra-national criminal justice institution, the ICC places some of its most critical functions at the disposal of its States Parties' processes and decisions' (*ibid.*: 151).

Yet for sovereigntists the obligation of state parties to cooperate with the ICC is a major issue:

> Throughout the Rome Conference our negotiators struggled to *preserve appropriate sovereign decision making in connection with obligations to cooperate with the court*. There was a temptation on the part of some delegates to require unqualified cooperation by states parties with all court orders, notwithstanding national judicial procedures that would be involved in any event. Such obligations of unqualified cooperation were unrealistic and would have raised serious *constitutional issues* not only in the United States but in many other jurisdictions. (Scheffer 1999: 15; emphasis added)

From Scheffer's point of view, it is not acceptable to invest a supra-state institution with the power to oblige a state to cooperate if this requirement clashes with the state's constitution. Hence, sovereigntists reject external authorities on the grounds that they claim to be above the domestic constitution, which figures as the only legitimate foundation of political authority. The notion of sovereignty as the highest legitimate authority is closely related to the constitution as the ultimate benchmark and point of reference for this authority. In short, advocates of this discourse understand sovereignty as 'constitutional sovereignty'.[25]

According to the sovereigntist discourse, the constitution is vested with an almost sacred character.[26] The sacred and foundational character of the US constitution becomes evident in the following statement by James Cunningham, US ambassador to the UN Security Council, in a 2003 Security Council debate on 'Justice and the rule of law': '*The United States of America is a nation founded*, not upon ethnicity or cultural custom or territory, but *upon law enshrined in our Constitution*. As a consequence, establishing and maintaining the rule of law has been an enduring theme of American foreign policy for over two centuries.'[27]

Symmetry as the basic feature of the sovereignty-based international order

The sovereigntist discourse is grounded in the assumption that the international order should be symmetrical. From the sovereigntist perspective, one of the core objections to the ICC is that the Rome Statute violates the 1969 Vienna Convention on the Law of Treaties because it allows for the prosecution of citizens of non-party states.[28] The Vienna Convention stipulates that a state has to express its consent to a treaty in order to be bound by it. According to Cassese, this Convention is inspired by the assumption of symmetry between states, regardless of their actual size and power: 'While the previous oligarchic structure allowed Great Powers formally to impose treaties upon lesser States, this is no longer permitted: coercion on a State to induce it to enter into an agreement is no longer allowed.' (2005: 171).[29] This assumption of symmetry is reflected in the following statement by Eric Rosand, US delegate to the UN General Assembly: 'First, however, let me reiterate that the United States respects the right of States to become party to the Rome Statute. At the same time, *we expect similar respect for our decision not to become party to the Rome Statute.*'[30] In the same vein, David Scheffer argued in one of the last meetings of the DipCon in Rome that US opposition to the ICC Statute – especially to the claim of jurisdiction over nationals of non-party states – is mainly due to the ICC Statute's violation of the Vienna Convention: '[T]he attempt to impose the jurisdiction of the Court on States which did not become parties to the Statute would violate an elementary rule set out in the Vienna Convention on the Law of Treaties.'[31]

At first sight, it might seem inconsistent that, in some cases, sovereigntists challenge the legitimacy of an international legal institution on the basis of other provisions of international law; given their belief that international law is generally subordinate to national legislation and to the constitution of a state. However, the point is that the Vienna Convention, despite the fact that it is an international legal treaty, expresses the principle of the sovereign independence and coexistence of states. Ruth Wedgwood, a US legal expert, makes this emphasis on sovereign independence explicit:

> All states claiming *territorial integrity* and *political independence* within the *Westphalian system* are bound to *respect the domestic governance of other countries,* including their legitimate exercise of public authority over criminal behaviour, limited by the jurisdictional rules of international law. But, one might argue, *states are not obliged to participate in an international body.* The genius behind the Rome Statute was to build a stable regime founded on state consent, rather than the peremptory authority of the Security Council. It may, then, seem in tension to prosecute third party nationals under that regime. (Wedgwood, 1999: 99; emphasis added)

The Vienna Convention was so frequently invoked by diplomats and legal experts engaging in the sovereigntist discourse that references to this Convention eventually also occurred in the context of sovereigntist media comments on the

ICC: 'The long-standing practice in diplomacy is that a country is not bound by any transnational treaty unless it first approves it.'[32] Sometimes media commentators refer to the principle of symmetry as laid down in the Vienna Convention as 'fairness', thereby decreasing the level of abstraction and complexity of the issue: '*Fairness*, too, is central. The United States should not be forced to submit to a treaty it has not ratified, no matter how much praise the agreement garners from governments, activists and U.N. leaders.'[33]

In keeping with the sovereigntist emphasis on symmetry among states, sovereigntists argue that if states exert influence on the domestic human rights policy of other states, this influence should be confined to exemplarism. Military intervention or other forms of interference are perceived as illegitimate. James Cunningham, for instance, repeatedly pointed out that the US is 'the unflagging champion of the rule of law'[34] and that '[n]o nation devotes more resources to the training in, and compliance with, the law of armed conflict than the United States'.[35] Because of its immaculate record of enforcing humanitarian and human rights law domestically, he hoped 'that other countries will follow our example in that area'.[36] Media commentators amplified this idea: 'No nation in all of history has been more concerned about good things, children, human rights and women, and lots more, than the United States.'[37] US diplomats dropped this stress on the US exemplary character for other states only after the abuses of Iraqi prisoners by US soldiers, mainly linked to the Abu Ghraib prison in Baghdad, became public in 2004.

Finally, sovereigntists criticise the ICC as being an asymmetrical institution that privileges state parties over non-party states. In this vein, David Scheffer argued in a meeting of the UN General Assembly's Sixth Committee that according to the ICC Statute, state parties have discretion over future amendments to the Statute which would be decided upon by the Assembly of States Parties, thereby excluding non-party states, even though their citizens would be affected by these amendments as well:

> Another fundamental concern of the United States Government was the way in which the Rome treaty provided for the adoption and application of amendments to crimes. In its current form, the amendment process for the addition of new crimes to the jurisdiction of the Court or revisions to the definitions of existing crimes in the treaty would create an extraordinary and unacceptable consequence. After the states parties decided to add a new crime or change the definition of an existing crime, any State that was party to the treaty could decide to immunize its officials from prosecution for the new or amended crime. Officials of non-parties, however, were subject to immediate prosecution. For a criminal court, that was an indefensible overreach of jurisdiction. Likewise, there would be some who would regard the idea that States parties could opt out of prosecution for war crimes for seven years, while non-parties could not, as an incentive to join the court. Criminal jurisdiction – individual criminal jurisdiction – should not be played with in that way.[38]

Anne Patterson reiterated this claim to symmetry between states parties and non-party states on the occasion of the vote on Council resolution 1593 (2005), referring the situation in Darfur to the ICC. The US insisted on exempting its citizens once again from the Court's jurisdiction over the situation in Darfur. Patterson justified the exemption before the Security Council as follows:

> Protection from the jurisdiction of the Court should not be viewed as unusual. Indeed, under article 124, even parties to the Rome Statute can opt out from the Court's jurisdiction over war crimes for a period of seven full years, and important supporters of the Court have in fact availed themselves of that opportunity to protect their own personnel. *If it is appropriate to afford such protection from the jurisdiction of the Court to States that have agreed to the Rome Statute, it cannot be inappropriate to afford protection to those that have never agreed.* It is our view that non-party States should be able opt out of the Court's jurisdiction, as parties to the Statute can, and the Council should be prepared to take action to that effect as appropriate situations arise in the future.[39]

Human rights: domestic enforcement and legal positivism

The sovereigntist concept of 'constitutional sovereignty' and the claims for an international order based on symmetry are closely related to a specific understanding of human rights. According to sovereigntism, the validity of human rights is bound to the domestic framework of states. Sovereigntists criticise the ICC in two ways: the strong sovereigntist criticism of the Court is that a suprastate institution is generally the wrong venue for the prosecution of crimes against international humanitarian and human rights law, whereas moderate sovereigntists charge the ICC of an overreach of jurisdiction. In this vein, some critics denounce the ICC as a neo-imperial project of European political elites in the framework of which the latter try to force their legal and moral convictions upon the majority of non-consenting states.

French legal expert Serge Sur is representative of the first category of critics of the ICC. He interprets the establishment of the ICC as a 'retrogression' in the development of humanitarian and human rights law. Sur's argument is worthy to be quoted at length:

> The retrogression in the protection of human rights has to be assessed in this context [the theoretical context of different groups of human rights]. This might be surprising to some or even sound provocative: is the ICC not driven by the concern of providing a better guarantee for the protection of human rights, i.e. the right to live, to dignity and the respect for the physical and moral integrity which every human being possesses and which have to be respected in any place and under any circumstances? ... Let us only notice that from this point of view, recent developments stressed human rights rather than *civil rights*. The latter are bound to a *nationality*, they apply to *individuals rooted in a state's legal order*, determined and defined by the exclusive and privileged relationship that they have to it. In a way, these are *fundamental rights*, which are grounded in a *particular and substantial link to a state* and which can only flourish within its framework. *They*

cannot be universal and identical for all, because they can only be exercised in relation to a given state. *They are defined and guaranteed only by the state and generally rest upon the condition of nationality*, or, marginally, of residence. … But to us it is uncontested that *civil rights* guarantee a more complete and more profound protection of individuals than *human rights, detached from any precise reference to a state and at risk to appear as universal as evanescent*. Stressing the latter whilst ignoring the former, which is the presently predominant doctrine, thus is not necessarily a progress. (Sur, 1999: 34; emphasis added)

Sur's emphasis on the state as the privileged venue for the enforcement of human rights reflects a rather common-sense assumption of the sovereigntist discourse. His dismissal of 'human rights', however, which he equates with negative freedom rights as generally 'evanescent' and his assertion that, for this reason, civil rights, i.e. positive participation rights, are superior to human rights, is not as widely shared within the context of sovereigntism. Rather, moderate sovereigntists criticise what they perceive as the ICC's lack of 'due process' structures. This charge points to the sovereigntist belief that negative freedom rights are best protected within the framework of the constitutional state. For moderate sovereigntists, negative freedom rights are as important as positive participation rights; however, the enforcement of both should be left to states. Once again, the legitimacy of enforcement rests upon the constitution: 'The U.S. Constitution amply provides for the prosecution of Americans who commit war crimes and defends those who are accused falsely. The United States should never cede the job of prosecuting its citizens to an unaccountable, politically motivated international body.'[40]

Moreover, the moderate position within the sovereigntist discourse does not insist on confining the enforcement of human rights to the framework of the state under any circumstances. According to proponents of this strand, several states could indeed agree upon prosecuting human rights offences jointly. In this case, they would establish a common institution characterised by a low degree of delegation and a high degree of state control (cf. Abbott *et al.*, 2000). It is important to note, however, that such an institution would not qualify as '*supra*-state', but rather as '*inter*-state', since it would not exercise power over participating states except for those competencies that states have explicitly delegated to it. Such an inter-state institution would leave a large margin of discretion to state parties. Moreover, it would have to be in accordance with the constitutions of state parties, and if not, provide for opt-out opportunities.

Against this background, it comes as no surprise that in the conflict over the establishment of the ICC, sovereigntists mainly challenged the legalistic discourse for linking human rights to the international society of states. Sovereigntists argue that this legalistic assertion figures as a mere cloak for the neo-imperialism of European political elites. This criticism is most prominent among media commentators:

Because *the ICC is a facet of the European elites' agenda of disparaging and diluting the sovereignty of nations*, it is especially ill-suited to this moment, when the primacy

of the nation-state needs to be affirmed. … Rather, the root of the European complaint of 'unilateralism' concerns the U.S. refusal to move 'up from' the defense
of national sovereignty. The ICC – 'up' there, untethered to the governance of
any nation or settled legal system – *presupposes, among much else, the universality
of a common conscience. That presupposition is refuted by the very nature of the ICC's
principal enthusiasts, the European elites* who are incorrigible tolerant of Yassar [*sic*]
Arafat's terrorism, but scandalized by U.S. 'unilateralism'.[41]

The charge of neo-imperialism becomes even more explicit in an article published in the French newspaper *Le Figaro* in 2002:

The ICC is *far from representing a 'project of the international community'* to which
the United States are 'unilaterally' opposed. In fact, *it is merely a project of the
European Union* for which the EU manages to gather the support of countries
that cannot be seriously considered as independent actors of international politics due to their small size or their extreme poverty. … The ICC is founded by
an international treaty: the Rome Statute. It is an evident principle of treaty law
which is explicitly confirmed by the 1969 Vienna Convention that treaties do
not create obligations on non-parties. It seems as if the Rome Statute pretends to
abandon this principle. … *The former anti-imperialists reconverted to 'humanitarian'
imperialists will rejoice in it.*[42]

Although sovereigntists lay the charge of 'humanitarian imperialism' only at
the legalistic discourse; in principle, they could also target the interventionist
discourse in as much as it also interprets human rights as universal. However,
given that both sovereigntists and interventionists opposed the Court, this
point presumably remained implicit for strategic reasons. Yet one implicit
hint at basic differences concerns the question of what source of international
law either discourse privileges, with sovereigntists emphasizing treaty law and
interventionists stressing customary law. Though both types of law in practice
complement each other and are interwoven, theoretically, they are based on
different ideas of how international law emerges: treaty law rests upon explicit
state consent, whereas customary law refers to the collectivity of states and is
almost unaffected by the disapproval of a single state.

Conclusion

Sovereigntists envisage a non-simultaneous development of international law
based on treaties. States whose moral and legal convictions converge can agree
on treaty-based inter-state institutions, but should respect the choice of other
states not to become parties to those treaties, if they do not share their normative underpinnings. According to the sovereigntist discourse, international
order should be based upon the principles of coexistence and non-intervention. Rule of law structures, by contrast, are viewed as being confined to the
domestic framework of states. Sovereigntists argue that the ICC undermines
the rule of law because it does not provide the adequate checks and balances

that domestic courts are subjected to.

In the sovereigntist discourse, states figure as the predominant units of world politics. Advocates of sovereigntism depict states as the major sources of political order and hold that this order is based on domestic democratic structures and an immediate congruency of rulers and the ruled. They dismiss the ICC as an indicator for a growing pressure on states from both the sub-state and the supra-state level. Moreover, sovereigntists link the notion of interest to the single state. They denounce the assertion of a collective interest of the international society of states as a mere cloak for the special interest of a group of states intending to increase its influence over others.

The sovereigntist concept of constitutional sovereignty emphasises the independence of states from one another and the absence of superior authorities above the state. According to this perspective, the domestic constitution of a state overrides the relevance of international law. The sovereigntist stress on independence and non-intervention into the domestic affairs of other states is closely related to the belief that international order should be based on symmetry.

Advocates of sovereigntism hold that human rights are best enforced within the political structures of states. According to this position, some states could indeed converge on the interpretation of human rights and create a joint institution for their enforcement, but it would be illegitimate to target citizens of non-party states. Doing so would represent an instance of neo-imperialism.

Notes

1 Broomhall defines universal jurisdiction as follows: 'Under universal jurisdiction, the fact that a crime did not occur within or have a discernible impact on the territory or security of a State (thus falling outside of territorial or protective principle jurisdiction) or that no national of the State perpetrated or was a victim of the act (active or passive personality jurisdiction) is no impediment to proceedings by that State's authorities. Where international law recognizes this form of jurisdiction, States have in effect acknowledged that any other State may or must investigate and prosecute a given crime, even absent the usual jurisdictional links' (2003: 106).

2 South Korea's proposal envisaged 'quasi-universal' jurisdiction for the Court by suggesting that at least *one* of the interested states had to express its consent to the Court's jurisdiction.

3 'Acceptance' means that the state in question either is party to the Rome Statute or that it accepts the ICC's jurisdiction *ad hoc*.

4 David J. Scheffer, DipCon 9th meeting (22 June 1998); U.N. Doc. A/CONF.183/C.1/SR.9, Vol. II, p. 195; emphasis added.

5 Bill Richardson, DipCon, 5th plenary meeting (17 June 1998); U.N. Doc. A/CONF.183/SR.5, Vol. II, p. 95; emphasis added.

6 George F. Will, 'U.S. Isn't Wary Enough of New World Court', *Seattle Post-Intelligencer* (14 July 2002); emphasis added.

7 James B. Cunningham, UN SC meeting 'Justice and the rule of law: the United Nations role' (24 September 2003); U.N. Doc. S/PV.4833, p. 21.

8 'A Court Without the US', *Washington Post* (21 July 1998).

9 'Bush Is Right to Reject Sway of International Criminal Court. If Soldiers Commit Crimes, Their Government Can Handle It', *Portland Press Herald* (2 July 2002).

10 George F. Will, 'U.S. Isn't Wary Enough of New World Court', *Seattle Post-Intelligencer* (14 July 2002); emphasis added.

11 James B. Cunningham, UN SC meeting 'Justice and the rule of law: the United Nations role' (24 September 2003); U.N. Doc. S/PV.4833, p. 20–21; emphasis added.

12 George F. Will, 'U.S Isn't Wary Enough of New World Court', *Seattle Post-Intelligencer* (14 July 2002) – emphasis added.

13 'Criminal Court or Rogue Court?', *Rocky Mountain News* (5 July 2002).

14 Eric Rosand, UN GA meeting (13 September 2004); U.N. Doc. A/58/PV.95, p. 6 – emphasis added.

15 Hubert Védrine, DipCon 6th plenary meeting (17 June 1998); U.N. Doc. A.CONF.183/SR.6, Vol. II, p. 101.

16 James B. Cunningham, UN SC meeting 'United Nations peacekeeping' (12 June 2003); U.N. Doc. S/PV.4772, p. 24; emphasis added.

17 Complementarity means that that if a national court is investigating or has been investigating a case, this case is inadmissible to investigation by the ICC.

18 Ibid.; emphasis added.

19 'Beware of International Traps', *Chattanooga Times Free Press* (8 July 2002).

20 'Criminal Court or Rogue Court?', *Rocky Mountain News* (5 July 2002); emphasis added.

21 Rome Statute of the International Criminal Court, Art. 27 (2); U.N. Doc. A/CONF.183/9.

22 Rome Statute of the International Criminal Court, Art. 98 (1); U.N. Doc. A/CONF.183/9.

23 David Scheffer is highly critical of this provision and blames it on the Bush Administration's overly rejectionist stance on the ICC. While Scheffer attempted to negotiated a 'fix' in the post-Rome Preparatory Commission sessions that would have allowed the US a critical engagement with the ICC without having to ratify the Rome Statute immediately, he criticises the Bush Administration for its 'short-sighted and anemic approach to the Preparatory Commission' (Scheffer, 2001–02: 63) and denounces its rejectionist posture as counter-productive. Scheffer's criticism highlights differences in the Clinton and Bush Administration's policy towards the ICC (cf. Ralph, 2007: 123ff.). Yet these differences should not obscure the fact that the discourses feeding into the different policies did not fundamentally change.

24 Anne W. Patterson, UN SC meeting 'Sudan' (31 March 2005); U.N. Doc. S/PV.5158, p. 3; emphasis added. In her statement, Patterson simultaneously drew upon interventionist arguments; see Chapter 4, 'The international society of states'.

25 Shinoda (2000) uses the term 'constitutional sovereignty' as well; however, his understanding differs from the way in which the term is used here. According to Shinoda, constitutional sovereignty incorporates merely the belief in 'higher or fundamental laws that rule even sovereigns' (*ibid.*: 19), meaning that sovereigns could be bound either by a state's constitution or by international law. My use of the term 'constitutional sovereignty', in contrast, is confined to the idea that a state's constitution provides the foundation of sovereignty and at the same time constrains the exercise of sovereign powers.

26 See Moravcsik (2005: 154ff.) for an overview and a critical discussion of the impact of US constitutional culture on US human rights policy.

27 James B. Cunningham, UN SC meeting 'Justice and the rule of law: the United Nations

role' (24 September 2003), U.N. Doc. S/PV.4833, p. 20; emphasis added.

28 It should be noted, however, that the US signed, but never ratified the Vienna Convention.

29 Nico Krisch, however, argues that state consent as such is no guarantee for symmetrical legal institutions: states may approve of legal provisions the content or the effects of which are highly asymmetric (2003a: 138).

30 Eric Rosand, UN General Assembly meeting (13 September 2004); U.N. Doc. A/58/PV.95, p. 5; emphasis added.

31 David Scheffer, DipCon 42nd meeting (17 July 1998); U.N. Doc. A/CONF.183/C.1/SR.42, Vol. II, p. 361.

32 'The Right to Say "No". The United States Should Not Be Forced to Submit to International Criminal Court', *Omaha World Herald* (23 June 2004).

33 *Ibid.*

34 James B. Cunningham, UN SC meeting 'Justice and the rule of law: the United Nations role' (24 September 2003), U.N. Doc. S/PV.4833, p. 21.

35 *Ibid.*, pp. 20–21.

36 *Ibid.*

37 'Beware of International Traps', *Chattanooga Times Free Press* (8 July 2002).

38 David J. Scheffer, UN General Assembly Sixth Committee (Legal) meeting (4 November 1998); U.N. Doc. A/C.6/53/SR.9, p. 8.

39 Anne W. Patterson, UN SC meeting 'Sudan' (31 May 2005); U.N. Doc. S/P.5158, p. 3; emphasis added.

40 Steve Barrett, 'U.S. Hardly Alone in Opposing the Court', *Chattanooga Times Free Press* (16 July 2002).

41 George F. Will, 'U.S. Isn't Wary Enough of New World Court', *Seattle Post-Intelligencer* (14 July 2002); emphasis added.

42 John Rosenthal, 'Les ambiguïtés de la Cour pénale internationale. Bush a raison de s'opposer à la CPI', *Le Figaro* (16 July 2002); emphasis added.

6 The progressivist discourse

The case of progressivism is a special and difficult case, as it only played a marginal role within the framework of the transatlantic debate over the ICC. The reason for this is that the progressivist discourse finds itself in a position that is fundamentally opposed to the ICC as an institution intended to fight impunity. In contrast to the progressivist discourse, both interventionism and sovereigntism challenge the final shape of the ICC but were not entirely opposed to the idea of an international criminal court as such. Rather, they opted for a different institutional design of the Court. Progressivists, however, contest the usefulness of the ICC project irrespective of its institutional design. Drawing on the democratic peace hypothesis, the progressivist discourse depicts the global promotion of democracy as the only possible path towards the establishment of a sustainable international order. Progressivists argue that the prosecution of offences against international criminal law may in effect hinder the possibility of democratisation. The reasoning behind this is very simple: the prospect of impunity could induce unelected military leaders to leave their offices and to yield to democratic forces. Viewed from a progressivist perspective, the establishment of the ICC decreases the chances of democratisation as authoritarian leaders, now threatened with prosecution, will cling to their offices for as long as possible. Moreover, the ICC could threaten peace processes more broadly: the risk of prosecution may keep warlords from the negotiating table, whereas the promise of amnesties has at times proven to be a valuable bargaining chip in the negotiation of peace agreements. Hence, the question of amnesties forms the only intersection of the progressivist discourse with the debate about the ICC. At the same time, the question of amnesties highlights the contradiction between progressivism and the ICC. According to a legal commentator, 'blanket amnesties could never warrant deference, as they are the *antithesis of the ICC*; even in situations of extreme political necessity, to accept a blanket amnesty would be for the ICC to succumb to blackmail' (Robinson, 2003: 481; emphasis added). In fact, at the Rome Conference, the issue of amnesties was marginalised – tabooed, one might even say – to such an extent that it was only mentioned three times and by delegates from states with a notoriously poor human rights record.[1] Delegates from other states did not pick up on the topic of amnesties and chose to ignore it instead.

This situation led to the following methodological difficulty: even though the problem of a potential tension between the aims of peace and justice occurred within the framework of the data collected concerning the debate about the ICC, the progressivist discourse remained marginal. The contributions with respect to the question of amnesties were too scarce to reconstruct the whole discourse on the basis of the collected material. Yet taking the discursive level of political conflicts seriously means that exploring what has *not* been said or written is often as important as analysing what has been said and written. Missing the progressivist discourse out would leave us with an incomplete picture of the debate over the ICC, even though it played only a marginal role in that debate. Therefore, additional data were collected. The challenge was to find a thematic focus that would help to restrict data collection and to proceed in a way comparable to the data collection concerning the ICC debate. Given the theoretical foundation of the discursive configuration of sovereignty and human rights, the requirement was to find a relatively coherent set of statements grounded in the assumption of an asymmetric international order while at the same time giving preference to the implementation of human rights within the domestic framework of states. The debates in 2000 over the reform of the UN and the foundation of the so-called 'Community of Democracies' matched these criteria. However, this is not to say that that was the only context in which the progressivist discourse plays a role. In fact, it is plausible to argue that it also occurs in other instances of US foreign policy as well as European foreign policy, in particular in the process of EU enlargement. Generally, the aim of this chapter is not to provide an exhaustive assessment of the progressivist discourse and its significance in international relations, but to illustrate its basic features in order to give a complete depiction of the discursive configuration of sovereignty and human rights.

The Community of Democracies represents a union of approximately 100 states. It was founded by, among others, the US, and its objective is the global promotion of democracy. The Community represents an 'invitation-only' club. According to the 'Criteria for Participation and Procedures' of the Community, '[i]nvitations to participate will be issued to genuine democracies and those countries undergoing democratic consolidation'.[2] The idea behind this structure is that only democratic states can legitimately and effectively contribute to the work of international organisations. This concept of linking the participation in supra-state fora to domestic democratic achievements also became popular in the context of the debate on the reform of the UN, especially in the US. Whilst proponents of progressivism refrained from promoting Woodrow Wilson's initial concept of a 'League of Democracies' that would consist of democratic states only (cf. Moravcsik, 1997: 545), since 2004 the Community of Democracies has convened a 'Caucus of Democracies' in UN bodies such as the General Assembly and the UN Commission on Human Rights. The Commission on Human Rights, in particular, had become a target of progressivist criticism, as notorious human rights violators – like Libya and Sudan – had been elected into the Commission, whereas the US had been voted out. This eventually resulted in the replacement of the Commission on Human Rights with the UN Human Rights Council, which features stricter membership rules (cf. Rahmani-Ocora, 2006; Scheipers, 2007).

From the outset, the Community of Democracies faced difficulties in winning recognition, which was probably due to the reluctance of European states – apart from the two of the Community's founding members, Poland and the Czech Republic – to support this project. The reason for European reserve towards the Community of Democracies is its exclusionary character. French diplomat Philippe Bossière expressed his disapproval of the concept by pointing out that 'democracy is by its very essence *inclusive* and respectful of the views of all'.

Four different types of data were collected for the reconstruction of the progressivist discourse. The Community of Democracies was debated in the UN General Assembly three times between 1999 and 2005. Moreover, the Community itself issued several formal documents: the final Warsaw Declaration 'Toward a Community of Democracies' (2000), the 'Criteria for Participation and Procedures' (2002) and the Seoul Action Plan (2002). In addition to this material, statements and remarks on the Community of Democracies by higher-ranking officials and staffers from the US Department of State were considered. Finally, data from the media were collected. The collection was restricted to three important periods: first, the coverage of the Community of Democracies foundational meeting in Warsaw (25 June–3 July 2000), secondly, the coverage of the second Community meeting in Seoul (10–18 November 2002) and thirdly, the coverage of the third Community meeting in Santiago (28 April–6 May 2005). It turned out, however, that the Community of Democracies was hardly mentioned, let alone debated, in European newspapers. As the US was one of the founding members of the Community, the US media coverage was more extensive, but only concerning the foundational meeting in Warsaw. For this reason, the time frame for the collection of media articles was extended to include the whole of July 2000. Generally, the issue of the Community of Democracies drew much less public attention than the ICC. None the less it is a valuable example of the progressivist discourse.

Table 6.1 summarises the main features of the progressivist discourse.

Construction of time	Sources of order	Features of order	Ontology/ basic units	Notion of interest refers to	Notion of sovereignty	Human rights refer to
Progress	Domestic democracy/ democratic peace	Asymmetry	Individuals/ civil society	Individuals/ democratic states	Popular sovereignty	Essence of humanity/ natural law

Table 6.1 Basic features of the progressivist discourse

The narrative of progressivism: international order as 'democratic peace'

Progress towards ubiquitous democratisation

The progressivist discourse bears some similarities to legalism in that both construct time in terms of progress. In doing so, both draw upon the Enlightenment tradition and its ideas about the rationalisation of political authority and the establishment of the rule of law. Yet the two discourses differ with respect to the framework in which this progressive development is supposed to take place: whilst the legalistic discourse emphasises the legalisation of international relations as the *telos* of progress, the progressivist discourse endorses an understanding of progress focused on the domestic structure of states. According to progressivists, the ultimate *telos* of progress is ubiquitous domestic democratisation. Consider in this respect the following speech by US Foreign Minister Condoleezza Rice at the Community of Democracies Opening Plenary in 2005 in Santiago:

> We at the Community of Democracies must use the power of our shared ideals to *accelerate democracy's movement to ever more places around the globe*. We must usher in an era of democracy that thinks of tyranny as we thought of slavery today: a moral abomination that could not withstand *the natural desire of every human being for a life of liberty and of dignity*.[3]

The progressivist belief in the achievability of ubiquitous democratisation emerges from the assumption that the desire for democracy and self-rule is an anthropological feature common to all humankind. The driving force behind progress towards democratisation is human nature. Yousif Ghafari, US delegate to the UN General Assembly, described the anthropological foundation that the Community of Democracies intends to foster as follows:

> While *citizens' desire for individual freedoms* can be repressed for a time by authoritarian and corrupt regimes, *history shows us that transition is possible – it is, in fact, inevitable*. That knowledge bolsters our support for the inalienable rights of freedom-loving people everywhere. Meeting that challenge will require strong cooperation among democratic nations and we stand with those Governments that respect human dignity.[4]

Given their assumption that the desire for democracy is so deeply rooted in human nature, progressivists perceive democratisation first and foremost as a development initiated by the domestic civil society of a state and not by external intervention:

> As more and more countries adopt democratic practices, the evidence continues to mount: *Democracy is not a foreign import or imposition*, but an inspiration to men and women all around the world who work for change within their own societies.
>
> Democratic ideals and values speak to a yearning fundamental to every human being – a yearning for freedom and dignity and a better life for themselves and

their children.[5]

The objective of international order: 'democratic peace'

The thesis of democratic peace is usually associated with the legacy of Kant and Wilson (cf. Cox, 2000; Risse-Kappen, 1994; Hurrell, 1990; Levy, 1988; Doyle, 1983). It is based on the assertion that democracies do not wage war against each other. Kant's 'Perpetual Peace' essay offers one possible explanation for this phenomenon: as soon as citizens of a state have influence on the political decision about war and peace within the framework of democratic self-government, war would be no longer available as an instrument of politics because the people as the potential bearer of the costs of war would not opt for their own detriment (Kant, 1995 [1795]).[6] Franceschet summarises the idea as follows: 'The DP [Democratic Peace] theorists thus express the classical liberal internationalist hope that the *external* sovereignty of states will be exercised with more restraint – and anarchy will thereby be mitigated – when *internal* sovereignty is located in the people' (2000: 284). The democratic peace thesis has not remained unchallenged. On the one hand, it has been criticised for its lack of explanatory power and precision. In this respect, scholars argue that the causal link between domestic democracy and external peacefulness cannot be convincingly established (cf. Layne, 1994; Risse-Kappen, 1995; Cohen, 1994). On the other hand, theorists of democratic peace have been challenged for too narrow a reading of Kant (Franceschet, 2000; C. Brown, 1992). The interpretation of democracy as a mere *domestic* political structure, Franceschet argues, 'only reinforces the statist framework of international relations, a grid that Kant himself realized cannot ultimately satisfy the conditions of individual freedom' (2000: 286).

Despite this criticism, the democratic peace thesis turns out to figure prominently within the progressivist discourse as the response to the question of what provides an adequate and sustainable fundament for international order. Progressivists assume that democratisation is not only beneficial for the citizens of the states in question, but also for the international order as a whole. This conviction is so central to the progressivist discourse that it is mentioned as one of the principles of the Community of Democracies, namely the assertion of 'the interdependence between peace, development, human rights and democracy'.[7]

In the same vein, US delegate to the General Assembly, Revius Ortique, depicted the correlation between domestic democracy and a peaceful international order as follows:

> Genuine democracy is not a function of a single election or a single document. It depends on many factors, such as the development of a strong civil society, an informed citizenry, a free press, a loyal opposition and respect for human rights and the rule of law. Without fear of justifiable contradiction, I declare to this

Assembly that *democratic Governments represent the best means of fostering* political stability, economic progress and *peaceful cooperation among states*.[8]

In sum, progressivists interpret democratisation, in the words of Maurice Halperin, US representative to the UN General Assembly, 'as the essential precondition for a more peaceful, prosperous, and just world'.[9] In this respect, the progressivist discourse seems at first sight reminiscent of the sovereigntist perspective: according to the latter, the maintenance of political order is primarily the task of states and their domestic institutions. However, whilst sovereigntism emphasises the peculiarities of every single domestic constitution and the principle of coexistence that is intended to facilitate inter-state relations under conditions of normative pluralism among states, progressivists argue that it is the similarities of domestic structures – i.e. the ubiquity of democracy – that will ultimately lead to global peace.

Challenging the objective of the ICC: amnesties in the context of the progressivist discourse

The main reason for the marginal role of the progressivist discourse in the debate over the establishment of the ICC is its incompatibility with the project of the Court as such. According to progressivists, the fight against impunity could potentially be an impediment to democratisation or peace processes more generally, as it rules out the possibility for authoritarian leaders to step down or for warlords to come to the negotiating table free from the threat of legal prosecution. Viewed from this perspective, unelected rulers would see the establishment of the ICC as a disincentive to yield power to the forces of peace and democracy. In contrast, the possibility of amnesties would be a decisive factor in facilitating peace processes and/or democratic transitions.

Legalists argue that one of the main purposes of the ICC is 'reconciliation'.[10] They expect that, for instance, after the end of a civil war, the awareness that those responsible for atrocities and offences will be prosecuted is a precondition for the reconciliation of the wider society. Progressivists, on the contrary, denounce prosecution as 'retribution' – even 'revenge' – and confront this with the call for amnesties, which they equate with reconciliation:

> The ability to give dictators a face-saving way out is an essential component of democratic change. Most societies, offered the choice between *looking backward for revenge* and *looking forward to democratic reconstruction*, have chosen the latter. … An International Criminal Court would take away that choice. An independent prosecutor, answerable to no state or institution, would have the power to indict a nation's former leaders and *overrule its national reconciliation process*.[11]

In a less radical way, US legal expert Ruth Wedgwood addresses the problem of mandatory prosecutions of former authoritarian leaders. She charges the delegates to the Rome Conference with not having discussed the problem of the admissibility of amnesties for crimes over which the ICC has jurisdiction:

Many of us hope that taking responsibility at an international level for the prosecution of gross human rights violations – including systematic war crimes, torture and disappearances – will increase the number of instances when a transition
can be stabilized without casting a blind eye to the past. There is less point in
threatening a barracks coup if a defendant is already in The Hague (or London)
awaiting trial; an international actor is not directly vulnerable to pressure. But
one must recognize that militaries can still attempt confrontation, *holding local
democracy hostage*, making plain what the cost of any prosecution may be.

What to do in such situations requires prudential judgment and high states-
manship. ... But no plenary discussion of this vexing problem was had in Rome.
... The Rome Statute omits any direct account of the problem of amnesties, and
the failure to acknowledge the legitimacy of considering local amnesties under
the Statute may prove troublesome. (Wedgwood, 1999: 96; emphasis added).

It remains questionable, however, whether it would have been possible to address the issue of amnesties in the Rome Statute. As one legal expert points
out, amnesties for grave violations of human rights represent the 'antithesis
of the ICC', 'because the very purpose of the International Criminal Court
is to ensure that perpetrators of genocide, crimes against humanity and war
crimes do not escape prosecution for their crimes' (Robinson, 2003: 481, 504).
According to others, the exclusion of amnesties under the ICC Statute is not
quite as definitive. Jessica Gavron (2002), for instance, argues that the establishment of an effective truth commission would satisfy the requirement of
complementarity under Article 17 of the Rome Statute, as long as the truth
commission is not intended to shield persons from criminal responsibility.

That the issue of amnesties is a major challenge has been confirmed by
the fact that it played a role in almost every investigation that the ICC has
started since its establishment. When in 2005 chief prosecutor Luis Moreno
Ocampo issued arrest warrants against the leaders of the Lord's Resistance
Army (LRA), Betty Bigombe, who was involved in the peace negotiations
in Uganda, said that this move would obstruct the peace talks and make a
surrender by the LRA unlikely (Apuuli, 2006: 185). The 2008 arrest warrant
against the Sudanese President Omar al-Bashir created an even greater uproar.
The African Union requested a suspension of the arrest warrant in order to
safeguard the protracted Sudanese peace negotiations. The Nigerian Foreign
Minister Ojo Maduekwe said that if al-Bashir were in fact arrested, Sudan
'could turn into one huge graveyard'.[12]

Against this background, some progressivist commentators are rather clear-
cut in their conclusion about the ICC: 'The ICC is a case of global do-goodism
gone wrong. It will hurt, rather than help, the cause of freedom. This is a case
where the opponents of "global justice" are on the side of democracy – and the
human rights campaigners are unwittingly in league with tyrants.'[13] This is
not to say, however, that the progressivist discourse is completely hostile to the
idea of holding political leaders accountable for potential offences. Yet there is
a crucial difference between the ICC as a legalistic project and the progressivist

perspective on prosecution with respect to the question *to whom* potential per-petrators should be held accountable: according to the Preamble of the Rome Statute, the central point of reference is the 'conscience of humanity' and 'the international community as a whole',[14] whereas the final Warsaw Declaration of the Community of Democracies specifies that accountability refers to 'the citizenry of the country'.[15] Thus, in the context of the progressivist discourse, jurisdictional responsibility exclusively relates to a state and its people rather than to a collective body outside or above the domestic framework of states. International criminal prosecutions not only risk the extension of civil war and oppression because they threaten warlords and unelected leaders with ac-countability, they also stymie democratisation at the level of civil society, as Adam Branch writes with respect to the ICC and Uganda:

> Corrective justice is not the only concept of justice; indeed, there is also the broader concept of *social or political justice*, in the sense of establishing a social and political order in which the fundamental injustices that led to conflict and violence have been rectified. ... Because such debate is essential for resolving the conflict and for furthering democracy in Uganda, the ICC intervention has had a wide-ranging effect of empowering an unaccountable international body to the detriment of domestic democratic processes. (Branch, 2007: 193–4)

Ontological features of the progressivist discourse: individuals as members of civil society

The progressivist discourse depicts individuals as the primary units of refer-ence for world politics. In this respect, it bears some similarities with the world society strand of legalism. In contrast to the latter, however, progressivists do not regard individuals as cosmopolitan citizens, but as citizens belonging to a particular polity. The notion of 'civil society' is of particular relevance to the progressivist discourse. Though progressivists take into account a certain degree of transnationalisation, their notion of civil society does not amount to the idea of a 'global civil society' (cf. C. Brown, 2001; Lipschutz, 1996; Walzer, 1995).

Individuals as basic ontological units in world politics

For progressivists, domestic democracy is the foundation of international or-der. The progressivist emphasis on domestic structures of states is at first sight reminiscent of the sovereigntist perspective, according to which the constitu-tions of states are a vital point of reference for the maintenance of international order. Yet for advocates of progressivism, it is not the constitution in which the domestic democracy of a state is rooted; rather, it is civil society. According to the progressivist perspective, in order to qualify as a democratic state, democ-racy has to emanate from civil society. The Warsaw Declaration emphasises the importance and indispensability of civil society:

> We will also promote civil society, including women's organizations, non-governmental organizations, labor and business associations, and independent media in their exercise of their democratic rights. Informed participation by all elements of society, men and women, in a country's economic and political life, including by persons belonging to minority groups, is fundamental to a vibrant and durable democracy.[16]

It comes as no surprise that civil society represents a major target of democratisation strategies envisaged by the Community of Democracies, since the progressivist discourse attributes such a significant role to individuals as participants of civil society. The Community's Seoul Plan of Action devotes several paragraphs to this topic. First, it calls for a focus on 'civic education' as a precondition for the emergence of a sustainable democracy:

> Recognizing that education at all levels is a fundamental component for ensuring citizens are aware of their rights and civic duties as members of a democratic society, equipped with the basic skills for effective participation in public affairs, and *that an educated citizenry is essential to the development, maintenance, and strengthening of democratic institutions and growth*, we intend to encourage States and all relevant levels of government in our respective countries to promote a *culture of democracy through education for democracy* ... [17]

Viewed from a progressivist perspective, 'democracy' is a cultural feature linked to the concept of 'civic culture' (cf. Almond and Verba, 1989).[18] In this respect, the progressivist discourse is clearly distinguished from sovereigntism, as the latter understands democracy as a formal structure rooted and embedded in the constitution of a state.[19]

A second progressivist strategy to strengthen civil society is the promotion of volunteerism. The assumption is that democracy is not located in any formal political structure, but in informal networks at different levels: 'Recognizing that active involvement in the community strengthens an individual, those served, and the community as a whole; contributes to a vibrant civil society; and encourages partnership among citizens, civil society organizations, and governments, we intend to promote volunteerism ...'[20]

As noted above, advocates of progressivism assume that the desire for democracy and individual freedom is an anthropological fact common to all human beings. Thus, if progressivists consider a state to be undemocratic and corrupt, this does not extend to its people. Rather, faced with undemocratic regimes, progressivists argue that these regimes can only persist by repressing the democratic aspirations of civil society. The question of how to cope with non-democratic states, however, turns out to be difficult. On the one hand, the Community of Democracies explicitly commits itself to the promotion of democratic norms and values. On the other, to impose such values externally would be undemocratic. US Under-Secretary of State Paula Dobriansky proves to be rather assertive when it comes to the question of how much interference in the domestic affairs of non-democratic states would be legitimate for the sake of democratisation:

> We must focus on a concrete agenda for strengthening democracy where it exists and for *encouraging it where it does not yet exist*. ... The Seoul Plan of Action should also incorporate the fact that *we bear these responsibilities not just for our own nations alone*. We also owe a duty to our neighbors and fellow democracies to help them fully realize these promises of democratic development. Therefore, we must work as individual actors, regional partners, and global stewards of democracy.[21]

The wording of the final Warsaw Declaration, in contrast, is much more modest:

> The Community of Democracies affirms our determination to work together to promote and strengthen democracy, recognizing that we are at differing stages in our democratic development. We will cooperate to consolidate and strengthen democratic institutions, *with due respect for sovereignty and the principle of non-interference in internal affairs*.[22]

A close reading of both the Warsaw Declaration and the Seoul Action Plan suggests that progressivists regard measures of capacity-building that target the civil society of non-democratic states as legitimate. In particular, NGOs figure prominently as 'global stewards of democracy', in Dobriansky's words. The Warsaw Declaration, for instance, states that the Community of Democracies will promote transnational 'people-to-people linkages'[23] and the Seoul Action Plan specifies that one of the strategies of democracy promotion consists of 'supporting non-governmental groups that inform citizens of their rights and responsibilities, that help engage citizens with their government, that advocate democratic values and that assist people in developing basic skills needed for effective participation in public affairs'.[24] The explicit way in which the progressivist discourse welcomes the involvement of NGOs in the process of democracy promotion represents a sharp distinction from the sovereigntist perspective, according to which NGOs undermine democracy rather than strengthening it.[25]

When it comes to the notion of interest, the progressivist discourse provides a rather inclusive response. Advocates of progressivism regard individuals as a significant point of reference for the construction of interest, since individuals are considered the primary units of reference for world politics. Revius Ortique, US representative to the UN General Assembly, argued that democratisation first and foremost serves the interest of individuals: 'We wish to bolster the increasingly widely supported view that democracy – government based on the will of the people, on the rule of law and on respect for human rights – offers *the best hope for all humanity*.'[26] Yet when taking into account the democratic peace thesis, which is an important part of the progressivist narrative, it becomes obvious that progressivists necessarily conceive of the interests of individuals, of states and of the international community (of democratic states, at least) as interrelated. For if democracy leads to a peaceful international order, individual democratic states as well as the community of democratic states evidently have an interest in democratisation. Accordingly, Ortique argues: 'Thus, the United States firmly believes that the *national interests* of every United Nations Member are best served by the growth of democracy throughout the world.'[27] Despite this interrelatedness of the interests of individuals, states and the international community, in his rather solemn closing remarks, Ortique leaves no doubt that the most significant point of reference in the context of the progressivist discourse is the individual:

> In closing, let me say that the United States is proud to support the movement of new or restored democracies. We continue to work with our partners in the United Nations and in other international organizations to help to transform democratic principles into reality *for people throughout the world. Human beings*, beyond the majestic mountains, across the serene valleys and broad plains and also in the overcrowded metropolises, all swell with pride, and *people of every hue and conviction* embrace this mighty movement in support of democratic freedoms, this movement in support of new or restored democracies *for peoples throughout the world*.

States and the supra-state level: international society as an 'invitation-only club'

The progressivist discourse distinguishes between two types of states: democratic and non-democratic. This distinction is institutionalised within the framework of the Community of Democracies itself. The Community is an invitation-only club. One hundred and six states were invited to the Warsaw foundational meeting in 2000, with all states having been identified as democratic beforehand. The Convening Group of the Community, which consists of ten states,[28] decides about the participation, i.e. classification, of states. Invitations depend on states' adherence to the Community's main principles. These principles are set out in the Community's 2000 'Criteria for Participation and Procedures', and include 'free, fair and periodic elections', 'multipartidism', the 'rule of law', the 'separation of powers', the 'respect for human rights' and fundamental freedoms and the 'right to full and non-discriminatory participation'.[29] The Community undertakes to monitor its participants' adherence to these standards and – in cases of non-compliance – to exclude them.[30] Potential new members, i.e. countries that have just started a transition to democracy, will first be invited as 'observers' – a status that demarcates a rite of passage (cf. van Gennep, 1986) from the non-democratic to the democratic category. Evidently, progressivists do not act on the assumption of a global international society, but rather a limited one amongst those states which qualify as democratic. The peculiarity of the progressivist discourse with regard to international society thus is that international society is seen as an exclusive 'club' with fixed criteria for participation.

The difficulty with such a bifurcation of international society lies, of course, in the question of how to decide which states qualify as democratic, given the vast differences between democracies, their historic developments and their cultural and regional contexts (cf. Lijphart, 1999; Schmidt, 2000). Members of the Community of Democracies are nevertheless confident that this is possible. Alexandr Vondra, Czech ambassador to the US, explained, for instance: 'With more than 100 countries, any common ground can be but a compromise, which is, after all, very much in the spirit of democracy.'[31] Whilst Vondra admits a high degree of diversity concerning the implementation of democracy, the wording of the Community's documents sounds less permissive. According to the 'Criteria for Participation and Procedures', variations in democratic structures are merely a temporal phenomenon. They are different stages on the preassigned way to democracy:

> The criteria should also reflect a balance between the Community of Democracies' aim to promote and strengthen democracy and the acknowledgement that its current participants are at differing stages in their democratic development.
> ...
> The fact that countries find themselves at different stages in their democratic development is to be considered. Nevertheless situations that raise a question regarding their commitment to democratic values will be evaluated by the CG [Convening Group]. *Different stages must not mean different criteria.*[32]

It comes as no surprise that the collision between the progressivist conviction that it is possible to draw a clear-cut line between democratic and non-democratic states on the one hand and the empirical variety of democratic structures on the other gave rise to criticism on the part of the media. Commentators complained that among the participants of the Community 'are dubious democracies like Peru and Haiti'.[33]

The progressivist idea of classifying states depending on whether or not they adhere to certain standards, including human rights, is at first sight reminiscent of the interventionist discourse. Indeed, both progressivism and interventionism endorse a kind of conditionality. Yet there is a crucial difference with regard to this conditionality. The interventionist version of conditionality is negative: if states do not comply with human rights standards, they lose their sovereignty prerogatives and intervention by external forces becomes legitimate. Progressivist conditionality, in contrast, is positive, i.e. those who meet certain conditions receive a reward: they are invited to join the Community of Democracies. As we shall see below, the differing conditionalities involved in the interventionist and the progressivist discourse are related to the feature of asymmetry that is common to both discourses.

Regarding the supra-state level, the basic conviction of progressivists is that cooperation of states on this level requires a substantial set of shared norms and values in order to be legitimate and effective. Advocates of progressivism often criticise the UN and its bodies – especially the General Assembly – for being ineffective and illegitimate because membership in the UN is universal and not restricted by specific requirements. According to the progressivist discourse, universal membership in supra-state organisations, first, undermines the legitimacy of those bodies and, second, renders them 'ineffective'.[34] Consider in this respect the following remarks by US Assistant Secretary of State Kim Holmes:

> Some say that, for their decisions to be truly democratic, international organizations must have universal membership, just like the United Nations General Assembly. They believe that expanding participation in bodies like the Security Council would vastly enhance the legitimacy of their decisions.
>
> Now, representation *is* a key element of democracy. But decisions do not become more democratic simply by having more member states involved in making them. *What makes a decision more democratic is whether those involved represent the voice and will of their people.* The legitimacy of their decisions will be questioned, for good reason, if this is not the case. Governments that do not respect the rule of law at home find it very easy to ignore the rule of law internationally.[35]

For Holmes, democracy at the supra-state level cannot be established by transferring democratic structures to that level; rather, it is primarily characterised as a delegation of the democratic will of a civil society via its government to the supra-state level. Moreover, according to Holmes, international law is not an independent source of order at the supra-state level, as she suspects that only democratic states comply with its provisions, whereas non-democratic states would be prone to ignoring it.

Following Holmes's perspective, the requirement of domestic democracy as a safeguard of supra-state legitimacy is particularly necessary with respect to the UN Commission of Human Rights:

> We see this played out most dramatically in the Commission on Human Rights (CHR). This year, members of the Commission included Cuba, Congo, China, Libya, Syria and Zimbabwe – widely recognized human rights abusers who care less about human rights than about preventing themselves from being sanctioned.
>
> ...
>
> If we want the Commission's decisions to be more democratic – more important, if we want its decisions to mean something *for the suffering people who look to it for help* – then the democratic members of the UN must take the lead. Countries that uphold the purposes and principles of the CHR should see that more democratic countries get elected to serve on it.[36]

In sum, progressivists are convinced that making membership of supra-state institutions dependent on domestic democratic structures and adherence to human rights standards not only enhances the effectiveness and the moral weight of those institutions, but is at the same time the only way to ensure that their decisions correspond to the will and the need of individuals.

Popular sovereignty and the embedding of human rights into the concept of democracy

Popular sovereignty

In his 1999 book *Representing Popular Sovereignty: The Constitution in American Political Culture*, Daniel Lessard Levin argues that the US constitution figures so prominently in US political culture because it is the symbolic embodiment of popular sovereignty. His thesis rests upon the fact that the constitution begins with the three words 'We the People': 'Beginning with the words, "We the People", the Constitution is a collective representation because it signifies the unified body of the nation, fusing that nation into a single text in which all members can find themselves represented' (Levin, 1999: 2). If Levin were right, constitutional sovereignty and popular sovereignty would be the same in as much as the constitution would merely serve as a symbol for the latter. Consequently, it would be difficult to maintain one of the crucial differences between the sovereigntist and the progressivist discourse; namely, the distinction between their respective notions of sovereignty.

In his empirical investigation of the US constitution's bicentennial, however, Levin encounters a paradox: although the constitution serves as a symbol of popular sovereignty, it induces neither active participation on the part of civil society nor the rebirth of civic virtues. Rather, Levin found evidence for an alienation of the citizenry from the constitutional system (*ibid.*: 101). He tries to explain this paradox in the conclusion of his book: 'One might easily argue that one of the most important attributes of the Constitution is the freedom it provides for citizens to engage in private pursuits. … One might even claim that an ethic of participatory democracy is incompatible with a Constitution that values representative democracy above direct democracy' (*ibid.*: 186–8). Levin is entirely right in pointing out different interpretations of democracy. However, these different concepts of democracy do not form a paradox at the heart of US *constitutional* culture. Rather, they clash because they belong to different notions of sovereignty that are embedded in different discourses. In his historical re-examination of sovereignty, Hideaki Shinoda argues in the same vein by contrasting popular sovereignty with constitutional sovereignty. With regard to the emergence of US sovereignty in the eighteenth century, he draws the conclusion that '[t]hese two pillars of the United States – popular sovereignty and the Constitution – represent the national and constitutional principles' (2000: 44), whereby the national principle equates sovereignty with the realisation of the true will of man and nation and the constitutional principle corresponds to the idea that sovereignty is constrained by formal rules (*ibid.*: 19).

The progressivist discourse refers to sovereignty as popular sovereignty. It draws upon Rousseau's concept of sovereignty, which is opposed to both Thomas Hobbes's idea of vesting the ruler with all sovereign powers and John

Locke's attempt to distinguish between the source of sovereignty – the people – and the location of sovereignty – the government (cf. Hinsley, 1986: 144ff.). According to US Assistant Secretary of State Kim Holmes, sovereignty not only emerges from the people, but also rests with them. Moreover, in order to establish and maintain popular sovereignty, the government of a state must not be removed from the people, but should remain close to it:

> True democracy rests in *popular sovereignty* – the voice and will of the people expressed through elections, and reflected in the maintenance of democratic institutions. *The closer government is to the people, then, the more democratic it will be and the more legitimate*. The further the centers of power are from the people – and the less accountable those centers are to the people – the less democratic they will be.[37]

Similarly, US Under-Secretary of State Paula Dobriansky argues that the involvement of civil society and the establishment of close links between government and non-governmental groups are important in order to sustain democracy:

> Forging closer ties between governments and non-governmental groups is vital to our success. Full democracy must be buttressed by a strong civil society that will hold governments accountable to their citizens. The public–private partnerships that we expect will emerge from Seoul will provide another aspect of support for democracy worldwide by helping to guarantee that governments remain transparent and responsible.[38]

In sum, proponents of progressivism endorse an understanding of sovereignty that ties in with a certain interpretation of democracy. Although the sovereigntist discourse stresses the existence of democratic structures as a precondition for the political legitimacy of institutions, the sovereigntist notion of democracy differs from the progressivist understanding of the term. From a sovereigntist perspective, democracy means representative democracy – the government represents the people and sovereignty is delegated from the people to the government.[39] Once sovereignty is removed from the people itself the constitution serves as a benchmark and constraint for sovereignty. This also implies that formal rules and structures – 'checks and balances' – figure most prominently within the framework of the sovereigntist discourse.

The progressivist notion of popular sovereignty, in contrast, envisages an understanding of democracy that is much more participatory. Democracy in the progressivist sense involves the active participation and even 'mobilisation' of civil society. Political leaders are considered to be directly accountable to the people and the will of the people is the main benchmark and constraint for the exercise of sovereignty (cf. Shinoda, 2000: 19).

Asymmetry based on different commitments to democracy

Both the progressivist and the interventionist discourse regard the current international order as asymmetric. There are, however, crucial differences between the progressivist and the interventionist perception of asymmetry. First, this concerns the theoretical foundation of asymmetry. According to advocates of interventionism, asymmetry is based on power inequalities between states. Within the framework of the progressivist discourse, in contrast, asymmetry between states emerges from variations in the commitment to democracy among these states. Thus asymmetry derives from different degrees of legitimacy of states and their governments.[40] In her speech to the 2005 meeting of the Community of Democracy, Condoleezza Rice emphasises this understanding of asymmetry:

> To advance our democratic consensus, all free nations must insist that *upholding democratic principles is the surest path to greater international status*. ... The democratic character of states must become the cornerstone of a *new, principled multilateralism*. The *real division in our world* is between those states that are committed to freedom and those who are not. International organizations like the Community of Democracies can help to *create a balance of power that favours freedom*.[41]

In contrast to the interventionist perspective, asymmetry in the progressivist sense is supposed to *result in* power inequalities, rather than being *based on* them. Rice proposes the creation of international institutions that would empower states that adhere to democratic standards, while at the same time disempowering those states that do not.

Second, the progressivist discourse distinguishes itself from the interventionist discourse when it comes to the question of whether it is possible to overcome asymmetry as the basic feature of international order. According to advocates of interventionism, asymmetry in the international order is a zero-sum game, meaning that even if the status of certain states changes within the international order, power inequalities still persist. Thus, for interventionists, asymmetry is an unchangeable feature of the international order. From a progressivist point of view, in contrast, international order could potentially move towards the Pareto frontier: all states would profit from ubiquitous democratisation. Asymmetry is not a necessary feature of international order; rather, it would become obsolete as soon as the process of democratisation is completed.

Third, and most importantly, the progressivist and the interventionist discourses differ concerning the policy instruments which they consider appropriate for the maintenance of international order. Interventionists argue that in order to prevent a major crisis or destabilisation of the international order, (military) intervention into the domestic affairs of other states can at times be necessary and legitimate. Progressivists, in contrast, are convinced that democracy cannot be imposed externally but has to emerge from the civil society of a country. When progressivists talk about relationships to third states, they speak a language of cooperation rather than interference. Among the policy instruments that they consider useful for the purpose of furthering democratisation are 'assistance' in building democratic institutions, 'democracy monitoring mechanisms', 'diplomatic engagement', 'sharing of experiences' and 'identifying best practices'.[42] Even though it is questionable whether the above-mentioned measures would not qualify as intervention into the domestic affairs of a state, the list of policy instruments reflects the progressivist preference for diplomatic means and/or positive incentives as opposed to military force. The progressivist discourse puts great emphasis on inducing sustainable transformations, whereas the interventionist repertoire of policy instruments seems more geared towards short-term crises in the international order.

However, intersections between the interventionist and the progressivist discourse are possible. One could argue that the two most recent military interventions led by the US – Afghanistan and Iraq – have been justified by a mixture of interventionist and progressivist arguments. However, progressivists have a peculiar interpretation of interventions in as much as they understand them as the self-liberation of a people from a repressive regime: 'With the help of the international community, *the men and women in Afghanistan have thrown off the dual yoke of oppression* by the Taliban and the terrorists.'[43]

Human rights: the domestic enforcement of natural law

According to the progressivist discourse, human rights and democracy are parts of a unified concept: democracy cannot be established without due respect for human rights and vice versa. This assumption is neither trivial nor uncontested. John Rawls, for instance, holds that universal human rights, which he equates with negative freedom rights, could be upheld even if a state does not on the whole feature democratic structures: 'Human rights are distinct from constitutional rights, or from the rights of liberal democratic citizenship, or from other rights that belong to certain kinds of political institutions, both individualist and associationist' (Rawls, 1999: 79–80). In contrast, progressivists emphasise the 'interdependence between ... human rights and democracy'.[44] From their perspective, freedom rights and participation rights are closely linked. This understanding becomes evident, for instance, from the list of 'democratic principles and practices' included in the Warsaw Declaration by the Community of Democracies. The list addresses both democratic structures and human rights standards. Both aspects are intertwined: the first item concerns democratic elections, followed by an enumeration of different freedom rights (freedom of opinion and expression, of religion, freedom of the media, freedom of peaceful assembly and association). Then the Warsaw Declaration addresses those rights the violation of which falls under the jurisdiction of the ICC: freedom from arbitrary arrest or detention and from torture. Next, it mentions the maintenance of democratic structures and the rule of law and then finishes by referring to the protection of human rights as stipulated in the Universal Declaration of Human Rights.[45] To the extent that the progressivist discourse depicts human rights and democracy as interrelated and restricts the establishment of democracy to the domestic level of states, it is evident that it also confines the implementation of human rights to the domestic realm of states.

Notwithstanding the progressivist preference for the implementation of human rights on the domestic level of states, progressivists align themselves with the natural law tradition in as much as they argue that being human *per se* implies bearing these rights.[46] The natural law approach seeks to ground human rights in certain religious or moral values. In the religious tradition, human rights are derived from a divine source; an argument that can be found, for instance, in Thomas Aquinas. The secular tradition of natural law draws upon the Enlightenment idea of universal reason and takes human nature, understood in essentialist terms, as the starting point (cf. van Hoof, 1983: 30ff.) The secular foundation of natural law started with Grotius, who was, however, still strongly influenced by the Spanish late scholastics. It is reflected in the works of Pufendorf, Wolff and Vattel (cf. Kimminich, 1985: 91ff.). Both traditions share two basic features. First, they seek to ground the validity of positive law in superior moral–legal ideals and evaluate the former against the latter. Secondly, they are based on a broad and inclusive conception of community, i.e. they aspire to the universal validity of these ideals.

By taking their inspiration from the natural law tradition, progressivists also adopt the aspiration of universality. However, this claim to universality leads to a paradox: on the one hand, democracy and human rights are claimed to refer to humanity as such, on the other, they serve as a framework for the construction of an *exclusive* identity of a group of 'decent' states that adhere to those values domestically and aim at promoting them globally. Consequently, the claim to universality serves as a demarcation against the deviant 'other' (Walker, 1993). It is the main source of justification for an asymmetric international order.

Moreover, the natural law perspective does not override the progressivist claim that human rights need to be enforced within the domestic framework of states:

> Liberty and human rights *may be universal values, but you need democratic self-government* – a social contract between people and their government – *to protect them.* If the power of government is expanded too much, human rights will inevitably be in danger. *Democratic self-governance, then, cannot be separated from human rights.* It is the main instrument by which human rights are preserved and advanced.[47]

Although the progressivist discourse shares the claim to the domestic enforcement of human rights with sovereigntism, their respective interpretations of human rights differ concerning the features of human rights as human rights *law*: whilst progressivists ground human rights in the natural law tradition and stress that they are inherent in all human beings by virtue of their humanity, sovereigntists conceptualise international human rights law as treaty law, thereby making its validity dependent on explicit state consent. Hence, sovereigntists explicitly reject the exclusionary nature of international society that progressivists regard as a vital tool for the purpose of democratisation.

Conclusion

The progressivist opposition to the ICC draws on the 'peace vs. justice' debate. In contrast to legalism, proponents of the progressivist discourse argue that the pursuit of justice can hinder the transition to peace in conflict-ridden societies. This is closely related to the extraordinary significance that the progressivist discourse attributes to democratisation. Whilst interventionists as well as sovereigntists are not hostile to the idea of an international criminal court as such, but opted for a different institutional design, progressivists fundamentally challenge the usefulness of the ICC. The reason for this, they argue, is that the ICC excludes the possibility of amnesties for crimes against international humanitarian and human rights law. According to advocates of progressivism, however, amnesties often facilitate peace processes and democratic transitions, whereas mandatory prosecution could jeopardise them.

Individuals as members of civil society provide the primary point of reference of the progressivist discourse. Civil society is considered the most important foundation of democracy. Moreover, the notion of interest also refers to individuals: if the desire for democratic self-rule is common to all human beings, democratisation will first and foremost benefit individuals. However, given that progressivists draw upon the democratic peace thesis, the interest of individuals, democratic states and the community of democratic states are conceived of as being convergent. According to progressivists, the international society of states is an exclusive community grounded in thick and advanced norms, most prominently democracy and human rights. This idea ties in with the assumption that the current international order is asymmetric. Democratic and non-democratic states should enjoy different statuses in this order.

Progressivists understand sovereignty in terms of popular sovereignty. In contrast to the constitutional notion of sovereignty emerging from the sovereigntist discourse, progressivists claim that the people represent both the source and the location of sovereignty. This leads to different conceptions of democracy: whilst the sovereigntist notion of constitutional sovereignty ties in with the concept of representative democracy, progressivists espouse the idea of participatory democracy. The progressivist understanding of human rights is intertwined with this concept of democracy. Negative freedom rights and positive participation rights are interwoven. In spite of the fact that progressivists draw upon the tradition of natural law and the claim to universal human rights that it implies, they favour the domestic level of states as the appropriate venue for the implementation of human rights.

Notes

1 Mr Abdullah (Afghanistan), DipCon 4th plenary meeting (16 June 1998); U.N. Doc. A/ CONF.183/SR.4, Vol. II, p. 87; Mr Fadl (Sudan), DipCon 5th meeting (18 June 1998); U.N. Doc. A/CONF.183/C.1/SR. 5, Vol. II, p. 168; Mr Bazel (Afghanistan), DipCon 11th meeting (22 June 1998), U.N. Doc. A/CONF/183/C.1/SR.11, Vol. II, p. 215.

2 Community of Democracies Convening Group, 'Criteria for Participation and Procedures' (27/09/2002), www.state.gov/g/drl/26085.htm (accessed August 2008).

3 Condoleezza Rice, 'Remarks at the Community of Democracies Opening Plenary', Santiago (28 April 2005); emphasis added.

4 Yousif Ghafari, UN GA plenary meeting (10 December 2004); A/59/PV.70, p. 19; emphasis added.

5 Paula J. Dobriansky, Remarks delivered by Under Secretary Dobriansky to the Community of Democracies on behalf of Secretary Powell, Seoul (11 November 2002); emphasis added.

6 The enlightened self-interest explanation is but one variety of the democratic peace hypothesis. Other approaches are based on institutional (Russett, 1993), economic (Doyle, 1983) or social-constructivist explanations (Risse-Kappen, 1995). For a detailed overview and critique, see Rosato (2003).

7 Final Warsaw Declaration: 'Toward a Community of Democracies', Warsaw (27 June 2000), http://state.gov/g/drl/rls/26811.htm.

8 Revius O. Ortique, UN GA plenary meeting (29 November 1999); A/54/PV.64, p. 10; emphasis added.

9 Maurice Halperin, UN GA plenary meeting (21 November 2000); A/55/PV.70, p. 12.

10 See Chapter 3.

11 Marc A. Thiessen, 'Prosecution a Bad Way to Remove a Dictator. The Ability to Give Dictators a Face-saving Way Out Is an Essential Component of Democratic Change', *Arkansas Democrat-Gazette* (16 July 2000); emphasis added.

12 Quoted in 'African Union Seeks to Delay Indictment Against Sudanese Leader', *International Herald Tribune* (21 July 2008).

13 Marc A. Thiessen, 'Prosecution a Bad Way to Remove a Dictator. The Ability to Give Dictators a Face-saving Way Out Is an Essential Component of Democratic Change', *Arkansas Democrat-Gazette* (16 July 2000).

14 Rome Statute of the International Criminal Court, Preamble; U.N. Doc. A/CONF.183/9.

15 Final Warsaw Declaration 'Toward a Community of Democracies', Warsaw (27 June 2000), www.state.gov/g/drl/rls/26811.htm (accessed August 2008).

16 *Ibid.*

17 Seoul Plan of Action 'Democracy: Investing for Peace and Prosperity', Seoul (12 November 2002), www.state.gov/drl/rls/15259.htm (accessed August 2008).

18 However, a crucial difference between Almond and Verba's account of 'civic culture' and the progressivist discourse is that the former depict civic culture as a mix of participatory and traditional attitudes (1989: 30), whereas the latter stresses the participatory aspect.

19 Cf. Chapter 5. As a more far-reaching genealogical hypothesis, it would be possible to claim that the progressivist discourse draws heavily upon a specific tradition of modernity. According to James Tully, Quentin Skinner's account of the 'Foundations of Modern Political Thought' rests on the central assumption that these foundations comprise 'one dominant ideology and one subordinate counter-ideology' (1988: 17). Tully calls the dominant ideology 'juridical' in as much as it comprises the idea that

political power 'is limited by the standard of right' – the central assumption of both the legalistic and the sovereigntist discourse. The subordinate ideology of republican humanism, in contrast, is based on the idea of virtues rather than laws (*ibid.*; cf. also Skinner 1978: Vol. I, 88ff.).

20 Seoul Plan of Action 'Democracy: Investing for Peace and Prosperity', Seoul (12 November 2002) www.state.gov.g/drl/rls/15259.htm (accessed August 2008).

21 Paula J. Dobriansky, 'Building better democracies and promoting democratic development: The Community of Democracies', Remarks at the Woodrow Wilson International Center for Scholars, Washington (18 October 2002); emphasis added.

22 Community of Democracies, Final Warsaw Declaration 'Toward a Community of Democracies', Warsaw (27 June 2000), www.state.gov/g/drl/rls/26811.htm (accessed August 2008); emphasis added.

23 *Ibid.*

24 Community of Democracies, Seoul Plan of Action 'Democracy: Investing for Peace and Prosperity', Seoul (12 November 2002), www.state.gov.g/drl/rls/15259.htm (accessed August 2008).

25 Cf. Chapter 5.

26 Revius O. Ortique, UN GA plenary meeting (29 November 1999); A/54/PV.64, p. 10; emphasis added.

27 *Ibid.*; emphasis added.

28 These are Chile, the Czech Republic, India, Mali, Mexico, Poland, Portugal, the Republic of Korea, South Africa, and the US.

29 Community of Democracies 'Criteria for Participation and Procedures' (2002), www.state.gov/g/drl/26085.htm (accessed August 2008).

30 *Ibid.*

31 James Morrison, 'Spirit of Democracy', *Washington Times* (28 July 2000).

32 Community of Democracies 'Criteria for Participation and Procedures' (2002), www.state.gov./g/drl/26085.htm (accessed August 2008); emphasis added.

33 Trudy Rubin, 'The Messy Reality of Democracy', *San Diego Union-Tribune* (1 July 2000).

34 Kim R. Holmes, 'Democracy and international organizations', Remarks to the World Federalist Association and Oxfam, Washington (5 December 2003).

35 *Ibid.*; emphasis added.

36 *Ibid.*; emphasis added.

37 *Ibid.*; emphasis added.

38 Paula J. Dobriansky, 'Building better democracies and promoting democratic development: The Community of Democracies', Remarks at the Woodrow Wilson International Center for Scholars, Washington (18 October 2002).

39 Cf. Chapter 5.

40 Gerry Simpson refers to this line of thought as 'liberal antipluralism' (2004: 76ff.). See also Kingsbury (1998: 621f.).

41 Condoleezza Rice, Remarks at the Community of Democracies Opening Plenary, Santiago (28 April 2005); emphasis added.

42 Community of Democracies, Seoul Plan of Action 'Democracy: Investing for Peace and Prosperity', Seoul (12 November 2002), www.state.gov.g/drl/rls/15259.htm (accessed August 2008).

43 Paula J. Dobriansky, Remarks delivered by Under-Secretary Dobriansky to the Community of Democracies on behalf of Secretary Powell, Seoul (11 November 2002); emphasis added.

44 Community of Democracies, Final Warsaw Declaration 'Toward a Community of

Democracies', Warsaw (27 June 2000); http://www.state.gov/g/drl/rls/26811.htm (accessed August 2008).

45 *Ibid.*

46 Cf. Chapter 6 'Progress towards ubiquitous democratisation'.

47 Kim R. Holmes, 'Democracy and international organizations', Remarks to the World Federalist Association and Oxfam, Washington (5 December 2003); emphasis added.

7 Conclusion

The transatlantic debate about the establishment of the ICC involves four discourses, each of which constructs the configuration of sovereignty and human rights in a specific way. To the extent that all four discourses claim to constitute the same object – the configuration of sovereignty and human rights – they form a discursive formation. Legalism is built on the assumption that sovereignty is a symmetrical concept and that human rights refer to humanity as a whole. Interventionism shares with legalism the idea that human rights have strong links to the supra-state level. However, according to the interventionist perspective, international order is asymmetric, with great powers playing an exceptional role in the maintenance of that order. Sovereigntism is diametrically opposed to interventionism. Sovereigntists opt for the institutionalisation and enforcement of human rights on the domestic level of states and hold that the sovereignty-based international order features a symmetric structure. Progressivism, finally, combines the idea of an asymmetric international order with the demand for the implementation of human rights within the domestic framework of states.

The scheme shown in Figure 7.1 visualises this discursive formation.

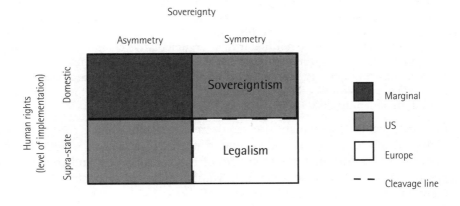

Figure 7.1 The transatlantic conflict over the ICC

The cleavage line in the conflict runs between the legalistic discourse, which was dominant among European actors on the one hand and the interventionist and the sovereigntist discourse in which most US actors engaged on the other. Progressivism played only a marginal role. This structure is puzzling in as much as all four discourses constitute the configuration of sovereignty and human rights in a specific way and are therefore at their very core incompatible with each other. Why did the US justify its position on the Court by drawing on two largely incompatible discourses? And how did this affect the dynamic of the transatlantic conflict over the ICC?

On the first question, the US political system grants the Senate a large share of influence over international law-making, since all international treaties have to be approved by a supermajority in the Senate. Therefore US political discourses relating to international law tend to flow from two different sources: the foreign policy elites in the State Department and the Pentagon on the one hand and members of the US Senate on the other. In the case of the ICC, the former were a main source of interventionist arguments and the latter mainly engaged in the sovereigntist discourse (Broomhall, 2001: 145ff.; Scharf, 1995–96: 171). In diplomatic statements, however, arguments inspired by both discourses were often put forward within the same statement.[1] This frequently led to the perception of inconsistency on the part of the US negotiation counterparts and observers: 'The muddle of arguments from the United States no doubt reflects some of the differences within Washington's policy-making community' (Schabas, 2004: 719).

The perceived inconsistency of the US position on the ICC is relevant with respect to the second question: how did the US simultaneous use of interventionist and sovereigntist arguments affect the dynamic of the transatlantic conflict? According to Frank Schimmelfennig (2003; 2000), consistency is one of the main requirements for an actor's perceived credibility in negotiations:

> The constraint of consistency applies, first, to the match between arguments and actions, second to the match between arguments used at different times and in different contexts, and third to the internal consistency between arguments. Rhetorical actors that do not honor their argumentative commitments in deed, reject warrants and grounds they accepted in earlier stages of the debate, are caught making contrary arguments before different audiences or are perceived to appeal to contradictory ideas to persuade a diffuse audience, will lose credibility. (Schimmelfennig, 2003: 221).

In short, actors who violate the requirement of consistency run the risk of being perceived as manipulating shared norms in a cynical way. In spite of the fact that Schimmelfennig's model of rhetorical action and the approach put forward in this book differ in certain theoretical respects,[2] the requirement of consistency seems to travel well between the two approaches. The core assumption of both approaches is that the discursive (or 'rhetorical', in Schimmelfennig's terminology) form of political interactions can have a decisive impact on the outcome of negotiations because this level has its own rules and its own mechanisms of empowerment and disempowerment. In this perspective, success in negotiations is not so much a matter of the material balance of power; it is a matter of winning the discursive battle.

Moreover, the requirement of consistency as a rule for discursive interactions seems to go some way to explain the US failure to impose its preferences on the institutional design of the ICC. For instance, the interventionist claim for privileges for great powers clashes with the sovereigntist emphasis on the sovereign equality of all states. It is plausible to argue that by engaging in two incompatible discourses simultaneously, interventionism and sovereigntism, the US violated this requirement and was in turn seen as using norms cynically. This assessment is in line with the accounts of several observers of the negotiation process, according to whom the US's negotiation counterparts had the impression that the US frequently used legal arguments as a cloak for concerns motivated by their national interest (Wippman, 2004: 167; Broomhall, 2001: 143; Weschler, 2000: 100f.). Even observers who were sympathetic to US concerns over the ICC felt that 'the administration failed to think through or effectively articulate its position on the court' (Wedgwood, 1998: 20). As a result, the US was perceived as an unreliable negotiation partner and seemed unable to strike compromises for fear that they might be rejected by US domestic political forces afterwards (Weschler, 2000: 101).

The US simultaneous use of interventionist and sovereigntist arguments and the resulting impression of inconsistency of the US position helped the legalistic discourse to acquire a hegemonic position. Observers agree that its proponents, the wider LMG and the European states within it, were perceived as a highly coordinated and credible group that provided 'leadership' throughout the negotiation process (Benedetti and Washburn, 1999: 27f.; Kirsch and Holmes, 1999: 11). It is plausible to assume that the rather consistent use of legalistic arguments[3] – an achievement that was facilitated by NGO efforts to rally LMG members around unified positions on specific topics – made the Europeans appear as more reliable and ultimately more credible negotiation partners. In contrast, the US use of two incompatible discourses also hindered the US in forging alliances with other opponents of the legalistic discourse, in particular with countries from the Non-Alignment Movement. Countries such as India, for instance, also oppose the ICC in its legalistic form. Yet they only drew upon sovereigntist arguments, whilst strongly objecting to the interventionist proposals to strengthen the role of the UN Security Council *vis-à-vis* the ICC – for quite obvious reasons, since non-permanent members of the UN Security Council would not profit from this interventionist demand (cf. Broomhall, 2003: 73; C. Brown, 2002: 221; Koskenniemi, 2004: 201).[4] As one legal expert argues, some developing countries even decided to align themselves with the legalistic stance because, faced with the choice of either transferring parts of their sovereignty to an independent ICC or making the ICC dependent on the Security Council, they considered the former to be the lesser evil: 'Perhaps the opposition to the Security Council provided a factor for coalition building that was more important than the acceptance of a restriction of sovereignty, which was necessary in the fight against impunity' (Weckel, 1998: 984).

The US position on the ICC: unilateralism, great power status or exceptionalism?

Accounts of the US stance on the ICC tend to fall into two camps: either they engage US unilateralism and superpower status as the main explanation, or they point out American exceptionalism. It should have become evident by now that both are to a certain extent right, though both fail to capture the US position fully.

Arguably, publications about 'US unilateralism' (Malone and Khong, 2003) or, alternatively, 'instrumental multilateralism' (Foot *et al.*, 2003) and the US ambivalent attitude towards international law (Krisch, 2003b, 2004) are legion. Scholars such as Robert Kagan (2003) have argued that the US, as the only remaining superpower in the post-Cold-War world order is far more concerned with safeguarding its room for manoeuvre in the sphere of security policy than Europe, which is seen to have turned into a post-modern Kantian 'paradise' of peace. This argument echoes the realist claim that great powers only support international legal institutions if these institutions promise to stabilise their predominant position in world politics. If international legal institutions, by contrast, are likely to result in the constraining of their possibilities to exercise power, and in particular if they affect their military capabilities, it is rational for major states to stay away from such legal entanglements (Waltz, 1979: 106, Scott, 2004). This prediction is rooted in the assumption that in an international system based on anarchy, the national interest of states is survival and safeguarding their political autonomy and control (Waltz, 1979: 117ff.).[5]

Yet the emphasis on great power politics and the instrumentalist understanding of international law is neither imperative nor ubiquitous among US political elites. Unlike the interventionist discourse, sovereigntism (and in a marginal role progressivism) do not include great power politics as a significant concept. If anything, the interventionist emphasis on the role of great powers indicates that realist tenets play an important part in US foreign policy (cf. Koskenniemi, 2002: 474ff.). The realist approach to explaining US opposition to the ICC and the interventionist discourse display striking similarities: both demand the primacy of politics over international law. Both perceive it as rational, as well as justified, for great powers to demand privileges if they commit themselves to international legal institutions. In short, interventionism and realism share a highly instrumentalist understanding of international law. This seems to confirm that realism is not only a theoretical approach in IR, but also a doctrine that provides orientation for policy makers. Some realists would not disagree:

> Realism has been particularly strong in both the International Relations field of academic enquiry and in the thinking of the United States Government since World War II and the United States has certainly succeeded in the realist quest for power. On this basis, it would seem reasonable to expect that realist thought may have influenced US policy and actions in relation to international law. (Scott, 2004: 78).

In contrast, accounts of the US position on the ICC that emphasise US exceptionalism seem to take the sovereigntist discourse at face value. They stress the specific US rights culture and the central and almost sacred role that the US constitution plays in this culture (cf. Kahn, 2005; McGoldrick, 2004). Alternatively, they argue that the US endorses a more traditional notion of sovereignty than European states, which have become socialised into 'pooling' their sovereignty in supra-state institutions, most notably the EU (Keohane, 2002). Ralph's account of the US opposition to the ICC as an attempt to safeguard a pluralist international society also draws on the notion of American exceptionalism (2007: 138ff.). Arguably, the central role of the constitution, the traditional understanding of sovereignty and the conception of international society as a pluralist society with a thin normative foundation are core elements of the sovereigntist discourse. However, they do not account for US efforts to bring the ICC within the remit of the UN Security Council or for the idea that the establishment of the ICC would hinder the US from performing its role as a custodian of international order, since both were inspired by interventionism. In sum, while both US great power status and American exceptionalism played a significant role with respect to the US position on the ICC, it is the inconsistency between the two lines of arguments and the two discourses, interventionism and sovereigntism, that had the greatest impact on the transatlantic conflict over the ICC.

The power of discourses

The legalistic discourse gained a hegemonic position in the course of the transatlantic debate over the ICC. Discursive hegemony is the assertion of normative superiority by one discourse, whereby that discourse successfully puts competing discursive options on the defence – as in the cases of interventionism and sovereigntism – or marginalises them – as in the case of progressivism. This section addresses the shifts in Britain's and France's position on the ICC as crucial events within the hegemonialisation of the legalistic discourse. The change in both countries' negotiating position can to a large extent be explained by the discursive power of the legalistic discourse. At the same time, this development also contributed to the consolidation of the discursive hegemony of legalism, which gained an increasing number of adherents. This is not to say that discursive hegemony simply means that diplomats of powerful countries engage in a certain discourse. Rather, a shift in the discursive position of an actor implies a change in the identity of the actor in question. By changing their position on the matter of the ICC and its institutional design, Britain and France at least partly abandoned their role as powerful international actors demanding legal privileges, or, particularly in the case of France as a nation eager to protect its sovereignty prerogatives. Instead, they acquired the legalistic identity of states that consider themselves equal to other states before the law and committed themselves to the idea of a peaceful international order through the legalisation of international politics.

Both Britain and France abandoned their reluctance towards an independent ICC (Britain in 1997; France shortly before the Rome Conference in 1998) and joined the LMG, thereby endorsing a legalistic stance. With the British and French shift of position, all EU member states took a unified stance on the ICC.[6] Not only did this probably contribute to the success advocates of legalism had in shaping the institutional design of the ICC according to their preferences, it also paved the way for making the global promotion of the ICC an explicit project of the EU's Common Foreign and Security Policy (CFSP) as of 2001. Whilst before that shift cleavages over the ICC matter criss-crossed Europe, Britain's and France's change of alliances transformed the establishment of the ICC into a 'Europe vs. the US' case (cf. Scheipers and Sicurelli, 2007).

In contrast to the unrelenting US opposition to the ICC, Britain's and France's shift of their negotiation position is indeed surprising and requires an explanation. Given that discourses are endowed with power and that they are able to empower actors, it would be consistent to assume that the reason for this development lay in the power of the legalistic discourse. To put so strong an assertion forward, however, it is necessary to discuss and assess alternative explanations. The field of IR theory provides four such alternative explanations: realism, liberal institutionalism, domestic-level approaches and approaches based on communicative action theory.

The realist explanation for the British and French shift of position is based on the assumption that the basic feature of anarchy in international relations provides strong incentives for power-balancing and self-help as the predominant strategy of states. Realism predicts that states will seek to safeguard high degrees of political autonomy and control, while at the same time aiming to reduce their dependence on others and their vulnerability to other states or international organisations. Viewed from a realist perspective, the ICC represents an organisation against the interference of which states – powerful ones in particular – should shield themselves. This is particularly true as the ICC potentially targets troops deployed in missions overseas, meaning that it touches upon security issues – the most sensitive field of foreign policy (cf. Waltz, 1979: 107). From a realist point of view, the decision to push for a strong and independent ICC would therefore be induced by a decrease in the power capabilities and thus in the degree of vulnerability of the concerned state.

Applied to the case of Britain and France, if both countries had considerably reduced the numbers of troops deployed overseas from 1997 onwards, it would have been perfectly rational for them to join the LMG. There is, however, no empirical evidence for such a development. The number of French and British troops deployed abroad, conversely, slightly increased in the period between 1997 and 1999.[7]

The liberal institutionalist approach shares the conception of states as rational utility maximisers with the realist theory, but it challenges the realist assumption that reducing dependence and refraining from inter-state cooperation is an imperative strategy under conditions of international anarchy. Rather, liberal institutionalists hold that even though the international system is anarchical, there are common rules and norms (Axelrod and Keohane, 1985: 226). Moreover, liberal institutionalists argue that the interests of states are not necessarily conflicting. States can also have mutual interests, in particular with respect to issues evolving from a high degree of interdependence among them (Keohane and Nye, 2001). The involvement of states in international organisations and regimes facilitates and furthers cooperation by 'chang[ing] the patterns of transaction costs and provid[ing] information to participants, so that uncertainty is reduced' (Axelrod and Keohane, 1985: 250, cf. also Oye, 1985; Keohane, 1989). With respect to the ICC, Caroline Fehl outlines two liberal institutionalist explanations: first, the establishment of the ICC was meant to address 'enforcement problems arising with prosecution in national courts', and second, it was intended to reduce the 'high transaction costs incurred in the more recently created system of "ad-hoc tribunals"' (2004: 368).

However, liberal institutionalists are not only interested in the circumstances that lead to the emergence of international organisations and regimes; they also address the question of the institutional design of these organisations (Korenemos et al., 2001). According to this perspective, the establishment and institutional design of international organisations involve a trade-off between costs and benefits for the involved actors, who will generate their negotiation positions on the basis of this calculation. Abbott and Snidal argue that there are two basic types of costs that actors have to weigh against the potential benefits of an institution and its specific design: 'sovereignty costs' and 'uncertainty costs' (2000: 436ff.). Sovereignty costs refer to the loss of political autonomy that legalisation implies. According to Abbott and Snidal, sovereignty costs are high when the institution in question incorporates a highly centralised and delegated mode of decision-making (*ibid.*: 437), which is clearly the case with respect to the ICC and the relatively strong and independent role of its chief prosecutor. Uncertainty costs indicate that states lack knowledge about future outcomes of an institution and its performance, which may also induce them to retain a high degree of control and oversight (Korenemos et al., 2001: 792).

From a liberal institutionalist perspective, the provision of additional information is crucial to explain shifts in the negotiation position of states. If states obtain new information on the potential benefits and the probable future performance of an institution and/or a particular choice of institutional design, this reduces uncertainty costs and may at the same time lead to a recalculation of the sovereignty costs involved. From a liberal-institutionalist perspective, one could hypothesise that the experience derived from the work of the two international criminal tribunals (ICTY and ICTR) provided both Britain and France with additional information and led to the shift in their position.

Though established by the UN Security Council, the chief prosecutors of the criminal tribunals were vested with rather large powers. At first sight, the performance of these tribunals seems to confirm the legalistic claim that concerns about politicised prosecutions initiated by an independent prosecutor were unfounded. The records of both tribunals suggest fairness and impartiality (Goldstone and Bass, 2000: 55f.).[8] At the same time, their record is far from immaculate: the ICTY was repeatedly suspected of having an anti-Serbian bias, as most of the defendants were Serbs (cf. Cassese, 2005: 456). Meanwhile in 1996 and 1997, the ICTR was charged of mismanagement, nepotism and corruption, which provoked UN Secretary-General Kofi Annan to demand an improvement of the situation in an official report and to appoint a new chief prosecutor for both tribunals and a new deputy prosecutor for the ICTR (Power, 2003). In addition, France in particular noticed that the establishment of international criminal tribunals can have unintended consequences for Western states: in December 1997, then French Defence Minister Alain Richard refused cooperation with the ICTY on the grounds that 'France [was] unwilling to expose its officers to possibly adversarial questioning that could implicate French military personnel in not stopping the war crimes they witnessed.'[9] The French refusal to cooperate with the ICTY on this occasion points to a rather high degree of suspicion about the tribunal and its prosecutor. In sum, the experience and information gained from the operation of the criminal tribunals are far from clear-cut. The fact that no politicised prosecutions, especially against citizens of OECD states, were initiated might have reduced uncertainties as to preferable institutional designs on the part of France and the UK, but this was probably neither the only nor the most important reason for their shift of position.

Moreover, the preceding chapters have indicated that the concept of sovereignty is far from unambiguous. Rather, sovereignty is a contested concept and its interpretation depends on the larger discursive context in which it is embedded. This casts doubt on the liberal institutionalist assumption that 'sovereignty costs' are neutral assets which can be calculated in a uniform way without taking into account the discursive contexts that inform actors' decisions. However, to do justice to liberal institutionalism: many of its proponents acknowledge that the way in which the concept of 'sovereignty' is understood affects actors' assessment of sovereignty costs, thereby potentially leading to different outcomes (Keohane, 2002; Abbott and Snidal, 2000: 441). This indicates potential ways in which constructivist insights can usefully complement rationalist theorising.

Approaches that put the significance of domestic factors for international politics to the fore, such as Robert Putnam's 'two-level game' (1988) or Andrew Moravcsik's liberal republicanism (1997),[10] represent a third option for explaining the case of Britain and France. According to these scholars, the major weakness of realist as well as liberal institutionalist approaches is that they reduce their perspective to the system level and regard states as unitary actors, thereby leaving aside the impact of preference formation on the domestic level. Moravcsik consequently replaces the concept of the state as a unitary actor with the notion of the state and its institutions as a 'transmission belt' that mediates between domestic political elites, interest groups and voters on the one hand and the international realm on the other (*ibid.*: 518). Four domestic factors are of crucial importance in this respect: the structure of domestic political institutions, powerful domestic groups such as governing coalitions and interest groups (*ibid.*: 530ff.), public opinion and the role of the head of government (Putnam, 1988: 456).[11] Viewed from a two-level game or liberal republican perspective, a shift in the negotiation position of a state primarily comes about due to shifts in its domestic power relations.

With respect to the UK, this approach does indeed bear some explanatory value: in the 1997 general election, the Labour party won a majority of seats in the parliament, thereby taking over power from the Conservatives. Whilst the latter did not even mention human rights in their party manifesto for the elections campaign, the Labour manifesto emphasised human rights and stated that the establishment of the ICC was an explicit objective of a Labour-led government.[12] In addition, Tony Blair, the new Prime Minister, appointed Robin Cook, whose commitment to the promotion of human rights was well known, as Secretary of State in his government. Without discussing the other potential domestic factors in more detail, it seems clear that the 1997 change of government in the UK had a great impact on the shift of Britain's negotiation position (cf. Deitelhoff and Burkard, 2005: 21). However, this is not to say that the power of the legalistic discourse remained ineffective or irrelevant in this case. Rather, the British case is an example of how the power of discourses and domestic factors work together: in their party manifesto, Labour had already made allusions to the legalistic discourse and emphasised its commitment to human rights, thereby clearly distinguishing itself from its Conservative counterparts. Thus, domestic factors do not only affect the discourse in which a state (represented by its national delegation) engages in international negotiations, but also vice versa: discourses that evolve in the international realm feed back into domestic politics and power struggles among domestic groups such as political parties.

The French case is more intriguing. In the 1995 presidential elections, Jacques Chirac was elected president. In the subsequent 1997 parliamentary elections, Chirac's party, the *Rassemblement pour la République* (RPR), lost a considerable number of seats in the *Assemblé Nationale*, which led to a *cohabitation* for the next electoral term. From 1997 to 2002, the *Parti Socialiste* (PS) was the largest party in the *Assemblé*. The PS was more open-minded on human rights issues than the conservative RPR,[13] however, given that the conduct of foreign policy represents the *domaine réservé* of the President and the French parliament largely lacks power in foreign policy issues and the negotiation and ratification of international treaties (Kessler, 1999: 23ff.), it is doubtful that the legislative elections had a considerable impact on France's shift of position in mid-1998. In contrast to the US institutional setting, which requires a Senate supermajority for the ratification of an international treaty, the French parliament generally does not have the role of a veto player when it comes to international law. In fact, the French parliament had the power to constrain the president's predominance in foreign policy issues only in one instance that touched upon the establishment of the ICC; namely, it had to pass implementing legislation in order to meet the requirements of the Rome Statute. But in this case, Chirac had to accommodate both houses, i.e. the *Assemblé*, with a left majority and the upper house, the *Sénat*, with a conservative majority. In addition, some of the senators took an explicitly sovereigntist stance on the matter, such as Charles Pasqua, who abstained from the vote. Thus, if one considers *Assemblé* and *Sénat* as veto players, they would block each other due to contradictory preferences. In sum, the French case does not provide evidence for the explanatory value of domestic-level approaches.

Finally, the communicative action approach offers an alternative explanation of why the UK and France changed their stance on the ICC. Thomas Risse claims that actors in international politics not only change their behaviour because they seek material gains or want to avert damage (bargaining), but also because they might be persuaded by the better argument (arguing) (2000: 8ff.). Risse's distinction between these two forms of action is based upon Habermas's theory of communicative action and posits that arguing is bound to several crucial preconditions: actors have to share a common life-world, they have to be willing to re-evaluate their preferences in the light of the statements of their negotiation counterparts and considerations of power and coercion have to take a back seat during negotiations (*ibid.*: 10f.). Although this perspective shares the concern with norms and communicative processes with the approach put forward in this study, there are crucial differences between the two accounts (cf. *ibid.*: 16f.): the 'better' argument could just as well be conceptualised as the more powerful argument. To the extent that discourses are vested with power, there is no communicative process that is void of power.

Risse and his collaborators try to maintain the distinction between decisions induced by argumentative persuasion and decisions affected by power, yet they only take into account material power. Within their theoretical framework, a change in the position of powerful actors is an indicator for the effects of arguing, as is a change in the position of actors whose material interests would suggest otherwise (Risse, 2000: 19; Ulbert *et al.*, 2004: 8). Both factors seem to apply to the British and the French case, as both are rather powerful countries (albeit not great powers as such) and both deployed a rather large number of troops abroad, so that their material interest would have suggested the importance of shielding themselves against prosecutions by the ICC. Were they simply persuaded?

The problem with the communicative action approach is that it proved to be impossible to eliminate aspects of power from the empirical picture. As Nicole Deitelhoff and Harald Müller have shown, in empirical settings, arguing and bargaining always occur simultaneously. It is impossible for the researcher clearly to establish which mode of action prevailed. In order to do so, one would have to extrapolate from the interaction of participants of a negotiation to the intentions and motivations of the involved actors (Deitelhoff and Müller, 2005: 171). Were they really persuaded by the better argument or coerced by the more powerful one? Did they aim to reap legitimacy gains? Did they back down for fear of being excluded? It is not possible to assess these questions empirically. Even if one is willing to concede that both Britain and France acted against their material interests in opting for a strong and independent ICC, this does not provide sufficient empirical evidence to infer that their decision represents an outcome of arguing, as the structural power of discourses as a causal factor still cannot be excluded.

This suggests that it is plausible to assume that the shift in France's and Britain's position resulted to a large extent from the hegemonic power of the legalistic discourse. Arguably, this discursive hegemony was facilitated and amplified by the fact that the legalistic discourse at some point became interwoven with the broader field of European integration discourses (Smith, 2003: 197). As Ian Manners argues, human rights are one of the EU's core norms and represent a vital part of the EU's external identity (2002). If the EU aims to promote them on a global scale this requires a minimum of unity over their interpretation and over preferences for their implementation among EU member states. In the long run, the staunch US opposition to the ICC might have even consolidated the unity among EU member states, as it offered a screen onto which the EU was able to project its distinctiveness as an actor in international relations (cf. Scheipers and Sicurelli, 2007).

Do we have to infer from the intimate linkage of the legalistic discourse with European integration discourses that the power of legalism is confined to the realm of the EU – and perhaps to accession candidates? The ratification record of the ICC Statute suggests otherwise: currently, 108 countries have ratified the Statute and 139 have signed it.[14] Arguably, the EU promotes the ICC towards third countries, particularly since this became an explicit goal of the CFSP in 2001. The 2001 EU 'Council Common Position on the ICC' stipulates that the EU and its member states commit themselves to push for further ratifications of the ICC Statute by 'raising the issue … in negotiations or political dialogues with third states, groups of states or regional organisations, whenever appropriate'.[15] This could raise the suspicion that the number of ratifications does not reflect the power of the legalistic discourse but rather the material interests of third states, which expect some kind of reward or favourable treatment by the EU by ratifying the ICC Statute.

Three factors cast doubt on this suspicion: first, a great number of non-European countries signed and ratified the Rome Statute before the EU launched its initiative. Many of these countries also refused to sign a BIA with the US, thereby accepting the loss of US military and economic aid provisions.[16] Second, the EU has a number of institutionalised relationships with third states that are not accession candidates. Since 1995, all these agreements have to include a conditionality clause that binds third states to abide by certain human rights standards (Smith, 2003: 111ff.). The ratification of treaties and statutes such as the Rome Statute, however, is not covered by the conditionality provisions, which mainly aim at preventing human rights violations by a government in the domestic realm of the state in question (*ibid.*).[17] Hence, if third states expect to cause certain effects concerning their relationship with the EU by way of ratifying the ICC Statute, this could only come about in an indirect way. The ratification of the Statute mainly affects the identity of the state in question. If this helps to build better relationships with the EU, this is proof of, rather than a challenge to, the power of discourses.

A related argument applies to the case of accession candidates. Whilst in the case of institutionalised relationships with third countries that are not accession candidates the ratification of the ICC Statute does not play an explicit role, this is different with respect to accession candidates. As mentioned above, the promotion of the ICC and the ratification of the Rome Statute is an explicit objective of the CFSP since 2001, as stipulated in a Council Common Position. Common Positions are part of the secondary legislation of the EU and are thus incorporated into the *acquis communautaire*, which all accession candidates have to adopt in order to acquire membership status of the EU. At present, all EU member states have accordingly ratified the Rome Statute.[18] There can be no doubt that accession candidates have strong material incentives – such as gaining influence on political decisions within the EU, economic and security benefits – for fulfilling all kinds of requirements set out by the EU in order to obtain EU membership. Hence, the decision of the accession candidates to ratify the ICC Statute can be well explained in rationalist terms, whereas this is not the case with respect to the EU member states' decision to opt for EU enlargement. On the contrary, the material interests of EU member states would have suggested opposing enlargement. As Frank Schimmelfennig argues, from the perspective of EU member states enlargement has to be understood as 'the expansion of international community' (2000: 47): norm-based arguments that depict the EU 'as the organization of the European liberal community of states' led to the self-entrapment of EU member states that eventually felt compelled to grant access to 'those countries that come to share its liberal values and norms' (*ibid.*: 48; cf. Fierke and Wiener, 1999). Rhetorical self-entrapment in this context refers to a process by which the strategic use of norm-based arguments leads to a situation in which actors find themselves bound and constrained by their previous commitments. If they deviated from previous commitments, this would come at risk of undermining one's legitimacy and credibility in the eyes of one's counterpart (Schimmelfennig, 2003: 221). According to Schimmelfennig, the rhetorical entrapment in constitutive values and the normative foundations of EU identity – such as liberal democracy, multilateralism and inclusiveness – enabled both the enlargement candidates and Western supporters of Eastern enlargement to transform EU enlargement into an issue of EU consistency and credibility, thereby successfully constraining the enlargement sceptics' room for manoeuvre (*ibid.*: 267ff.). This argument is also plausible when it comes to the ICC: the ratification of the ICC Statute by accession candidates represents one step towards the acquisition of a 'European' identity and an explicit commitment to 'European' norms – a strong case for membership. In sum, in the case of the accession states, it becomes evident that accession and the material gains it implies on the one hand and the acquisition of a 'European' identity on the other are interwoven.

International society: hegemony and anarchy

As the preceding chapters have shown, the most constitutive norms of international society – sovereignty and human rights – are far from being uncontested. Hedley Bull was aware of the issue of norm contestation and the problems it caused for the emergence and maintenance of international society (1995: 38ff.). However, he sought to solve the problem of achieving international order under conditions of normative pluralism by distinguishing between several types of norms. According to Bull, international society rests upon the basic and constitutive norm of sovereignty, which he regarded as undisputed, thus providing for the possibility of coexistence among states (*ibid.*). For Bull, to burden international society with more substantial and advanced norms such as human rights meant jeopardising international society and could possibly result in disorder. This categorisation of norms as 'thin' (basic and constitutive) and 'thick' (substantial and advanced) became firmly embedded into English School theorising (Buzan, 2004: 52ff.). The pluralist–solidarist debate mainly focuses on whether too much emphasis on 'thick' norms may undermine 'thin' norms or whether 'thin' norms need to be underpinned by 'thick' norms in order to be effective (*ibid.*: 30).

The findings of this study suggest that the recourse to 'thin' norms offers no respite from the norm contestation that Bull feared for its potentially disruptive effects on international society. Sovereignty is as much contested as human rights. What does this mean for the concept of international society?

Following Bull's perspective according to which norm contestation potentially leads to disorder and disintegration, this would mean that the transatlantic conflict over the ICC will have negative consequences for the stability and persistence of international society. Yet Bull's approach to the phenomenon of norm conflict entails shortcomings. His notion of conflict is close to the everyday usage of the term. It depicts conflict as something that separates and disrupts. In the context of sociology, however, conflict has been understood as a form of a social relationship (Stark, 2002: 248). Lewis Coser (1956) maintained that conflicts do not necessarily lead to the disruption and disintegration of social structures. They may as well lead to integration. Conflict over norms, in particular, can 'revitalise' the normative foundations of a social group, thereby rendering it more stable (*ibid.*: 155).

This perspective on conflicts ties in with the critical perspective advanced throughout this study. From a critical point of view, conflict is the norm rather than the exception. Norm conflict is inevitable because the meaning of norms is fluid and never entirely fixed. Moreover, conflict is the central venue for the construction of political identities (Diez, 2002). Most conflicts involve the articulation of identities by demarcating a boundary between the 'self' and the 'other' – a dynamic that captures their disintegrative potential. The EU, for instance, used the transatlantic debate over the ICC as a preferred venue for constructing its international identity by distinguishing itself from the US. At the same time, all actors involved in the transatlantic conflict over the ICC claimed to speak on behalf of the 'international society', thereby constructing and reproducing an encompassing identity under which all parties to the conflict are subsumed. Herein lies the integrative potential of the conflict.

According to Nicholas Wheeler and Tim Dunne, Bull's later writings can be read in this vein. They argue that in his later works, Bull revoked his former dismissal of human rights norms as a pillar of international society and espoused 'a non-foundationalist universalist ethic' (Wheeler and Dunne, 1998: 50). They explain that in contrast to John Vincent, who endorsed an essentialist understanding of human rights in the tradition of natural law, Bull's approach to human rights came close to Rorty's (1993) pragmatist understanding of human rights. According to Bull, human rights do not emerge from a human nature understood in essentialist terms, but were directed towards an 'imagined community of mankind' (quoted in Wheeler and Dunne, 1998: 51). By not asserting a certain understanding of human rights, one could reduce the acrimony of norm contestations and thereby minimise their disruptive potential. The content of the human rights concept would then be open to continued debate and conversation.

The pragmatist turn could easily be applied to the concept of sovereignty as well. Sovereignty would then gain its meaning from a similarly 'imagined community of states'. Moreover, the conflicts about human rights and sovereignty would probably not take place apart from each other. Rather, this study suggests that both norms are debated in conjunction. Viewed from this perspective, international society would no longer be an *entity*, but rather a *process* – an imagined community that is involved in a continued debate about its own normative foundations.

Finally, this also allows for a reinterpretation of the idea of the international society as an *anarchical* society. Viewed from this perspective, anarchy does not only indicate the lack of a central political authority – a world government. Rather, anarchy implies that the meaning of normative foundations of the international society – sovereignty and human rights – is fluid and subject to continuous contestation and conflict. Hegemonic interpretations may emerge, but they are likely to be challenged by counter-discourses, so that the anarchical condition of the international society will prevail.

Notes

1 See, for instance, David Scheffer, DipCon 29th meeting (9 July 1998); U.N. Doc. A/CONF.183/C.1/SR.29, Vol. II, p. 297.

2 The concept of rhetorical action posits that actors use arguments strategically. They present their policy preferences by appealing to a political community's shared norms, thereby signalling their conformity with the community's standard of legitimacy. However, their strategic use of arguments is constrained by the rigidity of community norms and (as mentioned above) the requirement of consistency. The main difference between the model of rhetorical action and the approach pursued in this book is that Schimmelfennig rejects 'the "oversocialized" view of actors whose identities and interests are determined by social structures' (2003: 198). Rhetorical actors pursue extra-discursive (material, rational) interests in a strategic way, but with rhetorical/discursive means. The approach put forward in this study, in contrast, is built on the assumption that actors' identities and interests are part of the discourse. Rationality, in this perspective, 'can be seen as a procedural norm associated with many of the identities of the polity, rather than as a fundamental logic of human action. To proceed in a rational manner is then a requirement of proper behaviour'. (March and Olsen, 1994: 253).

3 The major challenge to this consistency was the UK's and France's initial reluctance to endorse legalistic positions. Yet observers reported that at the Rome Conference 'Europe, minus France, was united within the Like-Minded Group. ... France joined with it voting for the statute after obtaining a final concession on the scope of the court's jurisdiction' (Benedetti and Washburn, 1999: 31).

4 The case of China is intriguing, in as much as China strongly pushed for emphasising state consent as the basis of jurisdiction of the ICC. That is, despite holding a veto in the Security Council, China did not side with the US interventionist arguments but took a sovereigntist position (McGoldrick, 2004: 437ff.).

5 For Waltz, power maximisation is not the prevailing strategy of states; rather, states aim at the maintenance of balance. Morgenthau and Herz, in contrast, hold that the struggle for survival implies power accumulation (Morgenthau, 1973: 28ff.; Herz, 1950: 157f.).

6 However, it is important to note that European unity was at times fragile. Both the negotiations on the ICC's jurisdiction and the European response to UN Security Council resolution 1483 indicate cracks in this unity (see Chapter 3).

7 In 1997, France deployed 7,500 troops in Bosnia and 1,500 troops in Central Africa. The latter withdrew in 1998. In 1999, France deployed a total of 11,800 troops on the territory of the former Yugoslavia. In 1997, Britain deployed 3,500 troops in Bosnia. In 1999, 10,000 troops were added in Kosovo and 1,000 in Sierra Leone. See Heyman (2001: 249ff., 809).

8   To be sure, Richard Goldstone was the first chief prosecutor of both tribunals, so that it should not take any wonder that he reaches this conclusion.

9   Charles Truehart, 'France Splits With Court over Bosnia; Generals Won't Testify in War Crimes Cases', *Washington Post* (16 December 1997).

10   See also Moravcsik's application of the domestic-level approach to the topic of European integration (1998). In the framework of this study, he focused on the interests of domestic producers and the macro-economic preferences of governing coalitions as the primary explanatory variable for European integration.

11   Owing to a lack of polls for the UK and France concerning the support of voters for the ICC, the aspect of public opinion cannot be assessed. Arguably, they would be of little use as polls usually only ask for support for an institution, but here we are interested in the details of institutional design.

12   'You Can Only Be Sure With the Conservatives', The Conservative Manifesto 1997, www.psr.keele.ac.uk/area/uk/man/con97.htm (accessed August 2008); 'New Labour Because Britain Deserves It Better', The Labour Manifesto 1997; www.psr.keele.ac.uk/area/uk/man/lab97.htm (accessed August 2008).

13   There were controversies about the ICC between the president and the parliament. For example, Chirac insisted on taking up the possibility of a seven-year opt-out for war crimes included in the Rome Statute at the instigation of France. A majority of the members of the *Assemblé Nationale* considered this unnecessary and thought it would even diminish France's reputation abroad, but Chirac remained unrelenting. This, however, only happened after the Rome Conference. Cf. Claire Tréant, 'Les Députés français examinent le projet de tribunal international', *Le Monde* (22 February 2000).

14   Cf. Coalition for the ICC, 'Ratification Chart for the ICC Statute' (16 August 2008); www.iccnow.org/documents/RatificationsbyUNGroup_18_July_08.pdf (accessed August 2008).

15   Council of the European Union, *Council Common Position of 11 June 2001 on the International Criminal Court* (2001/443/CFSP, Brussels, 12 June 2001). Cf. also Council of the European Union, *Council Conclusion on the International Criminal Court (ICC) and the draft US American Servicemembers' Protection Act, ASPA* (Brussels, 17–18 June 2002) and Council of the European Union, *Action Plan to Follow-up on the Common Position on the International Criminal Court* (Brussels, 4 February 2004).

16   In 2004, South Africa lost 7.6 million, Ecuador also 7.6 million, Peru 2.4 million, Uruguay 1.4 million and Malta 1.1 million US dollars. These figures relate to the suspension of military aid and thus do not yet include further cuts in the provision of economic support. See www.iccnow.org/documents/CountriesOpposedBIA_AidLoss_16Dec05.pdf?PHPSESSID=57952fb65871bd587f7c65ecc47c7fdd (accessed August 2008).

17   More recently, however, there was a move towards including the ICC in conditionality packages. Within the framework of the EU's 'Governance Initiative' for ACP countries, states that have ratified the ICC Statute can apply for additional legal and governance aid from the EU.

18   The Czech Republic represents an exception in as much as it signed, but has not yet ratified the Rome Statute. Though the Czech Republic initially aligned itself with the LMG, it repeatedly delayed ratification. The reasons for this are twofold: on the one hand, some sovereigntist voices within the Czech Republic point to constitutional questions and emphasise the difficulties of amending the relatively new Czech constitution in order to make it compatible with the ICC Statute; on the other, the perceived 'close ties' between the Czech Republic and the US play a role. However, it thereby exposes itself to sustained criticism from the EU, the Council of Europe and domestic NGOs.

Cf. League of Human Rights in the Czech Republic, 'Czech Republic: Impunity of Racially Motivated Attacks and Police Violence Still Prevails', document presented to the Association Council between the European Union and the Czech Republic (18 November 2002), www.fidh.org/IMG/pdf/cz1811a.pdf (accessed August 2008).

Appendix

Overview of the data

I *Diplomacy: analysed conferences and meetings*

DipCon[1]

4th plenary meeting (16 June 1998), U.N. Doc. A/CONF.183/SR.4.
5th plenary meeting (17 June 1998), U.N. Doc. A/CONF.183/SR.5.
6th plenary meeting (17 June 1998), U.N. Doc. A/CONF.183/SR.6.
2nd meeting (16 June 1998), U.N. Doc. A/CONF.183/C.1/SR.2.
3rd meeting (17 June 1998), U.N. Doc. A/CONF.183/C.1/SR.3.
4th meeting (17 June 1998), U.N. Doc. A/CONF.183/C.1/SR.4.
6th meeting (18 June 1998), U.N. Doc. A/CONF.183/C.1/SR.6
7th meeting (18 June 1998), U.N. Doc. A/CONF.183/C.1/SR.7.
8th meeting (19 June 1998), U.N. Doc. A/CONF.183/C.1/SR.8.
9th meeting (22 June 1998), U.N. Doc. A/CONF.183/C.1/SR.9.
10th meeting (22 June 1998), U.N. Doc. A/CONF.183/C.1/SR.10.
26th meeting (8 July 1998), U.N. Doc. A/CONF.183/C.1/SR.26.
29th meeting (9 July 1998), U.N. Doc. A/CONF.183/C.1/SR.29.
32nd meeting (10 July 1998), U.N. Doc. A/CONF.183/C.1/SR.32.
33rd meeting (13 July 1998), U.N. Doc. A/CONF.183/C.1/SR.33.
42nd meeting (17 July 1998), U.N. Doc. A/CONF.183/C.1/SR.42.
9th plenary meeting (17 July 1998), U.N. Doc. A/CONF.183/SR.9.

UN Security Council

'Civilians in armed conflict' (16 September 1999), U.N. Doc. S/PV.4046.
'International tribunal – Yugoslavia' (20 June 2000), U.N. Doc. S/PV.4174.
'United Nations peacekeeping' (12 June 2003), U.N. Doc. S/PV.4772.
'Liberia' (1 August 2003), U.N. Doc. S/PV.4803.
'Justice and the rule of law: the United Nations role' (24 September 2003), U.N. Doc. S/PV.4833.
'Civilians in armed conflict' (9 December 2003), U.N. Doc. S/PV.4877.
'Complex crises and UN response' (28 May 2004), U.N. Doc. S/PV.4980.
'Civilians in armed conflict' (14 June 2004), U.N. Doc. S/PV.4990.
'Justice and the rule of law: the United Nations role' (6 December 2004), U.N. Doc. S/PV.5052.
'Civilians in armed conflict' (14 December 2004), U.N. Doc. S/PV.5100.

'Sudan' (31 March 2005), U.N. Doc. S/PV.5158.

UN General Assembly
(24 September 1997), U.N. Doc. A/52/PV.9.
(8 December 1998), U.N. Doc. A/53/PV.83.
(29 November 1999), U.N. Doc. A/54/PV.64.
(21 November 2000), U.N. Doc. A/55/PV.70.
(13 September 2004), U.N. Doc. A/58/PV.95.
(10 December 2004), U.N. Doc. A/59/PV.70.

UN General Assembly/Sixth Committee (Legal)
(29 October 1996), U.N. Doc. A/C.6/51/SR.26.
(31 October 1996), U.N. Doc. A/C.6/51/SR.28.
(1 November 1996), U.N. Doc. A/C.6/51/SR.29.
(4 November 1996), U.N. Doc. A/C.6/51/SR.31.
(5 November 1996), U.N. Doc. A/C.6/51/SR.32.
(12 November 1996), U.N. Doc. A/C.6/51/SR.38.
(23 October 1997), U.N. Doc. A/C.6/52/SR.14.
(4 November 1998), U.N. Doc. A/C.6/53/SR.9.
(12 December 2000), U.N. Doc. A/C.6/55/SR.9.
(30 November 2004), U.N. Doc. A/C.6/59/SR.27.

II International law: considered journals (1998–2005)

American Journal of International Law (AJIL)
Archiv des Völkerrechts (AVR)
Europäische Grundrechte Zeitschrift (EuGRZ)
European Journal of International Law (EJIL)
Journal of International Criminal Justice (JICJ)[2]
Revue Générale de Droit International Public (RGDIP)
Stanford Journal of International Law (SJIL)
Zeitschrift für ausländisches öffentliches Recht und Völkerrecht (ZaöRV)

III Media: daily newspapers

Germany (search entry: *'international* strafgerichtshof*'*)
Frankfurter Allgemeine Zeitung
Frankfurter Rundschau
General-Anzeiger (Bonn)
Hamburger Abendblatt
Stuttgarter Zeitung
Süddeutsche Zeitung
tageszeitung
Welt am Sonntag

United Kingdom (search entry: *'international criminal court'*)
Evening News (Edinburgh)

Financial Times
Guardian
Herald (Glasgow)
Independent
Mirror
Observer
The Times

France (search entry: 'cour pénale internationale')

La Croix
Les Echos
Le Figaro
Libération
Le Monde
Sud Ouest

United States (search entry: *'international criminal court'*)

Arkansas Democrat-Gazette
Baltimore Sun
Buffalo News
Chattanooga Times Free Press
Dayton Daily News
Denver Post
Detroit Free Press
Fresno Bee
Herald Sun
Los Angeles Times
Miami Herald
New York Times
Omaha World Herald
Portland Press Herald
Post-Standard
Rocky Mountain News
San Diego Union-Tribune
San Francisco Chronicle
Salt Lake Tribune
Seattle Post-Intelligencer
St. Louis Post-Dispatch
Tampa Tribune
Tulsa World
USA Today
Washington Post
Washington Times

Data collection periods (media)

19–26 July 1998 (Adoption of the Rome Statute)
30 June–8 July 2002 (Entry into force of Rome Statute)
12–19 July 2002 (Adoption of Security Council Resolution 1422)
12–19 June 2003 (Adoption of Security Council Resolution 1487)

15 May–30 June 2004 (Failed renewal of Security Council Resolution 1487)
31 March–6 April 2005 (Adoption of Security Council Resolution 1593)

1 The legalistic discourse

a) Discursive arena of diplomacy (in chronological order)

Elizabeth Wilmshurst (UK), UN GA Sixth Committee meeting (31 October 1996), U.N. Doc. A/C.6/51/SR.28, p. 8.

Rolf Welberts (D), UN GA Sixth Committee meeting (1 November 1996), U.N. Doc. A/C.6/51/SR.29, p. 11.

Hartmut Hillgenberg (D), UN GA Sixth Committee meeting (5 November 1996), U.N. Doc. A/C.6/51/SR.32, p. 10.

Sir Franklin Berman (UK), UN GA Sixth Committee meeting (12 November 1996), U.N. Doc. A/C.6/51/SR.38, p. 6.

Klaus Kinkel (D), UN GA meeting (24 September 1997), U.N. Doc. A/52/PV.9, p. 10.

Rolf Welberts (D), UN GA Sixth Committee meeting (23 October 1997), A/C.6./52/SR.14, p. 9.

Edzard Schmidt-Jortzig (D), DipCon, 4th plenary meeting (16 June 1998), U.N. Doc. A/CONF.183/SR.4, Vol. II, p. 83.

Bill Richardson (US) DipCon, 5th plenary meeting (17 June 1998), U.N. Doc. A/CONF.183/SR.5, Vol. II, p. 95.

Sir Franklin Berman (UK), DipCon, 6th plenary meeting (17 June 1998), U.N. Doc. A/CONF.183/SR.6, Vol. II, p. 98.

Hubert Védrine (F), DipCon, 6th plenary meeting (17 June 1998), U.N. Doc. A/CONF.183/SR.6, Vol. II, p. 101.

Hans-Peter Kaul (D), DipCon, 3rd meeting (17 June 1998), U.N. Doc. A/CONF.183/C.1/SR.3, Vol. II, p. 146.

Hans-Peter Kaul (D), DipCon, 7th meeting (18 June 1998), U.N. Doc. A/CONF.183/C.1/SR.7, Vol. II, p. 184.

Marc Perrin de Brichambaut (F), DipCon, 8th meeting (19 June 1998), U.N. Doc. A/CONF.183/C.1/SR.8, Vol. II, p. 189.

Hans-Peter Kaul (D), DipCon, 10th meeting (22 June 1998), U.N. Doc. A/CONF.183/C.1/SR.10, Vol. II, p. 204.

Elizabeth Wilmshurst (UK), DipCon, 2[9th] meeting (9 July 1998), U.N. Doc. A/CONF.183/C.1/SR.29, Vol. II, p. 295.

Marc Perrin de Brichambaut (F), DipCon, 29th meeting (9 July 1998), U.N. Doc. A/CONF.183/C.1/SR.29, Vol. II, pp. 295–6.

Hans-Peter Kaul (D), DipCon, 29th meeting (9 July 1998), U.N. Doc. A/CONF.183/C.1/SR.29, Vol. II, p. 304.

Gerd Westdickenberg (D), DipCon, 33rd meeting (13 July 1998), U.N. Doc. A/CONF.183/C.1/SR.33, Vol. II, p. 325.

Sir Franklin Berman (UK), DipCon, 33rd meeting (13 July 1998), U.N. Doc. A/CONF.183/C.1/SR.33, Vol. II, p. 326.

Nancy Soderberg (US), UN GA meeting (8 December 1998), U.N. Doc. A/53/PV.83, p. 12.

Alain Dejammet (F), UN SC meeting: 'Civilians in armed conflict' (16 September 1999), U.N. Doc. S/PV.4046, p. 18.

Sir Jeremy Greenstock (UK), UN SC meeting: 'Civilians in armed conflict' (16 September 1999), U.N. Doc. S/PV.4046, p. 16.

Sir Jeremy Greenstock (UK), UN SC meeting: 'International tribunal – Yugoslavia' (20

June 2000), U.N. Doc. S/PV.4174, p. 7.

François Alabrune (F), UN GA Sixth Committee meeting (12 December 2000), U.N. Doc. A/C.6/55/SR.9, p. 3.

Michel Duclos (F), UN SC meeting: 'United Nations peacekeeping' (12 June 2003), U.N. Doc. S/PV.4772, p. 24.

Gunter Pleuger (D), UN SC meeting: 'United Nations peacekeeping' (12 June 2003), U.N. Doc. S/PV.4772, p. 25.

Gunter Pleuger (D), UN SC meeting: 'Liberia' (1/08/2003), U.N. Doc. S/PV.4803, p. 4.

Dominique Galouzeau de Villepin (F), UN SC meeting: 'Justice and the rule of law: the United Nations role' (24 September 2003), U.N. Doc. S/PV.4833, pp. 6–7.

Gunter Pleuger (D), UN SC meeting: 'Justice and the rule of law: The United Nations role' (24 September 2003), U.N. Doc. S/PV.4833, pp. 15–16.

Michel Duclos (F), UN SC meeting: 'Civilians in armed conflict' (9 December 2003), U.N. Doc. S/PV.4877, p. 20.

Wolfgang Trautwein (D), UN SC meeting: 'Civilians in armed conflict' (9 December 2003), U.N. Doc. S/PV.4877, p. 25.

Wolfgang Trautwein (D), UN SC meeting: 'Complex crises and UN response' (28 May 2004), U.N. Doc. S/PV.4980, p. 26.

Wolfgang Trautwein (D), UN SC meeting: 'Civilians in armed conflicts' (14 June 2004), U.N. Doc. S/PV.4990, pp. 23–4.

Gunter Pleuger (D), UN SC meeting: 'Justice and the rule of law: the United Nations role' (6 October 2004), U.N. Doc. S/PV.5052, p. 8.

Jean-Marc De La Sablière (F), UN SC meeting: 'Justice and the rule of law: The United Nations role', (6 October 2004), U.N. Doc. S/PV.5052, pp. 20–1.

Jean-Marc De La Sablière (F), UN SC meeting: 'Civilians in armed conflict' (14 December 2004), U.N. Doc. S/PV.5100, pp. 13–14.

Sir Emyr Jones Parry (UK), UN SC meeting: 'Civilians in armed conflict' (14 December 2004), U.N. Doc. S/PV.5100, p. 17.

Gunter Pleuger (D), UN SC meeting: 'Civilians in armed conflict', (14 December 2004), U.N. Doc. S/PV.5100, p. 18.

Jean-Marc De La Sablière (F), UN SC meeting: 'Sudan' (31 March 2005), U.N. Doc. S/PV.5158, p. 8.

Sir Emyr Jones Parry (UK), UN SC meeting: 'Sudan' (31 March 2005), U.N. Doc. S/PV.5158, p. 7.

b)   *Discursive arena of international legal experts (in alphabetical order)*

Blanke, Hermann-Josef and Claus Molitor (2001) 'Der Internationale Strafgerichtshof', *AVR* 39, 142–69.

Carrillo-Salcedo, Juan-Antonio (1999) 'La cour pénale internationale: l'humanité trouve une place dans le droit international', *RGDIP* 103:1, 23–8.

Cassese, Antonio (1999) 'The statute of the International Criminal Court: some preliminary reflections', *EJIL* 10:1, 144–71.

Charney, Jonathan I. (1999) 'Progress in international criminal law?', *AJIL* 93:2, 452–64.

Condorelli, Luigi (1999) 'La Cour pénale internationale. Un pas géant (pourvu qu'il soit accompli…)', *RGDIP* 103:1, 7–21.

Hafner, Gerhard, Kristen Boon, Anne Rbesame and Jonathan Huston (1999) 'A response to the American view as presented by Ruth Wedgwood', *EJIL* 10:1, 108–23.

Heselhaus, Sebastian (2002) 'Resolution 1422 (2002) des Sicherheitsrates zur Begrenzung der Tätigkeit des Internationalen Strafgerichtshofs', *ZaöRV* 62, 907–40.

Lattanzi, Flavia (1999) 'Competence de la Cour pénale internationale et consentement des états', *RGDIP* 103:2, 425–44.

Meron, Theodor (1998) 'War crimes law comes of age', *AJIL* 92:3, 462–8.

Reisman, W. Michael (2004) 'Learning to deal with rejection: The International Criminal Court and the United States', *JICJ* 2:1, 17–18.

Robinson, Darryl (2003) 'Serving the interests of justice: Amnesties, truth commissions and the International Criminal Court', *EJIL* 14:3, 481–505.

Stahn, Carsten (1998) 'Zwischen Weltfrieden und materieller Gerechtigkeit: Die Gerichtsbarkeit des Ständigen Internationalen Strafgerichtshofs (IntStGH)', *EuGRZ* 25, 577–91.

Weckel, Philippe (1998) 'La cour pénale internationale. Présentation générale', *RGDIP* 102:4, 983–93.

Zimmermann, Andreas (1998) 'Die Schaffung eines ständigen Internationalen Strafgerichtshofes. Perspektiven und Probleme vor der Staatenkonferenz in Rom', *ZaöRV* 58, 47–108.

c) *Discursive arena of the media (in chronological order)*

Anthony Lewis, 'U.S. denied its heritage in failing to embrace world court', *St. Louis Post-Dispatch* (21 July 1998).

Kenneth Roth, 'Human rights, American wrongs: Europe must resist the US obduracy that is threatening to undermine the International Criminal Court', *Financial Times* (1 July 2002).

'Justice for all at the ICC', *Financial Times* (2 July 2002).

'L'amérique, la justice et la paix', *Les Echos* (2 July 2002).

Paul Meunier, 'La Cour sans les grands', *Sud Ouest* (2 July 2002).

'For the sake of justice, US should rethink its objection to international court', *Herald* (2 July 2002).

'Contempt for the law', *San Francisco Chronicle* (2 July 2002).

Christian Semler, 'Wider die Logik der Erpresser', *tageszeitung* (5 July 2002).

Erich Rathfelder, 'Bosnien braucht Europa. Die USA gefährden mit ihrem Verhalten den Frieden auf dem Balkan', *tageszeitung* (5 July 2002).

'Die Souveränität der Staaten bleibt unberührt. Vereinte Nationen. Wahre Gründe des US-Widerstands gegen den Internationalen Strafgerichtshof sind unklar', *General-Anzeiger* (8 July 2002).

Bassir Pour Afsane, 'Le débat à l'ONU sur la Cour pénale internationale confirme l'isolement des Etats-Unis. Un troisième proposition de compromis, présentée par les Americains, maintient l'exigence d'un régime d'exemption général pour leurs GI', *Le Monde* (12 July 2002).

Franz-Josef Hutsch, 'Recht des Stärkeren statt Stärke des Rechts', *Hamburger Abendblatt* (15 July 2002).

Stefan Ulrich, 'Der amerikanische Verrat', *Süddeutsche Zeitung* (15 July 2002).

Andreas Zumach, 'Keine Spur von Europas Stärke', *tageszeitung* (15 July 2002).

Cokie and Steven Roberts, 'A double standard can bite you back', *Tulsa World* (16 July 2002).

Terry Olson, 'Une défense de la Cour pénale internationale', *Le Figaro* (19 July 2002).

Andreas Zumach, 'Erpressung lohnt sich. Internationales Strafgericht: Bundesregierung knickt ein', *tageszeitung* (14 June 2003).

Steve Crawshaw, 'Why the US needs this court contempt for justice: America's rejection of the International Criminal Court is a threat to its own security', *Observer* (15 June

2003).

Clare Short, 'What's next on the horizon for UN?', *Evening News* (16 June 2003).

William Bourdon, 'La par belle aux bourreaux. La justice pénale internationale est minée par les pays décideurs qui œuvrent pour leur impunité', *Libération* (11 June 2004).

Steve Crawshaw and Richard Dicker, 'Britain's flawed position on the global court', *Financial Times* (22 June 2004).

Jean-Christophe Ploquin, 'Soudan. Darfour. Difficile justice', *La Croix* (1 April 2005).

'Sudan: Saving Darfur', *Guardian* (1 April 2005).

Bernd Pickert, 'Für Darfur reicht der Fortschritt nicht. Sicherheitsrat bricht US-Widerstand gegen Strafgerichtshof', *tageszeitung* (1 April 2005).

Matthias Rüb: 'In der Substanz unverändert. Washington läßt dennoch die UN-Resolution zu Darfur passieren', *Frankfurter Allgemeine Zeitung* (2 April 2005).

Adrian Zielcke, 'Ein Durchbruch. Ahndung von Kriegsverbrechen', *Stuttgarter Zeitung* (2 April 2005).

'Genocide: Sudan's obvious crime', *Seattle Post-Intelligencer* (5 April 2005).

'An end to the nightmare', *St. Louis Post-Dispatch* (5 April 2005).

2 The interventionist discourse

a) Discursive arena of diplomacy (in chronological order)

François Legal (F), UN GA Sixth Committee meeting (29 October 1996), U.N. Doc.A/C.6/51/SR.26, p. 10.

David J. Scheffer (US), UN GA Sixth Committee meeting (31 October 1996), U.N. Doc. A/C.6/51/SR.28, p. 11.

Marc Perrin de Brichambaut (F), UN GA Sixth Committee meeting (4 November 1996), U.N. Doc. A/C.6/51/SR.31, p. 7.

Clive Crook (US), UN GA Sixth Committee meeting (5 November 1996), U.N. Doc. A/C.6/51/SR.32, p. 4.

Damien Loras (F), UN GA Sixth Committee meeting (23 October 1997), U.N. Doc. A/C.6/52/SR.14, p. 3.

Bill Richardson (US), UN GA Sixth Committee meeting (23 February 1998), U.N. Doc. A/C.6/52/SR.13, p. 5.

Béatrice le Frapper du Hellen (F), DipCon, 2nd meeting (16 June 1998), U.N. Doc. A/CONF.183/C.1/SR.2, Vol. II, p. 141.

Bill Richardson (US), DipCon, 5th plenary meeting (17 June 1998), U.N. Doc. A/CONF.183/SR.5, Vol. II, p. 95.

Hubert Védrine (F), DipCon, 6th plenary meeting (17 June 1998), U.N. Doc. A/CONF.183/SR.6, Vol. II, p. 101.

François Alabrune (F), DipCon, 6th meeting (18 June 1998), U.N. Doc. A/CONF.183/C.1/SR.6, Vol. II, p. 177.

Elizabeth Wilmshurst (UK), DipCon, 6th meeting (18 June 1998), U.N. Doc. A/CONF.183/C.1/SR.6, Vol. II, p. 177.

Marc Perrin de Brichambaut (F), DipCon, 29th meeting (9 July 1998), U.N. Doc. A/CONF.183/C.1/SR.29, Vol. II, p. 296.

David J. Scheffer (US), DipCon, 29th meeting (9 July 1998), U.N. Doc. A/CONF.183/C.1/SR.29, Vol. II, p. 297.

David J. Scheffer (US), DipCon, 9th plenary meeting (17 July 1998), U.N. Doc. A/CONF.183/SR.9, Vol. II, p. 126.

David J. Scheffer (US), UN GA Sixth Committee meeting (4 November 1998), U.N. Doc.

A/C.6/53/SR.9, p. 8.

Richard Holbrooke (US), UN SC meeting 'Civilians in armed conflict' (16 September 1999), U.N. Doc. S/PV.4046, pp. 13–14.

David J. Scheffer (US), UN GA Sixth Committee meeting (12 December 2000), U.N. Doc. A/C.6/55/SR.9, p. 5.

James Cunningham (US), UN SC meeting 'United Nations peacekeeping' (12 June 2003), U.N. Doc. S/PV.4772, p. 23.

Gunter Pleuger (D), UN SC meeting 'Liberia' (1 August 2003), U.N. Doc. S/PV.4803, p. 4.

John D. Negroponte (US), UN SC meeting 'Liberia' (1 August 2003), U.N. Doc. S/PV.4803, p. 5.

James Cunningham (US), UN SC meeting 'Justice and the rule of law: The United Nations role' (24 September 2003), U.N. Doc. S/PV.4833, p. 20.

John C. Danforth (US), UN SC meeting 'Justice and the rule of law: The United Nations role' (6 October 2004), U.N. Doc. S/PV.5052, p. 18.

Eric Rosand (US), UN GA Sixth Committee meeting (30 November 2004), U.N. Doc. A/C.6/59/SR.27, p. 2.

Stuart Holliday (US), UN SC meeting 'Civilians in armed conflict' (14 December 2004), U.N. Doc. S/PV.5100, p. 20.

Anne W. Patterson (US), UN SC meeting 'Sudan' (31 March 2005), U.N. Doc. S/PV. 5158, p. 3.

Additional material (in alphabetical order)

Richard N. Haass (US State Department Director, Policy Planning Staff), 'Sovereignty: Existing Rights, Evolving Responsibilities', Remarks to the School of Foreign Service and the Mortara Center for International Studies, Georgetown University, Washington, DC (14 January 2003). http://www.state.gov/s/p/rem/2003/16648.htm (accessed 7 April 2006).

Stewart Patrick (US State Department Policy Planning Staff), 'The Role of the U.S. Government in Humanitarian Intervention', Remarks to the 43rd Annual International Affairs Symposium, 'The Suffering of Strangers: Global Humanitarian Intervention in a Turbulent World', Lewis and Clark College, Portland, Oregon (5 April 2004), http://www.state.gov/s/p/rem/31299.htm (accessed 7 April 2006).

b)   Discursive arena of international legal experts (in alphabetical order)

Danner, Allison Marston (2003) 'Enhancing the legitimacy and accountability of prosecutorial discretion at the International Criminal Court', *AJIL* 97:3, 510–52.

Mundis, Daryl A. (2003) 'The Assembly of States Parties and the institutional framework of the International Criminal Court', *AJIL* 97:1, 132–47.

Scheffer, David J. (1999) 'The United States and the International Criminal Court', *AJIL* 93:1, 12–22.

Wedgwood, Ruth (1999) 'The International Criminal Court: An American view', *EJIL* 10:1, 93–107.

c)   Discursive arena of the media (in chronological order)

'A court without the US', *Washington Post* (21 July 1998).

Fred Hiatt, 'The trouble with the war-crimes court', *Washington Post* (26 July 1998).

Robert Kagan, 'Europeans courting international disaster', *Washington Post* (30 June 2002).

'For the sake of justice, US should rethink its objection to international court', *Herald* (2 July 2002).

'International Criminal Court. Bush tries shock therapy on U.N.', *Herald-Sun* (2 July 2002).

'Court politics', *The Times* (2 July 2002).

Michael Caplan, 'ICC hopes to give peace a chance', *The Times* (2 July 2002).

'Bush right to reject sway of International Criminal Court. If soldiers commit crimes, their government can handle it', *Portland Press Herald* (2 July 2002).

'Joining international court would be grave error for U.S.', *Tampa Tribune* (6 July 2002).

Herbert Kremp, 'Sonderrecht für die USA? Im Streit um den Internationalen Strafgerichtshof will Washington aus gutem Grund nicht einlenken', *Welt am Sonntag* (7 July 2002).

Michael Nakoryakov, 'U.S. may dislike world court, but staying outside won't help', *Salt Lake Tribune* (14 July 2002).

Georg F. Will, 'U.S. isn't wary enough of new world court', *Seattle Post-Intelligencer* (14 July 2002).

'Nach dem Kompromiß', *Frankfurter Allgemeine Zeitung* (15 July 2002).

Stephen J. Hadley, 'Tribunal is threat to USA', *USA Today* (15 July 2002).

Ian Buruma, 'Why we must share America's dirty work', *Guardian* (16 July 2002).

Steve Barrett, 'Don't let foreign court try U.S. troops', *Chattanooga Times Free Press* (17 June 2003).

'The right to say "no". United States should not be forced to submit to International Criminal Court', *Omaha World Herald* (23 June 2004).

'The Pentagon and "lawfare"', *Washington Times* (24 June 2005).

A noble compromise', *The Times* (2 April 2005).

3 The sovereigntist discourse

a) Discursive arena of diplomacy (in chronological order)

Damien Loras (F), UN GA Sixth Committee meeting (23 October 1997), U.N. Doc. A/C.6/52/SR.14, p. 3.

Bill Richardson (US), DipCon, 5th plenary meeting (17 June 1998), U.N. Doc. A/CONF.183/SR.5, Vol. II, p. 95.

Jamison S. Borek (US), DipCon, 3rd meeting (17 June 1998), U.N. Doc. A/CONF.183/C.1/SR.3, Vol. II, p. 152.

Hubert Védrine (F), DipCon, 6th plenary meeting (17 June 1998), U.N. Doc. A/CONF.183/SR.6, Vol. II, p. 101.

David J. Scheffer (US), DipCon, 4th meeting (17 June 1998), U.N. Doc. A/CONF.183/C.1/SR.4, Vol. II, p. 159.

François Alabrune (F), DipCon, 5th meeting (18 June 1998), U.N. Doc. A/CONF.183/C.1/SR.5, Vol. II, p. 164.

Marc Perrin de Brichambaut (F), DipCon, 8th meeting (19 June 1998), U.N. Doc. A/CONF.183/C.1/SR.8, Vol. II, pp. 189–90.

Mr. Scheffer (US), DipCon, 9th meeting (22 June 1998), U.N. Doc. A/CONF.183/C.1/SR.9, Vol. II, p. 195.

Fred Dalton (US), DipCon, 26th meeting (8 July 1998), U.N. Doc. A/CONF.183/C.1/SR.26, Vol. II, p. 280.

Marc Perrin de Brichambaut (F), DipCon, 29th meeting (9 July 1998), U.N. Doc. A/CONF.183/C.1/SR.29, Vol. II, p. 296.

David J. Scheffer (US), DipCon, 29th meeting (9 July 1998), U.N. Doc.A/CONF.183/C.1/

SR.29, Vol. II, p. 297.

David J. Scheffer (US), DipCon, 32nd meeting (10 July 1998), U.N. Doc. A/CONF.183/C.1/SR.32, Vol. II, p. 322.

Mr. Scheffer (US), DipCon, 42nd meeting (17 July 1998), U.N. Doc. A/CONF.183/C.1/SR.42, Vol. II, p. 361.

David J. Scheffer (US), DipCon, 9th plenary meeting (17 July 1998), U.N. Doc. A/CONF.183/SR.9, Vol. II, p. 126.

David J. Scheffer (US), UN GA Sixth Committee meeting (4 November 1998), U.N. Doc. A/C.6/53/SR.9, p. 8.

Nancy Soderberg (US), UN GA meeting (8 December 1998), U.N. Doc. A/53/PV.83, p. 11.

François Alabrune (F), UN GA Sixth Committee meeting (12 December 2000), U.N. Doc. A/C.6/55/SR.9, p. 3.

David J. Scheffer (US), UN GA Sixth Committee meeting (12 December 2000), U.N. Doc. A/C.6/55/SR.9, p. 5.

James Cunningham (US), UN SC meeting 'United Nations peacekeeping' (12 June 2003), U.N. Doc. S/PV.4772, p. 23.

James Cunningham (US), UN SC meeting 'Justice and the rule of law: The United Nations role' (24 September 2003), U.N. Doc. S/PV.4833, pp. 20–1.

Eric Rosand (US), UN GA meeting (13 September 2004), U.N. Doc. A/58/PV.95, p. 5.

John C. Danforth (US), UN SC meeting 'Justice and the rule of law: The United Nations role' (6 October 2004), U.N. Doc. S/PV.5052, p. 18.

Eric Rosand (US), UN GA Sixth Committee meeting (30 November 2004), U.N. Doc. A/C.6/59/SR.27, p. 2.

Stuart Holliday (US), UN SC meeting 'Civilians in armed conflict' (14 December 2004), U.N. Doc. S/PV.5100, p. 20.

Anne W. Patterson (US), UN SC meeting 'Sudan' (31 March 2005), U.N. Doc. S/PV. 5158, p. 3.

b) Discursive arena of international legal experts (in alphabetical order)

Danner, Allison Marston (2003) 'Enhancing the legitimacy and accountability of prosecutorial discretion at the International Criminal Court', *AJIL* 97:3, 510–52.

Scheffer, David J. (2005) 'Article 98(2) of the Rome Statute: America's original intent', *JICJ* 3:2, 333–53.

Scheffer, David J. (2004) 'How to turn the tide using the Rome Statute's temporal jurisdiction', *JICJ* 2:1, 26–34.

Scheffer, David J. (1999) 'The United States and the International Criminal Court', *AJIL* 93:1, 12–22.

Sur, Serge (1999) 'Vers une cour pénale internationale: la convention de Rome entre les ONG et le Conseil de sécurité', *RGDIP* 103:1, 29–45.

Wedgwood, Ruth (2005) 'Address to the Cornell International Law Journal Symposium: Milošević and Hussein on Trial', *CILJ* 38:3, 779–87.

Wedgwood, Ruth (1999) 'The International Criminal Court: An American view', *EJIL* 10:1, 93–107.

c) Discursive arena of the media (in chronological order)

'A court without the US', *Washington Post* (21 July 1998).

Fred Hiatt, 'The trouble with the war-crimes court', *Washington Post* (26 July 1998).

'Bush right to reject sway of International Criminal Court. If soldiers commit crimes, their government can handle it', *Portland Press Herald* (2 July 2002).

'Criminal court or rogue court?', *Rocky Mountain News* (5 July 2002).
'Joining international court would be grave error for U.S.', *Tampa Tribune* (6 July 2002).
'Beware of international traps', *Chattanooga Times Free Press* (8 July 2002).
Georg F. Will, 'U.S. isn't wary enough of new world court', *Seattle Post-Intelligencer* (14 July 2002).
Stephen J. Hadley, 'Tribunal is threat to USA', *USA Today* (15 July 2002).
John Rosenthal, 'Les ambiguitiés de la Cour pénale internationale. Bush a raison de s'opposer à la CPI', *Le Figaro* (16 July 2002).
Steve Barrett, 'U.S. hardly alone in opposing the court', *Chattanooga Free Press* (16 July 2002).
Steve Barrett, 'Don't let foreign court try U.S. troops', *Chattanooga Times Free Press* (17 June 2003).
'The right to say "no". United States should not be forced to submit to International Criminal Court', *Omaha World Herald* (23 June 2004).

4 The progressivist discourse

a) Discursive arena of diplomacy (in chronological order)

Revius O. Ortique (US), UN GA meeting (29 November 1999), U.N. Doc. A/54/PV.64, pp. 9–11.
Maurice Halperin (US), UN GA meeting (21 November 2000), U.N. Doc. A/55/PV.70, pp. 11–12.
Yousif Ghafari (US), UN GA meeting (10 December 2004), U.N. Doc. A/59/PV.70, p. 19.

Additional material

Community of Democracies, 'Final Warsaw Declaration: Toward a Community of Democracies' (27 June 2000), http://www.state.gov/g/drl/rls/26811.htm (accessed 7 April 2006).
Community of Democracies, 'Criteria for Participation and Procedures' (12 September 2000), http://state.gov/g/drl/26085.htm (accessed 7 April 2006).
Community of Democracies, 'Seoul Plan of Action – Democracy: Investing for Peace and Prosperity' (12 November 2002), http://state.gov/g/drl/rls/15259.htm (accessed 7 April 2006).
Paula J. Dobriansky (US State Department Under Secretary for the State of Global Affairs), 'Building Better Democracies and Promoting Democratic Development: The Community of Democracies', Remarks at the Woodrow Wilson International Center for Scholars, Washington, DC (18 October 2002), http://www.state.gov/g/rls/rm/2002/14516.htm (accessed 7 April 2006).
Paula J. Dobriansky (US State Department Under Secretary for the State of Global Affairs), 'Remarks Delivered by Under Secretary Dobriansky to the Community of Democracies on Behalf of Secretary Powell', Remarks to the Roundtable on Consolidating Democratic Institutions at the Community of Democracies Ministerial Meeting, Seoul, Korea (11 November 2002), http://www.state.gov/g/rls/rm/2002/16254.htm (accessed 7 April 2006).
Kim R. Holmes (US State Department Assistant Secretary for International Organization Affairs), 'Democracy and International Organizations', Remarks to the World Federalist Association and Oxfam, Washington, DC (5 December 2003), URL: http://www.state.gov/p/io/rls/rm/2003/26949.htm (accessed 7 April 2006).

b)   Discursive arena of international legal experts

Wedgwood, Ruth (1999) 'The International Criminal Court: An American view', *EJIL* 10:1, 93–107.

c)   Discursive arena of the media (in chronological order)

Trudy Rubin, 'The messy reality of democracy', *San Diego Union-Tribune* (1 July 2000).
Marc A. Thiessen, 'Prosecution a bad way to remove a dictator. The ability to give dictators a face-saving way out is an essential component of democratic change', *Arkansas Democrat-Gazette* (16 July 2000).
James Morrison, 'Spirit of democracy', *Washington Times* (28 July 2000).

Notes

1   I only analysed those meetings that have been attended by delegates from the four countries under consideration.
2   The first volume of this journal was published in 2003.

References

Abbott, Kenneth W., Robert O. Keohane, Andrew Moravcsik, Anne-Marie Slaughter and Duncan Snidal (2000) 'The concept of legalization', *International Organization* 54:3, 401–19.

Abbott, Kenneth W. and Duncan Snidal (2000) 'Hard and soft law in international governance', *International Organization* 54:3, 421–56.

Allott, Philip (1990) *Eunomia: New Order for a New World* (Oxford: Oxford University Press).

Almond, Gabriel A. and Sidney Verba (1989) *The Civic Culture: Political Attitudes and Democracy in Five Nations* (Newbury Park, CA: Sage).

Alvarez, José E. (2003) 'Hegemonic international law revisited', *American Journal of International Law* 97:4, 873–87.

Apuuli, Kasaija Phillip (2006) 'The ICC arrest warrants for the Lord's Resistance Army leaders and peace prospects for Northern Uganda', *Journal of International Criminal Justice* 4:1, 179–87.

Arendt, Hannah (1986) *The Origins of Totalitarianism* (London: André Deutsch).

Armstrong, David (1999) 'Law, justice and the idea of a world society', *International Affairs* 75:3, 547–61.

Arsanjani, Mahnoush H. (1999) 'The Rome Statute of the International Criminal Court', *American Journal of International Law* 93:1, 22–43.

Ashley, Richard K. (1988) 'Untying the sovereign state: a double reading of the anarchy problematique', *Millennium: Journal of International Studies* 17:2, 227–62.

Axelrod, Robert and Robert O. Keohane (1985) 'Achieving cooperation under anarchy: Strategies and institutions', *World Politics* 38:1, 226–54.

Badie, Bertrand (2002) *Souveränität und Verantwortung: Politische Prinzipien zwischen Fiktion und Wirklichkeit* (Hamburg: Hamburger Edition).

Barkin, J. Samuel (1998) 'The evolution of the constitution of sovereignty and the emergence of human rights norms', *Millennium: Journal of International Studies* 27:2, 229–52.

Barnett, Michael and Raymond Duvall (2005) 'Power in international politics', *International Organization* 59:1, 39–75.

Bartelson, Jens (1995) *A Genealogy of Sovereignty* (Cambridge: Cambridge University Press).

Bedont, Barbara and Katherine Hall Martinez (1999) 'Ending impunity for gender crimes under the International Criminal Court', *Brown Journal of World Affairs* 6:1, 68–85.

Beetham, David (1999) *Democracy and Human Rights* (Cambridge: Polity).

Benedetti, Fanny and John L. Washburn (1999) 'Drafting the International Criminal Court Treaty: Two years to Rome and an afterword on the Rome Diplomatic Conference', *Global Governance* 5:1, 1–37.

Bennett, W. Lance (1994) 'The news about foreign policy', in W. Lance Bennett and David L. Paletz (eds), *Taken by Storm: The Media, Public Opinion, and US Foreign Policy in the Gulf War* (Chicago: University of Chicago Press), 12–40.

Bennett, W. Lance and David L. Paletz (eds) (1994) *Taken by Storm: The Media, Public Opinion, and US Foreign Policy in the Gulf War* (Chicago: University of Chicago Press).

Boli, John and George M. Thomas (1997) 'World culture in the world polity: a century of international non-governmental organization', *American Sociological Review* 62:2, 171–90.

Boltanski, Luc (1999) *Distant Suffering: Morality, Media and Politics* (Cambridge: Cambridge University Press).

Bonacker, Thorsten and André Brodocz (2001) 'Im Namen der Menschenrechte: Zur symbolischen Integration der internationalen Gemeinschaft durch Normen', *Zeitschrift für Internationale Beziehungen* 8:2, 179–208.

Branch, Adam (2007) 'Uganda's civil war and the politics of ICC intervention', *Ethics and International Affairs* 21:1, 179–98.

Brands, H. W. (1998a) 'Exemplary America versus interventionist America', in Robert L. Hutchings, *At the End of the American Century: America's Role in the Post-Cold War World* (Baltimore, MD: Johns Hopkins University Press), 29–50.

Brands, H. W. (1998b) *What America Owes the World: The Struggle for the Soul of Foreign Policy* (Cambridge: Cambridge University Press).

Breau, Susan C. (2008) 'The constitutionalization of the international legal order', *Leiden Journal of International Law* 21:4, 545–61.

Broomhall, Bruce (2001) 'Toward U.S. acceptance of the International Criminal Court', *Law and Contemporary Problems* 64:1, 141–51.

Broomhall, Bruce (2003) *International Justice and the International Criminal Court: Between Sovereignty and the Rule of Law* (Oxford: Oxford University Press).

Brown, Bartram S. (1999) 'U.S. objections to the statute of the International Criminal Court: A brief response', *New York University Journal of International Law and Politics* 31:4, 855–91.

Brown, Bartram S. (2002) 'Unilateralism, multilateralism and the International Criminal Court', in Stewart Patrick and Shepard Forman (eds), *Multilateralism and US Foreign Policy: Ambivalent Engagement* (Boulder, CO: Lynne Rienner), 323–44.

Brown, Chris (1992) '"Really existing liberalism" and international order', *Millennium: Journal of International Studies* 21:3, 313–28.

Brown, Chris (2001) 'Cosmopolitanism, world citizenship and global civil society', in Simon Caney and Peter Jones (eds), *Human Rights and Global Diversity* (London: Frank Cass), 7–26.

Brown, Chris (2002) *Sovereignty, Rights and Justice: International Relations Theory Today* (Cambridge: Polity).

Brownlie, Ian (2003) *Principles of Public International Law* (Oxford: Oxford University Press).

Buzan, Barry (1993) 'From international system to international society: Structural realism and regime theory meet the English school', *International Organization* 47:3, 327–52.

Buzan, Barry (2004) *From International to World Society? English School Theory and the Social Structure of Globalisation* (Cambridge: Cambridge University Press).

Camilleri, Joseph A. and Jim Falk (1992) *The End of Sovereignty? The Politics of a Shrinking and Fragmenting World* (Aldershot: Edward Elgar).

Caney, Simon (2006) *Justice Beyond Borders: A Global Political Theory* (Oxford: Oxford University Press).

Carr, Edward Hallett (1964) *The Twenty Years' Crisis 1919–1939* (New York: Harper &

Row).

Cassese, Antonio (1999) 'A follow-up: forcible humanitarian countermeasures and opinion necessitates', *European Journal of International Law* 10:4, 791–9.

Cassese, Antonio (2005) *International Law* (Oxford: Oxford University Press).

Chalaby, Jean K. (1996) 'Beyond the prison-house of language: Discourse as a sociological concept', *British Journal of Sociology* 47:4, 684–98.

Chayes, Abram and Antonia Handler Chayes (1995) *The New Sovereignty: Compliance with International Regulatory Agreements* (Cambridge, MA: Harvard University Press).

Clark, Ann-Marie (1995) 'Non-governmental organizations and their influence on international society', *Journal of International Affairs* 48:2, 507–25.

Cohen, Raymond (1994) 'Pacific unions: a reappraisal of the theory that "democracies do not go to war with each other"', *Review of International Studies* 20:3, 207–23.

Connolly, William E. (1983) *The Terms of Political Discourse* (Oxford: Martin Robertson).

Coser, Lewis (1956) *The Functions of Social Conflict* (Glencoe, IL: Free Press).

Cox, Michael (2000) 'Wilsonianism resurgent? The Clinton administration and the promotion of democracy', in Michael Cox, G. John Ikenberry and Takashi Inoguchi (eds), *American Democracy Promotion: Impulses, Strategies, and Impacts* (Oxford: Oxford University Press), 218–40.

Cranston, Maurice W. (1973) *What are Human Rights?* (London: Bodley Head).

Cryer, Robert (2006) 'Sudan, resolution 1593, and international criminal justice', *Leiden Journal of International Law* 19:1, 195–222.

Deitelhoff, Nicole (2007) 'The discursive construction of legal norms and institutions: Law and politics in the negotiation on the International Criminal Court', *Comparative Research in Law & Political Economy Research Paper 32* (Toronto: University of York).

Deitelhoff, Nicole and Eva Burkard (2005) *Europa vor Gericht: Die EU-Außenpolitik und der Internationale Strafgerichtshof* (Frankfurt/Main: Hessische Stiftung Friedens- und Konfliktforschung).

Deitelhoff, Nicole and Harald Müller (2005) 'Theoretical paradise – empirically lost? Arguing with Habermas', *Review of International Studies* 31:1, 167–79.

Diez, Thomas (1999) *Die EU lesen* (Opladen: Leske + Budrich).

Diez, Thomas (2002) 'Die Konflikttheorie postmoderner Theorien internationaler Beziehungen', in Thorsten Bonacker (ed.), *Sozialwissenschaftliche Konflikttheorien: Eine Einführung* (Opladen: Leske + Budrich), 187–204.

Diez, Thomas and Richard Whitman (2002) 'Analysing European integration: reflecting on the English school – scenarios for an encounter', *Journal of Common Market Studies* 40:1, 43–67.

Donnelly, Jack (2002) *Universal Human Rights in Theory and Practice* (Ithaca, NY: Cornell University Press).

Doty, Roxanne L. (1996) *Imperial Encounters: The Politics of Representation in North–South Relations* (Minneapolis: University of Minnesota Press).

Doyle, Michael W. (1983) 'Kant, liberal legacies and foreign affairs', *Philosophy and Public Affairs* 12, 205–35.

Economides, Spyros (2001) 'The International Criminal Court', in Karen E. Smith and Margot Light (eds), *Ethics and Foreign Policy* (Cambridge: Cambridge University Press), 112–28.

Fairclough, Norman (1995a) *Critical Discourse Analysis: the Critical Study of Language* (London: Longman).

Fairclough, Norman (1995b) *Media Discourse* (London: Arnold).

Fairclough, Norman (2003) *Analysing Discourse: Textual Analysis for Social Research* (London: Routledge).

Falk, Richard A. (1995) 'The world order between inter-state law and the law of humanity: the role of civil society institutions', in Daniele Archibugi and David Held (eds), *Cosmopolitan Democracy: an Agenda for a New World Order* (Cambridge: Polity), 163–79.

Fehl, Caroline (2004) 'Explaining the International Criminal Court: A "practice test" for rationalist and constructivist approaches', *European Journal for International Relations* 10:3, 357–94.

Fierke, Karen M. and Antje Wiener (1999) 'Constructing institutional interest: EU and NATO enlargement', *Journal of European Public Policy* 6:5, 721–42.

Finnemore, Martha and Stephen J. Toope (2001) 'Alternatives to "legalization": Richer views of law and politics', *International Organization* 55:3, 743–58.

Foot, Rosemary, Neil MacFarlane and Michael Mastaduno (2003) 'Conclusion: instrumental multilateralism in US foreign policy', in Rosemary Foot, Neil Macfarlane and Michael Mastaduno (eds), *US Hegemony and International Organizations: The United States and Multilateral Institutions* (Oxford: Oxford University Press), 264–96.

Franceschet, Antonio (2000) 'Popular sovereignty or cosmopolitan democracy? Liberalism, Kant and international reform', *European Journal of International Relations* 6:2, 277–302.

Frost, Mervyn (1996) *Ethics in International Relations: A Constitutive Theory* (Cambridge: Cambridge University Press).

Frost, Mervyn (2000) 'Reply to Peter Sutch's "Human rights as settled norms: Mervyn Frost and the limits of Hegelian human rights theory"', *Review of International Studies* 26:3, 477–83.

Gallie, W. B. (1956) 'Essentially contested concepts', *Proceedings of the Aristotelian Society, New Series* 56, 167–98.

Gavron, Jessica (2002) 'Amnesties in the light of developments in international law and the establishment of the International Criminal Court', *International and Comparative Law Quarterly* 51:1, 91–117.

George, Jim (1994) *Discourses of Global Politics: A Critical (Re)Introduction to International Relations* (Boulder, CO: Lynne Rienner).

Giddens, Anthony (1985) *A Contemporary Critique of Historical Materialism, Vol: II: The Nation State and Violence* (Cambridge: Cambridge University Press).

Glaser, Barney G. and Anselm S. Strauss (1967) *The Discovery of Grounded Theory: Strategies for Qualitative Research* (Chicago: Aldine de Gruyter).

Glasius, Marlies (2005) *The International Criminal Court: A Global Civil Society Achievement* (London: Routledge).

Goldstone, Richard J. and Gary Jonathan Bass (2000) 'Lessons from the international criminal tribunals', in Sarah B. Sewall and Carl Kaysen (eds), *The United States and the International Criminal Court: National Security and International Law* (Lanham, MD: Rowman & Littlefield), 51–60.

Gong, Gerrit W. (1984) *The Standard of "Civilization" in International Society* (Oxford: Clarendon).

Gordenker, Leon and Thomas G. Weiss (1996) 'Pluralizing global governance: Analytical approaches and dimensions', in Leon Gordenker and Thomas G. Weiss (eds), *NGOs, the UN, and Global Governance* (Boulder, CO: Lynne Rienner), 17–47.

Guzzini, Stefano (1993) 'Structural power: The limits of neorealist power analysis', *International Organization* 47:3, 443–78.

Habermas, Jürgen (1994) *Faktizität und Geltung:Beiträge zu einer Diskurstheorie des Rechts und des demokratischen Rechtsstaats* (Frankfurt/ Main: Suhrkamp).

Hall, Christopher Keith (1998a) 'The third and fourth sessions of the UN Preparatory

Committee on the Establishment of an International Criminal Court', *American Journal of International Law* 92:1, 124–33.

Hall, Christopher Keith (1998b) 'The sixth session of the UN Preparatory Committee on the Establishment of an International Criminal Court', *American Journal of International Law* 92:3, 548–56.

Hallin, Daniel C. (1986) *The "Uncensored War": The Media and Vietnam* (Berkeley: University of California Press).

Heins, Volker (2002a) 'Der Mythos der globalen Zivilgesellschaft', in Christiane Frantz and Annette Zimmer (eds), *Zivilgesellschaft international: Alte und neue NGOs* (Opladen: Leske + Budrich), 83–101.

Heins, Volker (2002b) *Weltbürger und Lokalpatrioten: Eine Einführung in das Thema Nichtregierungsorganisationen* (Opladen: Leske + Budrich).

Henkin, Louis (1995) 'Human rights and state "sovereignty"', *Georgia Journal of International and Comparative Law* 25:1–2, 31–45.

Herz, John H. (1950) 'Idealist internationalism and the security dilemma', *World Politics* 2:2, 157–80.

Heyman, Charles (ed.) (2001) *Jane's World Armies* 9 (Coulsden: Jane's Publishing).

Hinsley, F. H. (1986) *Sovereignty* (Cambridge: Cambridge University Press).

Holsti, Kalevi J. (1996) *The State, War, and the State of War* (Cambridge: Cambridge University Press).

Hurrell, Andrew (1990) 'Kant and the Kantian paradigm in International Relations', *Review of International Studies* 16:3, 183–205.

Ignatieff, Michael (2003) *Human Rights as Politics and Idolatry* (Princeton, NJ: Princeton University Press).

Jackson, Robert (1990) *Quasi-States: Sovereignty, International Relations and the Third World* (Cambridge: Cambridge University Press).

Jackson, Robert (2000) *The Global Covenant: Human Conduct in a World of States* (Oxford: Oxford University Press).

Jacobson, David (2001) 'The global political culture', in Mathias Albert, David Jacobson and Yosef Lapid (eds), *Identities, Borders, Orders: Rethinking International Relations Theory* (Minneapolis: University of Minnesota Press), 161–80.

Kagan, Robert (2003) *Paradise and Power: America and Europe in the New World Order* (New York: Atlantic Books).

Kahn, Paul W. (2005) 'American exceptionalism, popular sovereignty, and the rule of law', in Michael Ignatieff (ed.), *American Exceptionalism and Human Rights* (Princeton, NJ: Princeton University Press), 198–222.

Kant, Immanuel (1995 [1795]) *Zum ewigen Frieden: Ein philosophischer Entwurf* (Stuttgart: Reclam).

Kaul, Hans-Peter (1998). 'Special note: The struggle for the International Criminal Court's jurisdiction', *European Journal of Crime, Criminal Law and Criminal Justice* 6:4, 48–60.

Keck, Margaret E. and Kathryn Sikkink (1998) *Activists Beyond Borders: Advocacy Networks in International Politics* (Ithaca, NY: Cornell University Press).

Keene, Edward (2002) *Beyond the Anarchical Society: Grotius, Colonialism and Order in World Politics* (Cambridge: Cambridge University Press).

Keohane, Robert O. (1989) *International Institutions and State Power: Essays in International Relations Theory* (Boulder, CO: Westview Press).

Keohane, Robert O. (2002) 'Ironies of sovereignty: the European Union and the United States', *Journal of Common Market Studies* 40:4, 743–65.

Keohane, Robert O. and Stanley Hoffmann (1990) 'Conclusion: Community politics and institutional change', in William Wallace (ed.), *The Dynamics of European Integration*

(London: Pinter), 276–300.

Keohane, Robert O. and Joseph S. Nye (2001) *Power and Interdependence* (New York: Longman).

Kessler, Marie-Christine (1999) *La politique étrangère de la France: Acteurs et processus* (Paris: Presses de Sciences Po).

Kimminich, Otto (1985) 'Die Entstehung des neuzeitlichen Völkerrechts', in Iring Fetscher and Herfried Münkler (eds), *Pipers Handwörterbuch der politischen Ideen, Bd: 3* (Munich: Piper).

Kingsbury, Benedict (1998) 'Sovereignty and inequality', *European Journal of International Law* 9:4, 599–625.

Kirsch, Philippe and Holmes, John T. (1999) 'The Rome Conference on an International Criminal Court: The negotiating process', *American Journal of International Law* 93:1, 2–12.

Korenemos, Barbara, Charles Lipson and Duncan Snidal (2001) 'The rational design of international institutions', *International Organization* 55:4, 761–800.

Koselleck, Reinhard (1992) *Kritik und Krise: eine Studie zur Pathogenese der bürgerlichen Welt* (Frankfurt/Main: Suhrkamp).

Koskenniemi, Martti (2002) *The Gentle Civilizer of Nations: The Rise and Fall of International Law, 1870 – 1960* (Cambridge: Cambridge University Press).

Koskenniemi, Martti (2004) 'International law and hegemony: A reconfiguration', *Cambridge Review of International Affairs* 17:2, 197–218.

Krasner, Stephen D. (1993) 'Westphalia and all that', in Judith Goldstein and Robert O. Keohane (eds), *Ideas and Foreign Policy: Beliefs, Institutions, and Political Change* (Ithaca, NY: Cornell University Press), 235–64.

Krasner, Stephen D. (1999) *Sovereignty: Organized Hypocrisy* (Princeton, NJ: Princeton University Press).

Kratochwil, Friedrich (1986) 'Of systems, boundaries, and territoriality: An inquiry into the formation of the state system', *World Politics* 39:1, 27–52.

Kratochwil, Friedrich (1995) 'Sovereignty as *dominium*: Is there a right of humanitarian intervention?', in Gene M. Lyons and Michael Mastaduno (eds), *Beyond Westphalia? State Sovereignty and International Intervention* (Baltimore, MD: John Hopkins University Press), 21–42.

Krebs, Ronald R. and Patrick Thaddeus Jackson (2007) 'Twisting tongues and twisting arms: The power of political rhetoric', *European Journal of International Relations* 13:1, 35–66.

Kress, Claus (2007) 'The crime of aggression before the first review of the ICC Statute', *Leiden Journal of International Law* 20:4, 851–65.

Krisch, Nico (2003a) 'More equal than the rest? Hierarchy, equality and US predominance in international law', in Michael Byers and Georg Nolte (eds), *United States Hegemony and the Foundations of International Law* (Cambridge: Cambridge University Press), 135–75.

Krisch, Nico (2003b) 'Weak as constraint, strong as tool: The place of international law in U.S. foreign policy', in David M. Malone and Yuen Foong Khong (eds), *Unilateralism and U:S: Foreign Policy* (Boulder, CO: Lynne Rienner), 41–69.

Krisch, Nico (2004) 'Amerikanische Hegemonie und liberale Revolution im Völkerrecht', *Der Staat* 43:3, 267–97.

Laclau, Ernesto (1990) *New Reflections on the Revolution of our Time* (London: Verso).

Laclau, Ernesto and Lillian Zac (1994) 'Minding the gap: The subject of politics', in Ernesto Laclau (ed.), *The Making of Political Identities* (London: Verso), 11–37.

Layne, Christopher (1994) 'Kant or Cant – the myth of democratic peace', *International*

Security 19:2, 5–49.

Levin, Daniel Lessard (1999) *Representing Popular Sovereignty: The Constitution in American Political Culture* (Albany: State University of New York Press).

Levy, David S. (1988) 'Domestic politics and war', *Journal of Interdisciplinary History* 18:4, 653–73.

Lijphart, Arend (1999) *Patterns of Democracy: Government Forms and Performance in Thirty-Six Countries* (New Haven, CT: Yale University Press).

Linklater, Andrew (1998) *The Transformation of Political Community* (Cambridge: Polity).

Lipschutz, Ronnie D. (1996) 'Reconstructing world politics: The emergence of global civil society', in Rick Fawn and Jeremy Larkin (eds), *International Society after the Cold War* (Basingstoke: Macmillan), 101–31.

Lohmann, Georg (1999). 'Menschenrechte zwischen Moral und Recht', in Stefan Gosepath and Georg Lohmann (eds), *Philosophie der Menschenrechte* (Frankfurt/Main: Suhrkamp), 62–95.

Luban, David (1980) 'Just war and human rights', *Philosophy and Public Affairs* 9:2, 160–81.

Lueger, Manfred (2001) *Auf den Spuren der sozialen Welt: Methodologie und Organisierung interpretativer Sozialforschung* (Frankfurt/Main: Peter Lang).

Lukes, Steven (2005) *Power: A Radical View* (London: Palgrave Macmillan).

Lyons, Gene M. and James Mayall (2003) 'Stating the problem of group rights', in G. M. Lyons and J. Mayall (eds), *International Human Rights in the 21st Century: Protecting the Rights of Groups* (Lanham, MD: Rowman & Littlefield), 3–19.

MacIntyre, Alasdair (1985) *After Virtue: A Study in Moral Theory* (London: Duckworth).

Maguire, Peter (2000) *Law and War: An American Story* (New York: Columbia University Press).

Malone, David M. and Yuen Foong Khong (eds) (2003) *Unilateralism and U:S: Foreign Policy: International Perspectives* (Boulder, CO: Lynne Rienner).

Manners, Ian (2002) 'Normative power Europe: A contradiction in terms?', *Journal of Common Market Studies* 40:2, 235–58.

March, James G. and Johan P. Olsen (1994) *Institutional Perspectives on Political Institutions* (Oslo: ARENA).

Mayall, James (2000) *World Politics: Progress and Its Limits* (Cambridge: Polity).

McDougall, Carrie (2007) 'When law and reality clash: The imperative of compromise in the context of the accumulated evil of the whole: Conditions for the exercise of the International Criminal Court's jurisdiction of the crime of aggression', *International Criminal Law Review* 7:2–3, 277–333.

McGoldrick, Dominic (2004) 'Political and legal responses to the ICC', in Dominic McGoldrick, Peter J. Rowe and Eric Donnelly (eds), *The Permanent International Criminal Court: Legal and Policy Issues* (Oxford: Hart), 389–451.

Merom, Gil (2003) *How Democracies Lose Small Wars: State, Society, and the Failures of France in Algeria, Israel in Lebanon, and the United States in Vietnam* (Cambridge: Cambridge University Press).

Meyer, Michael (2001) 'Between theory, method, and politics: Positioning of the approaches to CDA', in Ruth Wodak and Michael Meyer, *Methods of Critical Discourse Analysis* (London: Sage), 14–31.

Milliken, Jennifer (1999) 'The study of discourse in International Relations: A critique of research and methods', *European Journal of International Relations* 5:2, 225–54.

Moghalu, Kingsley Chiedu (2008) *Global Justice: The Politics of War Crimes Trials* (Stanford, CA: Stanford University Press).

Moravcsik, Andrew (1997) 'Taking preferences seriously: A liberal theory of international politics', *International Organization* 51:4, 513–53.

Moravcsik, Andrew (1998) *The Choice for Europe: Social Purpose and State Power from Messina to Maastricht* (Ithaca, NY: Cornell University Press).

Moravcsik, Andrew (2005) 'The paradox of US human rights policy', in Michael Ignatieff (ed.), *American Exceptionalism and Human Rights* (Princeton, NJ: Princeton University Press), 147–97.

Morgenthau, Hans J. (1973) *Politics among Nations: The Struggle for Power and Peace* (New York: Knopf).

Morrow, Raymond A. (1994) *Critical Theory and Methodology* (London: Sage).

Nardin, Terry (1983). Law, Morality, and the Relations of States (Princeton, NJ: Princeton University Press).

Nussbaum, Martha C. (2000) *Women and Human Development: The Capabilities Approach* (Cambridge: Cambridge University Press).

Oye, Kenneth A. (1985) 'Explaining cooperation under anarchy: Hypotheses and strategies', *World Politics* 38:1, 1–24.

Parsons, Anthony (1993) 'The United Nations and the national interests of states', in Adam Roberts and Benedict Kingsbury (eds), *United Nations, Divided World: The UN's Role in International Relations* (Oxford: Clarendon), 47–60.

Power, Samantha (2003) 'Rwanda: The two faces of justice', *New York Review of Books* 50:1, 47–50.

Price, Richard and Christian Reus-Smit (1998) 'Dangerous liaisons? Critical international theory and constructivism', *European Journal of International Relations* 4:3, 259–94.

Putnam, Robert D. (1988) 'Diplomacy and domestic politics: The logic of two-level games', *International Organization* 42:3, 427–60.

Rahmani-Ocora, Ladan (2006) 'Giving the emperor real clothes: The UN Human Rights Council', *Global Governance* 12:1, 15–20.

Ralph, Jason (2005) 'International society, the International Criminal Court and American foreign policy', *Review of International Studies* 31:1, 27–44.

Ralph, Jason (2007) *Defending the Society of States: Why America Opposes the International Criminal Court and its Vision of World Society* (Oxford: Oxford University Press).

Rawls, John (1999) *The Law of Peoples* (Cambridge, MA: Harvard University Press).

Reichertz, Jo (2003) *Die Abduktion in der qualitativen Sozialforschung* (Opladen: Leske + Budrich).

Rengger, Nicholas J. (1995) *Political Theory, Modernity, and Postmodernity: Beyond Enlightenment and Critique* (Oxford: Blackwell).

Reus-Smit, Christian (1999) *The Moral Purpose of the State: Culture, Social Identity, and Rationality in International Relations* (Princeton, NJ: Princeton University Press).

Reus-Smit, Christian (2001) 'Human rights and the social construction of sovereignty', *Review of International Studies* 27:4, 519–38.

Reus-Smit, Christian (2004) 'The politics of international law', in Christian Reus-Smit (ed.), *The Politics of International Law* (Cambridge: Cambridge University Press), 14–44.

Risse, Thomas (2000) '"Let's argue!" Communicative action in world politics', *International Organization* 54:1, 1–39.

Risse, Thomas (2002) 'Transnational actors and world politics', in Walter Carlsnaes, Thomas Risse and Beth A. Simmons (eds), *Handbook of International Relations* (London: Sage), 255–74.

Risse, Thomas and Kathryn Sikkink (1999) 'The socialization of international human rights norms into domestic practices: an introduction', in Thomas Risse, Stephen C. Ropp and Kathryn Sikkink (eds), *The Power of Human Rights: International Norms and Domestic Change* (Cambridge: Cambridge University Press), 1–38.

Risse-Kappen, Thomas (1994) 'Wie weiter mit dem "demokratischen Frieden"?', *Zeitschrift für Internationale Beziehungen* 1:2, 367–79.

Risse-Kappen, Thomas (1995) 'Democratic peace – warlike democracies? A social constructivist interpretation of the liberal argument', *European Journal of International Relations* 1:4, 491–518.

Roach, Stephen C. (2005) 'Arab states and the role of Islam in the International Criminal Court', *Political Studies* 53:1, 143–61.

Robinson, Piers (2000) 'The CNN effect: can the news media drive foreign policy?', *Review of International Studies* 25:2, 301–10.

Rodgers, Daniel T. (1982). 'In search of progressivism', *Reviews in American History* 10, 113–32.

Rorty, Richard (1993) 'Human rights, rationality, and sentimentality', in Stephen Shute and Susan Hurley (eds), *On Human Rights: The Oxford Amnesty Lecture* (New York: Basic Books), 111–35.

Rosato, Sebastian (2003) 'The flawed logic of democratic peace', *American Political Science Review* 97:4, 585–602.

Rosenau, James N. (1990) *Turbulence in World Politics: A Theory of Change and Continuity* (Princeton, NJ: Princeton University Press).

Rosenau, James N. (1995) 'Sovereignty in a turbulent world', in Gene M. Lyons and Michael Mastaduno (eds), *Beyond Westphalia? State Sovereignty and International Intervention* (Baltimore, MD: John Hopkins University Press), 191–227.

Rudolph, Christopher (2001). 'Constructing an atrocities regime: The politics of war crimes tribunals', *International Organization* 55:3, 655–91.

Ruggie, John G. (1986) 'Continuity and transformation in the world polity: Toward a neorealist synthesis', in Robert O. Keohane, *Neorealism and Its Critics* (New York: Columbia University Press), 131–57.

Rumelili, Bahar (2004) 'Constructing identity and relating to difference: understanding the EU's mode of differentiation', *Review of International Studies* 30:1, 27–47.

Russett, Bruce M. (1993) *Grasping the Democratic Peace: Principles for a Post-Cold War World* (Princeton, NJ: Princeton University Press).

Schabas, William A. (2001) *An Introduction to the International Criminal Court* (Cambridge: Cambridge University Press).

Schabas, William A. (2004) 'United States hostility to the International Criminal Court: It's all about the Security Council', *European Journal of International Law* 15:4, 701–20.

Scharf, Michael P. (1995–96) 'The politics of establishing an international criminal court', *Duke Journal of Comparative and International Law* 6:1, 167–73.

Scharf, Michael P. (1999) 'The politics behind the U.S. opposition to the International Criminal Court', *New England Comparative and International Law Journal* 5, www.nesl.edu/intljournal/VOL5/SCHARF.HTM (accessed 19 August 2008).

Scheffer, David J. (2001–2) 'Staying the course with the International Criminal Court', *Cornell International Law Journal* 35:1, 47–100.

Scheipers, Sibylle (2007) 'Civilization vs toleration: The new UN Human Rights Council and the normative foundations of the international order', *Journal of International Relations and Development* 10:3, 219–42.

Scheipers, Sibylle and Daniela Sicurelli (2007) 'Normative power Europe: A credible utopia?', *Journal of Common Market Studies* 45:2, 435–57.

Schimmelfennig, Frank (2003) *The EU, NATO and the Integration of Europe: Rules and Rhetoric* (Cambridge: Cambridge University Press).

Schimmelfennig, Frank (2000). 'The community trap: Liberal norms, rhetorical action, and the eastern enlargement of the European Union', *International Organization* 55:1, 47–80.

Schmidt, Manfred G. (2000) *Demokratietheorien: Eine Einführung* (Opladen: Leske + Budrich).

Scholte, Jan Aart (2000) *Globalization: A Critical Introduction* (London: Palgrave).

Schuster, Matthias (2003) 'The Rome Statute and the crime of aggression: A Gordian knot in search of a sword', *Criminal Law Forum* 14:1, 1–57.

Scott, Shirley V. (2004) 'Is there room for international law in *realpolitik*? Accounting for the US "attitude" towards international law', *Review of International Studies* 30:1, 71–88.

Shinoda, Hideaki (2000) *Re-examining Sovereignty: From Classical Theory to the Global Age* (Basingstoke: Macmillan).

Shklar, Judith N. (1986). *Legalism: Law, Morals and Political Trials* (Cambridge, MA: Harvard University Press).

Shklar, Judith N. (1998) *Political Thought and Political Thinkers* (Chicago, IL: University of Chicago Press).

Shue, Henry (1996) *Basic Rights: Subsistence, Affluence, and US Foreign Policy* (Princeton, NJ: Princeton University Press).

Sikkink, Kathryn (1993) 'Human rights, principled issue-networks, and sovereignty in Latin America', *International Organization* 47:3, 411–41.

Simpson, Gerry (2004) *Great Powers and Outlaw States: Unequal Sovereigns in the International Legal Order* (Cambridge: Cambridge University Press).

Skinner, Quentin (1978) *Foundations of Modern Political Thought, Vol: I: The Renaissance* (Cambridge: Cambridge University Press).

Smith, Karen E. (2003) *European Union Foreign Policy in a Changing World* (Cambridge: Polity).

Spiro, Peter J. (2000) 'The new sovereigntists: American exceptionalism and its false prophets', *Foreign Affairs* 79:6, 9–15.

Stark, Carsten (2002) 'Die Konflikttheorie von Georg Simmel', in Thorsten Bonacker (ed.), *Sozialwissenschaftliche Konflikttheorien: Eine Einführung* (Opladen: Leske + Budrich), 83–97.

Torfing, Jacob (1999) *New Theories of Discourse: Laclau, Mouffe, and Žižek* (Oxford: Blackwell).

Tully, James H. (1988) *Meaning and Context: Quentin Skinner and His Critics* (Cambridge: Cambridge University Press).

Ulbert, Cornelia, Thomas Risse and Harald Müller (2004) *Arguing and Bargaining in Multilateral Negotiations: Final Report to the Volkswagen Foundation* (Berlin and Frankfurt/Main: FU Berlin and HSFK).

Vagts, Detlev F. (2001) 'Hegemonic international law', *American Journal of International Law* 95:4, 843–8.

van Gennep, Arnold (1986) *Übergangsriten* (Frankfurt/ Main: Campus).

van Hoof, G. J. H. (1983) *Rethinking the Sources of International Law* (Deventer: Kluwer).

Vincent, R. John (1986) *Human Rights and International Relations: Issues and Responses* (Cambridge: Cambridge University Press).

von Hebel, Hermann and Darryl Robinson (1999) 'Crimes within the jurisdiction of the Court', in Roy S. Lee (ed.), *The International Criminal Court: The Making of the Rome Statute: Issues, Negotiations, Results* (The Hague: Kluwer), 79–126.

Walker, R. B. J. (1993) *Inside/Outside: International Relations as Political Theory* (Cambridge: Cambridge University Press).

Walker, R. B. J. (2000) 'Both globalisation and sovereignty: Re-imagining the political', in Paul Wapner and Lester Edwin Ruiz, *Principled World Politics: The Challenge of Normative International Relations* (Lanham, MD: Rowman & Littlefield), 23–34.

Waltz, Kenneth N. (1979) *Theory of International Politics* (New York, NY: McGraw-Hill).

Walzer, Michael (1995) 'The concept of civil society', in Michael Walzer (ed.), *Toward a Global Civil Society* (Oxford: Providence), 7–27.

Walzer, Michael (2000) *Just and Unjust Wars: A Moral Argument with Historical Illustrations* (London: Basic Books).

Wæver, Ole (1995) 'Securitization and desecuritization', in Ronnie D. Lipschutz (ed.), *On Security* (New York: Columbia University Press), 46–86.

Wæver, Ole (2004) 'Discursive approaches', in Thomas Diez and Antje Wiener (eds), *European Integration Theory* (Oxford: Oxford University Press), 197–215.

Weber, Cynthia (1995) *Simulating Sovereignty: Intervention, the State and Symbolic Exchange* (Cambridge: Cambridge University Press).

Wedgwood, Ruth (1998) 'Fiddling in Rome: America and the International Criminal Court', *Foreign Affairs* 77:6, 20–4.

Weller, Marc (2002) 'Undoing the global constitution: UN Security Council action on the International Criminal Court', *International Affairs* 78:4, 693–712.

Weschler, Lawrence (2000) 'Exceptional cases in Rome: The United States and the struggle on the ICC', in Sarah B. Sewall and Carl Kaysen (eds), *The United States and the International Criminal Court: National Security and International Law* (Lanham, MD: Rowman & Littlefield), 85–111.

Wheeler, Nicholas J. (2000) *Saving Strangers: Humanitarian Intervention in International Society* (Oxford: Oxford University Press).

Wheeler, Nicholas J. (2001) 'Humanitarian vigilantes or legal entrepreneurs: Enforcing human rights in international society', in Simon Caney and Peter Jones (eds), *Human Rights and Global Diversity* (London: Frank Cass), 139–62.

Wheeler, Nicholas J. and Timothy Dunne (1996) 'Hedley Bull's pluralism of the intellect and solidarism of the will', *International Affairs* 72:1, 91–107.

Wheeler, Nicholas J. and Timothy Dunne (1998) 'Hedley Bull and the idea of a universal moral community: Fictional, primordial or imagined?', in B. A. Roberson (ed.), *International Society and the Development of International Relations Theory* (London: Pinter), 43–58.

Williams, Paul R. and Francesca Jannotti Pecci (2004) 'Earned sovereignty: Bridging the gap between sovereignty and self-determination', *Stanford Journal of International Law* 40:1, 1–21.

Wippman, David (2004) 'The International Criminal Court', in Christian Reus-Smit (ed.), *The Politics of International Law* (Cambridge: Cambridge University Press), 151–88.

Wodak, Ruth (2001) 'What CDA is about – a summary of its history, important concepts and its developments', in Ruth Wodak and Michael Meyer (eds), *Methods of Critical Discourse Analysis* (London: Sage), 1–13.

Wodak, Ruth and Michael Meyer (eds) (2001) *Methods of Critical Discourse Analysis* (London: Sage Publications).

Yee, Albert S. (1996) 'The causal effects of ideas on policies', *International Organization* 50:1, 69–108.

Zaller, John (1994) 'Strategic politicians, public opinion, and the Gulf crisis', in W. Lance Bennett and David L. Paletz (eds), *Taken by Storm: The Media, Public Opinion, and US Foreign Policy in the Gulf War* (Chicago: University of Chicago Press), 250–72.

Index